AN ANNOYANCE OF NEIGHBOURS

LIFE IS NEVER DULL WHEN YOU HAVE NEIGHBOURS!

DR ANGELA LIGHTBURN

Matador
9 Priory Business Park,
Wistow Road, Kibworth Beauchamp,
Leicestershire. LE8 0RX
Tel: (+44) 116 279 2299
Fax: (+44) 116 279 2277
Email: books@troubador.co.uk
Web: www.troubador.co.uk/matador

ISBN 978 1785892 028

British Library Cataloguing in Publication Data.
A catalogue record for this book is available from the British Library.

Printed and bound in the UK by TJ International, Padstow, Cornwall
Typeset in 11pt Aldine by Troubador Publishing Ltd, Leicester, UK

Matador is an imprint of Troubador Publishing Ltd

"Everyone should have two neighbours,
One to talk to and one to talk about."

ANON

"Great minds discuss ideas;
Average minds discuss events;
Small minds discuss people."

ELEANOR ROOSEVELT

About the author

The author has lived all over the country and has had man
neighbours over the years. Shared flats in converted hous
led to own purpose-built flat in block, followed by s
in suburbia, then detached cottage on a lane and final
rural isolation, each step of the way carefully plann
reduce the number of neighbours. She now knows
of the locals than when she lived anywhere else.

Along the way she picked up a degree in Psy
a PhD in Applied Psychology and a Dip
Insurance (don't ask), so knows a thing or
human behaviour, and along with the experi
and time has an unparalleled insight into un
and coping with neighbours. She knows th
sometimes finds it hard to put into practic

She has seen it all, possibly done a goo
the T-shirt and written this book. It is a w
peak at the neighbours from behind t
net curtains of life. She hopes it mak
you enjoy reading it as much as she h
it. When you next catch sight of your
start to visualise them in a complete
warned – they might have read thi

Contents

The Psychology Of Neighbourly Relations (Or Why We Hate The Neighbours)

The collective noun for neighbours is an 'annoyance' or a 'nerve', and we all know just how annoying and frazzling on the nerves neighbours can be! Everybody has neighbours and all of us have stories to tell about their noisy, selfish, nuisance behaviour and, just occasionally, a heart-warming story about a genuinely altruistic neighbour. This is a humorous collection of neighbour stereotypes, not meant to be taken too seriously or literally. After reading it, you will be able to classify your neighbours and learn how to handle them so that they cause you the least hassle. Or at the very least you will be able to laugh at them behind their backs.

We all have neighbours unless you're rich enough to own 1,000 hectares with a house in the middle of it, and no footpaths or roads crossing it, and if you're reading this then I can presume that you are not one of them. Even so, every property has its boundaries and there will always be someone complaining about a fence, a straying animal or overgrown vegetation blocking their view.

An online poll asked, "Have you ever had an

annoying neighbour?" 85% reported having annoying neighbours and regularly think up ideas to annoy them back. Only 6% said they had lovely neighbours and 9% admitted to being the annoying neighbour.

Long running feuds with neighbours can last for years and end up in a full-blown stand-off with neither party willing to let go nor remedy the situation. Chances are that it started with a petty squabble but now no one can remember what it was about, just that they feel that they are the aggrieved party.

Halifax Home Insurance carried out a survey of 2,000 homebuyers in 2010 and found that nearly 1 in 10 people claimed to have moved house because of the neighbours, with aggressive behaviour in connection with boundaries and parking coming top, closely followed by noise. Of the latter, most was due to loud music, children, TVs blaring out, barking dogs, DIY, noisy vehicles at unsocial hours or shouting and rows. Oh, and 3% said that their neighbours were guilty of noisy sex! General disrepair, untidiness and mess made a few others move and nosy neighbours had caused some to up sticks and go to live somewhere else. Makes you wonder what they were trying to hide.

Nobody selling their house because of the neighbours is likely to tell their potential buyers that this is their reason for moving, even though they are legally obliged to mention any disputes in which they have been involved. Unless it results in a fight attended by the police or ends up in court, most people consider the odd neighbourly spat to be perfectly normal, and not worthy of mention. Anyway, the new people might get on famously with your uncouth, belligerent next door neighbour!

Sherlock Holmes famously told Dr Watson to "Go to the nearest public house. That is the centre of country gossip." And it is sound advice which you should consider when looking at property, especially if it is in an unfamiliar area. For sure, there might be a lull in the conversation when you walk in, but letting the locals know you are thinking of moving to the vicinity, and oiling the wheels with a pint or two, will soon break down the barriers. You will learn a lot about the local area and its residents, such as the night shift worker who gets home at 6am, the once a year model aircraft extravaganza and the local who is the county yodelling champion, so they don't come as a surprise and you can have some peace of mind when deciding whether to move in. Googling the neighbours can also inform you as to what they do for a living, and Facebook, Twitter and Instagram can tell you a lot about their hobbies and habits.

First impressions are important in any sphere of life, and how many of us consider the neighbours or ask about them when looking at a potential new home? You can pick your friends and find your dream home but you can't pick your neighbours. In this frantic modern life where families consist of commuting adults working crazy hours, and parents who are afraid to let their children play outside for fear of germs or perverts, it is becoming increasingly common to realise that you've lived in your house for 5 years and never met the neighbours. Lucky you! Because if you did get to know them, the likelihood is that they'd fit into one or more neighbour stereotypes. We very quickly make a judgement when we meet people for the first time and most of us probably consider ourselves good judges of character. We assess someone from their unspoken signs and signals – their clothes, the way they walk, the colour of their paintwork, state of the garden, style of house, make of car, body language and other non-verbal clues as well as their behaviour and facial expressions and this is before they have uttered a single word, pleasant or otherwise! It has been estimated that 94% of our communication is non-verbal. Even if you don't understand a word of the language being spoken, you can make a pretty good guess from the tone of voice and accompanying gestures as to what it's all about! And just because they are friendly, courteous and make good eye contact doesn't mean they are not psychopaths and will not turn into the neighbours from hell.

In order to tell if someone is not what they seem on first meeting, you have to observe them in different situations, watch and listen over a period of time. If you do all the talking, you'll miss the important stuff that gives them away. If they tell you that they are pillars of the local church or in the police or armed forces, or an important figure in the community or wider society, you can experience what is known as 'icon intimidation' which can hamper or skew your judgement. Trust your instincts! Say for example that you have had an accident, or are laid up with an illness, feeling low and vulnerable. A neighbour might phone to see how you are, spending less than a minute enquiring after your health, and quickly curtail the conversation. The impression you are left with is that they couldn't give a toss and have just gone through the motions because it was expected. They clearly can't be bothered to walk the short distance to your house, where they would not have been able to get away so expediently. Neither do they offer any help, however insincerely meant. It gives the impression of someone totally uncaring although nothing nasty has been said and some might see it as a kind deed. It isn't. They have simply ticked the box and gone back to their cosy life. You can see from this example that from events like this we make assumptions that may or may not be true, and can lose perspective. Even if future evidence contradicts our opinions, the suspicions or feelings that have been planted by one negative event or an out of character remark become very difficult to change. If some time has elapsed since the initial episode, we have had time to brood on the details and the feelings coalesce into an ingrained dislike. Every time we see them, we are reminded of the incident. If we have also repeated (and probably embellished) the story to others, then it becomes blown up out of all proportion and impossible to rectify. The unsuspecting neighbour becomes persona non grata because of perhaps one uncharacteristic transgression or mistake but, because we don't know them well, we extrapolate that this is how they always are, which exacerbates the problem, and behave towards them accordingly.

So how do you spot potentially bad neighbours when looking for somewhere to live? Don't just look at the immediate neighbours' houses; check out the properties on the approaches and at different times of the day and days of the week. A quiet street on a Monday morning may look and sound very different on a Saturday night.

1. Look for signs of neglect – unmown grass, weedy gardens, drainpipes hanging off, peeling paintwork, cracked windows, litter and rubbish, and abandoned vehicles in the driveway.
2. Lots of cars parked outside mean lots of inhabitants or visitors, coming and going at all hours, banging car doors, and revving engines.
3. Dogs tied up outside may mean noise from their barking. People who neglect pets often have no respect for people either.
4. That ideal flat over a dress shop may not be so desirable when the shop changes ownership or goes out of business and becomes a fast food restaurant or a massage parlour.
5. If there is a vacant plot next door, think about what might be built on it in the future. You might not be bothered about living next door to a building site for a few months if the result is houses that enhance the locality. But supposing it became a landfill site or a distribution centre operating all hours or that idyllic field becomes a motorbike scrambling venue, significantly increasing the noise, pollution and local traffic in a predominantly rural area? Always get local

authority searches done and read them thoroughly. You underestimate yourself if you think they will be couched in language that you won't understand. Only a fool signs a legal document without having read and understood the implications of every clause and condition. An article in the national newspapers told the story of how a couple went ahead and bought a beautiful house near a church in a pretty village without properly reading the paperwork, only to find out that they were liable for £100,000 of chancel repairs. Caveat emptor!

6. Ditto vacant buildings. They can attract a variety of nefarious activities that can devalue your home or make it unsaleable, including squatters not necessarily of the human kind.

7. Use ALL your senses. When house-hunting you may come across your dream property in an enviable location, reasonably priced because the owners are keen to sell. Why? No one wants to buy it because of the pungent smell of pigs from an intensive rearing unit next door.

Ignoring the signs is one of the most common mistakes house-hunters make. It is easy to wax lyrical about the roses round the door, the Jacuzzi bath, the walk-in wardrobes, the perfect location and the reasonable price, but disregard those nuisance neighbours and you may live to regret it. Bad neighbours lower a property's value or make it impossible to sell, and make life miserable. Moving again is a very expensive and stressful business even if you can find a buyer. We may depend on services such as motorways, power lines and sewage farms but no one wants to live near them.

And how about the neighbours themselves? There are well-documented signs to be aware of when talking to your neighbour – do they suddenly shout abuse at someone else while in the middle of a perfectly innocuous conversation with you? Do they tend to blame everyone else for their failures and predicaments rather than taking responsibility for their actions? Do they maliciously slag off other people behind their backs? Do they interrupt you when you're talking or constantly manoeuvre the conversation back to themselves all the time, showing a lack of empathy? These traits may not appear straight away and certainly not all at the same time, which is why many new neighbours get along for a while until they discover something they don't like, or an incident makes them wary. Then they start thinking, and that's when the small things start to add up. If one neighbour assumes a zero tolerance stance, things can get seriously mean! If you are uncertain as to their motives, ask them how they feel about a sensitive subject. Their response will tell you a good deal about their attitudes and compassion for others, including you.

Most people make themselves more accessible to others who they consider to be their equals and generally keep more of a distance from those they consider to be inferior, perhaps in class or education, and conversely also those they perceive as being superior: intellectually, financially, culturally or socially. In other words, we prefer to socialise with people who are just like us.

But why is it that so few of us know who our neighbours are and wouldn't recognise them if we met them away from home? There are a variety of reasons, and many of them are the result of changes in society and the way we live our lives today. In the past, when safety nets of social welfare didn't exist, people were much more dependent upon their family and neighbours for mutual aid and support in hard times. In Victorian times, social security and the compensation culture were nonexistent. If you were off work for a period, the neighbours would leave a casserole or some vegetables from their garden on the kitchen table or a bucket of coal at the back door, and the vicar would surreptitiously leave a few coins beside the clock on the mantelpiece. This saved you from starvation and the workhouse, and you were forever grateful. You would have done exactly the same for someone else in need. There but for the grace of God and all that...

Years ago, most towns, cities and villages had relatively stable communities. Now, many more people live in flats with no communal areas and the pressure on land means houses are being built without front gardens for people to potter in and exchange greetings with passers-by and neighbours. These days, people work longer hours, which may include anti-social shifts at nights and weekends, and may even work away for part, or all, of the working week. In any case, the time spent commuting is getting longer, as more people work outside their local environment. Getting home at 9pm or later and having to be on the 6.45 train the next morning are not conducive to a social life during the week. Gripes about the work-life balance abound.

Gone are the days when all the local men worked at the factory, mine or farm and knew each other as colleagues as well as neighbours and the women stayed at home to look after the children and socialised with each other on a daily basis. We are now more likely to befriend work colleagues than neighbours as we inevitably spend more time with them, have more in common and be of a similar age, despite possibly living many miles apart.

Where cars are used for at least part of the journey to work, some parents may drop children off at school (or more than one school) on the way to their place of employment. The harassed working parent often does not have the luxury of the walk and a leisurely chat at the school gate. Less walking means fewer opportunities to converse with or even greet the neighbours. Children are also likely to be ferried by car to their social activities after school and in holiday time due to fear of crime and a lack of reliable public transport.

The decline in use of places where people previously used to gather such as churches, public baths, pubs, village shops, post offices, launderettes and social clubs has limited the opportunities for neighbours to come across each other to exchange pleasantries and make friends. Much of this is to do with the change in the means of communication as more and more of us socialise at a distance by digital means such as Skype, the internet and mobile phones, and the interactions are more likely to be on a one-to-one basis. More diverse populations mean that sometimes there may be language or cultural barriers to getting to know the neighbours.

There are many more choices as to how to spend our dwindling free time, from going to the gym, where there is more testosterone fuelled competition than possibilities to make friends, to online gaming. With on-demand services, DVDs and ever more sophisticated recording devices, we tend to make our own entertainment rather than looking to people to provide it. It is encouraging that allotments are now so popular that there are waiting lists as these are places where people who live fairly close to each other can interact and have a common activity to bring them together and share knowledge, experiences and skills while leaning on a spade or over a cup of tea together huddled in a shed.

The breakdown of the extended family means that grandparents may be hundreds, if not thousands, of miles away, still working or having an active retirement travelling and enjoying sports and hobbies. Mobility for economic reasons of employment means that people tend not to stay in the same place for as long as their parents or grandparents would have done. This means that people have less of a stake in the local community and tend to be less willing to get involved. This is a complaint shared by people living in places where many of the houses are second homes, that the owners are not friendly and show no interest in becoming involved in local activities, even when they are there.

Modern life, on the whole, is just not conducive to creating neighbourly communities with their diverse and heterogeneous mix, and it could be said that the way we live actively discourages and undermines attempts to communicate with the neighbours. Increasingly, relationships are, somewhat cynically and selfishly, deliberately chosen for their benefit to the individual rather than simply happening due to physical proximity. Neighbours might share a common locality but they are unlikely to work together, socialise together or have similar interests. The exception to this might be those who work permanently from home, stay-at-home parents caring for children, other home-based carers and the elderly and retired for whom neighbourly relations carry more value.

Although by nature we are a social bunch, cheek by jowl living in vast cities and long days spent in the close proximity of others on trains, buses, underground and at work, traffic jams and crowds of people wherever we go mean that our personal space is often violated. This can be very stressful and unhealthy, so it is no wonder that, in what is left of our spare time, we like to have some privacy, and will fight to preserve and protect it. Fifty years ago, doors used to be left unlocked and neighbours would call in uninvited and be welcomed. That is simply not the case in most communities today. Mistrust and the value of privacy have seen to that. If people want to know what neighbourliness is in this day and age they watch EastEnders or Coronation Street or Emmerdale, which are totally unrepresentative of the vast majority of neighbourhoods. Interestingly, other countries have similar programmes. In France, they have a TV show 'Nos

Chers Voisins' (Our Dear Neighbours) whose trademark is the pettiness, rivalries and scheming that goes on in a fictional apartment block. You can't help feeling that there is a sense of voyeurism in these programmes, and that people can watch and make judgements about others without the messy business of getting involved.

Despite all this, research has almost unanimously shown that neighbourliness brings benefits, and that getting on with the neighbours makes people happier and consequently their lives are richer for it. Most people get a feeling of satisfaction from being able to help a neighbour solve a problem, be it the loan of equipment, a helping hand with some DIY or feeding the cat in their absence and have no expectation of the favour being reciprocated. They do it out of altruism and if it results in friendliness and the return of the favour sometime then that's a bonus. Problems arise when someone becomes resentful when the favour is not reciprocated or they feel they are being used unfairly or the borrowed item is returned damaged.

Neighbourliness should become more important as more of us live alone due to divorce, death or simply from personal choice, and support from public agencies declines. Having supportive neighbours can alleviate loneliness, depression and low self-esteem, boost confidence, health and trust, and contributes to a sense of worth and belonging.

Before moving on to our neighbour characters, let's look at Arthur Schopenhauer's parable of the winter porcupines, written in 1851.

"On a cold winter's day, a group of porcupines huddled together trying to keep warm in the freezing weather. After a while they started to feel the stabs of each other's quills and shuffled apart. But gradually they began to get cold again so were forced to move closer together to share their warmth until their quills forced them to move apart again. This went on for some time until finally they discovered the optimum distance from one another that provided both a maximum of warmth and a minimum of pain. In human beings, loneliness makes us yearn for company. This brings people together, but their many disagreeable qualities and intolerable faults drive them apart again. Eventually they find a happy medium where they can coexist, by following the unwritten laws of politeness and good manners. Everyone learns to keep the right distance from each other. The metaphorical need for warmth is only partially satisfied, but the pain of the quills is kept to a minimum for both parties."

The story is, of course, an analogy for the problems we all have with relationships, including those with our neighbours. Too close a relationship can feel claustrophobic and an invasion of privacy but no interaction at all risks loneliness and isolation. All relationships need to find the right balance, but unfortunately this can mean different things to different people and this disparity, be it real or imagined, can often be the cause of those neighbourly misunderstandings and disputes. What is perceived as helpful assistance by one person can be seen as gross interference by someone else.

Whole academic tomes have been written on the subject of neighbourly relations. The work of Philip Abrams, published in 1986 in a book by Martin Bulmer entitled 'Neighbours', was the first major study of its kind since the 1960s. It concentrated on neighbourhood care as an important example of informal social care. Interestingly, it concluded that "pure goodness of heart" was rarely a motive for helping others.

There are numerous quotes about neighbours in literature and from famous individuals, mostly derogatory, and you'll find a good few of them here, one at the beginning of each character, chosen for their appropriateness and pertinence. To claim to be a definitive overview of neighbourly relations would be presumptuous, but amongst the quotes, stories and observations you should catch a glimpse of someone you know, and perhaps give a wry smile of recognition. No doubt you could add some funny or hair raising stories of your own. "There's nowt so queer as folk" so they say and they don't come much stranger than neighbours. If there was a continuum from 1 to 100, someone, somewhere has a neighbour for every point on the scale, from the out and out anti-social, aggressive neighbour to the supportive neighbour who spontaneously offers exactly the right help at precisely the right time. This book is a mixture of apocryphal legends, personal experience, myth, stereotypes, stock characters, hearsay, invention, exaggeration, fact, fiction and academic research.

So, next time you toss a snail over the fence, think about those neighbours who complain that they can't understand why their garden is so full of pests eating their precious plants and consider which of the following caricatures best suits them. Then you can refer to them as a number 17 or a 38, even in their earshot, so they don't know what you are talking about. Why not pick a nickname for them from the comprehensive list or make up an applicable one of your own? And don't forget to scrutinise their front door and its trappings for some insight into the occupants' personalities after reading the chapter on doors and doormats, knobs and knockers. You might think of yourself as the ideal neighbour, but the quiz will reveal what sort of neighbour you really are!

If you don't recognise some of the more unpleasant characters in this book, then think yourself lucky. You just haven't come across them – yet.

Meet The Neighbours

A flag system has been provided as follows:

Green: relaxing to be with, trustworthy, warm, sympathetic, empathic, accommodating, well-meant, well-intentioned, gracious, kind. Lucky you!

Amber: two-faced, blow hot and cold, wry, cynical, sarcastic, fond of gossip. Be careful, be wary, be vigilant, be on your guard, watch your back, and be careful what you tell them.

Red: toxic, septic, virulent, pestiferous, deadly, poisonous, obnoxious, odious, malevolent, spiteful, invidious, duplicitous, untrustworthy, malicious, enjoy others' misfortunes, bitter, jealous, liars and cheats. Avoid.

After reading about the following neighbourhood characters, you may or may not agree with this classification. After all, one man's meat is another man's poison.

1. The Angelic Grandma Neighbour
: Green Flag

"You can only be a good neighbour if you have good neighbours." Howard E Koch

Her name will be Winifred or Gladys, Doris or Joan and woe betide you if you try to shorten it. Most people refer to her by her surname. Widowed and living alone in the most idyllic cottage with roses round the door and real antique furniture, her cottage smells of lavender and furniture polish. There is a photo of her late husband proudly holding a silver cup in front of a display of vegetables and another of the two of them in the sunshine of a summer's day at the seaside. He looks a kindly soul and she tells you that they lived here all their married life and never had an argument. Her grey hair is pulled back into a neat bun and she has a beatific smile carefully in place. She is always nicely if not expensively dressed, preferring skirts and blouses to tracksuits and trousers, and wears sensible shoes. The brass door knocker is kept well-polished. She reminds you of your own grandmother, but nicer. There is a son in Australia, whom she idolises, but who never visits even on the odd occasion when he is in the country on business. If she is lucky he rings her on her birthday and at Christmas, but can't talk for long because he is Very Busy or Just Going Out.

Agatha Christie novels are her favourite reading matter – "I do like a good murder!" – and she solves the crime long before the end. She is gentile and proud and reminiscent of another era long gone. Not once have you heard her swear. She comes across as a bit stiff and likes to do everything the proper way. But she's not averse to a sherry or two at Christmas and likes a choice piece of gossip, but secrets are safe with her. She is very private and not very sociable, turning down all your well-meant invitations to get-togethers ("You don't want me there!"). You can trust her to babysit, feed the cat, take a valuable parcel in or keep an eye on the house while you're away. She is no trouble and never asks for a return favour.

You see her shopping on her own locally, wicker basket in the crook of her arm. The kettle is always on, tea is served in proper hand-painted bone china cups and the cakes are homemade. In the summer you never leave without a bunch of sweet peas, a jar of jam or some fruit and vegetables from the garden. Sugar is served using sugar tongs and you've seen a pair of grape scissors in the fruit bowl. She will listen to your rants about work and family without criticising, judging or telling you a story about someone she knows to whom the same thing happened and how they dealt with it, and always manages to say the right thing. "Now, tell me all about it and we'll see what can be done" is a favourite.

She loves to hear about your family and where you have been on holiday, so don't forget to send her a postcard. She doesn't have a computer but has embraced modern technology in so far as she has acquired a mobile phone, although it's never turned on and she keeps losing it. An elderly car stands on the drive in showroom condition.

In many ways she is the Perfect Neighbour. Sadly, she is too proud to ask for help and when you discover she has died, you realise that you hardly knew her at all.

You may think that you know just how to handle this easy neighbour, but in reality she is handling you. Be kind to her. Adopt her. She may keep you at a distance and be very self-sufficient but at times she may be a little lonely, so go out of your way, within the boundaries that she will accept, to be especially generous to her. Neighbours like this are rare. Don't take them for granted and show your appreciation, even if they will only accept your thanks (and don't forget to thank them as they were brought up to respect good manners), because one day they will not be there and the neighbours from hell may move in!

2. The Stingy Neighbour
: Red Flag

> "THE MEASURE OF YOUR LIFE WILL NOT BE IN WHAT YOU ACCUMULATE, BUT IN WHAT YOU GIVE AWAY." DR WAYNE DYER

The Stingy Neighbours are not poor; they are just mean with money. There is a thin line between frugality and stinginess, and while most people are careful, this neighbour is known to be a skinflint. We've all identified the person who is the last to the bar to get a round in or, worse, leaves before it's their turn, but this neighbour takes tightfistedness to a whole new level.

You know the type. They send their starving kids round to yours at tea time, and keep asking you to pick their kids up from school but never return the favour because it costs them in fuel. If you are throwing a party they will either bring nothing or present you with a very cheap bottle of wine, and then proceed to drink your expensive stuff and eat all the food you've laid on. They're well-known at local gallery openings for making a beeline for the free booze and nibbles. They steal all the soap and shampoo samples from places they stay and you know where they took their holidays because their bathroom towels have the resort's name on them, and you suspect that they reuse dental floss. They will happily confide that they wash their clothes while taking a shower and that you can rinse and reuse paper towels.

If you go out for a meal, they're the one at the end of the evening calculating what their food cost them and putting down the exact amount in cash on the table, and they don't include a tip. When you are leaving, you notice that they have bags full of paper napkins, cutlery or even the restaurant's toilet rolls. They have been known to visit the supermarket at the end of the day and go bin-diving for food thrown out for being past its sell-by date.

They won't buy a poppy from the door to door seller in November, because they saved the one from last year. And they have never bought a copy of the Big Issue. On Hallowe'en they turn out the lights and sit in the dark rather than have to give away sweets to the trick-or-treaters.

They won't pay for babysitters. Instead they invite a young couple round so they can watch a DVD claiming that they are doing them a favour by giving them somewhere to go for free. If you happen to mention that you are going shopping they will give you a long list of things to get for them and then conveniently forget to pay you. Inviting you round for a cuppa is a rare event, but if they do you discover that they reuse teabags and although you just bought them whole milk, they claim they only have skimmed because they water it down to make it go further. On the table there's a bowl full of all those free sachets of tomato sauce, salt and sugar, liberated from the local chippy. On Sundays they go to the 'All you can eat' places to get their money's worth. They have been known to collect and eat road kill.

At work they look in everyone's pots of pens for odd coins and will park miles away just to avoid paying a 50p parking fee, or bum lifts off neighbours even if it's out of their way. For their kids' lunches, they spread butter round the outside of each slice of bread and only add filling to the middle so it looks OK and they claim it doesn't taste any different. The accompanying bottle may look like an expensive brand but is full of tap water. In the supermarket they're the ones with fists full of coupons and vouchers holding everyone up at the checkout.

Christmas cards to other neighbours are considered a waste of money. Their justification for being mean-spirited and miserly is to ask "Why send cards to people you see every day?" Envelopes received are reused if the stamp hasn't been franked.

Lint that collects in the filter of the tumble dryer is saved and used to stuff cushions or given to the hamster for bedding. Nothing is wasted if it can be used or sold. Their children told you that their parents sold their baby teeth to the ivory trade and that they lie about their ages to get them into attractions free of charge.

Their house is furnished from Freecycle and the contents of local skips and they turn all the radiators down and wear six layers of clothes in the winter, claiming it's better for you. They cut their own hair and it shows.

3. The Absent Minded Professor Neighbour
:Green Flag

"I am not absent minded. It is the presence of mind that makes me unaware of everything else." G K Chesterton

Quirky and super intelligent, this neighbour is easily recognised by his appearance alone. He can be seen walking down the street in his slippers wearing a moth-eaten cardigan buttoned up unevenly or worn inside out. He (and it is almost always a he) is reputed to have worked in academia many moons ago. An enigmatic character, often much maligned and misunderstood. You may laugh at him and treat him as a figure of fun but sometimes he can be quite insensitive to others' feelings and bluntly say things others would regret and turn into an eccentric nuisance. His grasp of dates and times is often tenuous as evidenced by his piano playing, which is exquisite but not appreciated at 4am. In his inattention to the details of everyday life, he just forgets that other people have to sleep and go to work. Underneath it all he is harmless and benevolent – if he has a telescope, you can be sure that he is genuinely looking at the stars.

He gets his reputation from his capacity to ignore the mundane and is so engrossed in his own world that he fails to notice anything else. Often oblivious to events going on around him, you may spot him walking down the road in the rain absorbed in reading a book. He delights in telling you that there are grass snakes in his compost heap and you have seen him dissecting owl pellets on the kitchen table. He spends hours looking for things that he has put down and can't find and will have something he would love to show you or give you if only he knew where he last had it. Three times last week you had to help him look for his house keys which you found in his own front door lock. He will suddenly appear in your kitchen, looking for his glasses which will be perched on his head. If he has genuinely lost them, and wants to go out, he will drive anyway. All the other neighbours who know him will pull over if they see him coming. He thinks this is out of kindness or respect, but the other drivers simply see it as self-preservation.

Don't be offended if, while talking to you, he suddenly breaks off and wanders away muttering to himself. He's had another cerebral idea and wants to explore its possibilities immediately. Talking to him can be fascinating if you have the time. He can mesmerise his audience through the sheer beauty of his prose and knowledge, if he feels like it. Then he will abruptly depart with a farewell salutation, getting your name mixed up with someone else's.

Your children love going round to his place as there are weird and wonderful stuffed animals and he shows them experiments that go bang. And he would be great on your pub quiz team if he ever remembers when and where it is. Fermat's Last Theorem holds no fear for him. He has never heard of the Kardashians but he is fairly certain that it is a settlement of villages in ancient Persia. His own offspring got used to being the last to be picked up from school because he forgot the time or even that he had any children.

He likes to walk as he says it gives him time to think, but please offer him a lift if you happen to see him out and about as he has probably forgotten where he parked his car or even overlooked the fact that he took it at all.

4. The Good Life Neighbour
: Green Flag

"I USED TO LIKE MY NEIGHBOURS UNTIL THEY PUT A PASSWORD ON THEIR WI-FI." ORIGIN UNKNOWN

Modelling themselves on the 1970s TV series *The Good Life*, they are the Barbara and Tom of suburbia, living on next to nothing by growing their own fruit and vegetables, planted in accordance with the appropriate phases of the moon, keeping chickens and making their own soap and entertainment. Their motto is 'Reuse, recycle, repair'. Their garden furniture is upcycled from old pallets and they call it their shabby chic look. When they tell you their toilet paper is recycled they are not joking.

They differ from the Organic Neighbour in that they have no income and have to barter for everything they can't grow, make, beg, borrow or steal from other neighbours, or they have to go without. They can often be spotted upside down rummaging in the skips behind the village hall after the latest jumble sale or prowling the high street charity shops on a Sunday night, and making off with stuff left by kind people who think their unwanted junk will be sold to help relieve world poverty.

They try to be self-sufficient by selling their excess produce at the gate, or bartering it for toothpaste and chocolate. Transport is either Shanks pony or an uncharacteristically top-of-the-range bicycle bought when they were on the corporate treadmill. Their philosophy extends to their reading matter which must be on sustainably sourced paper. You will be bombarded with earnest conversations about peak oil and the transition movement, which they are trying to get going in the area without much success, and dire predictions of what will happen when the food supplies run out.

Be gentle with them – they are trying to save the planet on your behalf, after all. It is useless to point out that the planet will be here long after humankind is extinct, or that unless he stands at the gate brandishing that murderous-looking scythe of his, he will be trampled underfoot in the stampede to get to his cabbages if the food supplies really do run out. These guys are searching for meaning to their lives and believe wholeheartedly in what they are doing.

On the other hand, as their property deteriorates year by year, the numbers of ramshackle sheds made of scrounged materials increases and the smells become ever more noxious as they experiment with making energy from methane, you realise that they are seriously devaluing your property.

Their electricity supply was cut off long ago and foraging for wood in suburbia is never easy so you may find that this is a fad unlikely to survive a bitterly cold winter. They will reluctantly concede, rejoin the rat race and things will get back to normal. Alternatively, as their house insurance provider has refused to accept a large load of manure as payment for the policy and they use candles (homemade of course) for light, it is just possible that they will accidentally set fire to the place, and maybe yours as well. An anonymous phone call to Environmental Health should improve the situation for you and may make them see sense, sell to the developers looking for a nice suburban brownfield site (in which case you'll have noisy builders next door for months) and decamp to a smallholding in rural Wales.

5. The Hippie Neighbour
: Green Flag

"TURN ON, TUNE IN, DROP OUT." TIMOTHY LEARY

Ah, the hippie. A benign character of middle years who lives in the spirit of the 1960s when life was a great deal simpler. Greeting you with "Peace, man" and its customary digital accompaniment, their long hair is now streaked with grey. They go by the names of Star, Echo or Zen and have called their children Freedom, Ocean and Butterfly. You can recognise their house as the one with a green man sculpture by the front door.

The modern world passes them by as they float through life in their djellabas, tie-dyed kaftans and bell-bottomed jeans, with their flowing locks secured only by a headband. The sound of beaded necklaces heralds their arrival and the pungent scent of patchouli lingers in the air when they've gone. Vanity and sartorial elegance are ignored as they go about in their sandals and socks. To keep a roof over their heads they make salves and offer homeopathic remedies made from herbs, the recipes for which they have gleaned from James Wong's book 'Grow Your Own Drugs'. They sell them at local farmers' markets, alongside twinkly crystals, joss sticks, books on spirituality, new age culture and all things Wicca. They advertise private tarot and palm readings, and those who believe they have the gift will offer themselves as psychic profilers, paranormal investigators and water diviners.

If you get an invitation, go round and marvel at their eclectic and colourful home. Don't turn down the offer of a cuppa – it'll be made with real tea leaves. But when you have finished it, they will snatch it away, swirl the contents three times (anticlockwise) and dramatically turn it upside down onto the table. Then they will examine the remaining contents in the cup and inform you that they are a window onto another world which they can intuitively interpret through the ancient art of tasseomancy. That's tea leaf reading to you and me.

They are still living life in the most environmentally conscious way they can, on or near a ley line if possible, and are great advocates of solar power and geothermal heat pumps, biomass plants, wind turbines and wave farms. However, they are undecided about the clean benefits of nuclear energy bearing in mind the production and use of nuclear weapons, the potential for radioactive contamination and the problems of storing waste for thousands of years while it decays. These days they eat granola and quinoa, reminisce about Woodstock and wax lyrical about Jimi Hendrix, The Grateful Dead and String Cheese. The joke that says they wave their hands in front of their faces when dancing to keep the music out of their eyes still applies.

Modern hippies work for themselves so that they can take the summer off and afford all those festival tickets. They may appear to denigrate capitalism and be anti-materialistic, but the more astute or dodgy have acquired a Volvo estate and deal in antiques, vintage tat, design hippie chic clothing ranges for children or have become exclusive interior designers to well-heeled London boho clients.

They are free spirits. They keep the pagan festivals of Imbolc, Beltane, Lammas and Samhain, and are to be found at the sacred places in between the realms of Earth, Sea and Sky at litha and yule solstices. Nothing fazes them and even death holds no fear as they age and prepare for The Last Great Adventure.

As next door neighbours go, you could do a lot worse. If you shout at them they'll smile benevolently and offer to tune your chakras. Accept the offer – you'll feel a lot better for taking on some of their philosophy of life. Meditation is, after all, a free shower for the mind. Just be wary if you see a laburnum tree or foxgloves amongst their flowerful garden, allegedly planted with bees and butterflies in mind.

6. The Crazy Cat Lady Neighbour
: Green Flag

"The more I see of people, the more I love my cat!" Origin unknown

Once upon a time a little girl was given two kittens and that was the Crazy Cat Lady's starter kit (excuse the pun!). This lady is dedicated to our feline friends and is part of the local cat rescue group, going out at night laden with cages, traps and cat food on an excursion to some derelict factory on an industrial estate where she's had a tip-off that there is a colony of ferals being fed on ham sandwiches. A couple of times a year you'll be asked to look after her clowder of cats while she's off to some exotic island – not for a holiday, you understand, but on a 'snip trip' catching and neutering the strays. When not giving a very good imitation of St Gertrude of Nivelles, the patron saint of cats, our ailurophile can be found at the cat shelter doing some volunteering such as 'befriending' or 'socialising' the inmates, checking out prospective owners' homes, or manning a stall raising money for our beleaguered moggies.

Her garden is the one with the sad little row of headstones where past furry friends have been laid to rest with due ceremony. They are adorned with candles, flowers and plaques with dates and messages saying something about the character of each one. She believes that they are waiting for her and that one day they will all cross the Rainbow Bridge together. You're likely to tread in something cat related as you walk up her gravel path and tap on the door using the lucky black cat door knocker. When she opens the door she'll have a grin like the Cheshire Cat and a tabby draped around her neck. Tea is served from a cat-shaped teapot into cat-themed mugs. But be sure to take a close look at the butter if you are offered a scone or a crumpet – those little striations in the butter exactly match the backward-pointing spikes called papilla on a cat's tongue. There are cats on the tea towels, cat ornaments on the mantelpiece and she wears cat jewellery on her coat. If you're invited to sit down, it will be on a sofa marked by cat-sized indentations, and the cushions will be covered in pictures of cats and moulted fur. Whether you like it or not, several large cats will make a beeline for you, and after a spat between them, the fattest will deign to make a nest on your knee, by turning a circle several times, pumping your flesh with its claws and then settling like a concrete weight and about as easy to shift. If it's feeding time there will be cats on every surface, mewing pathetically, waiting for their tea and trying to trip you up as they mill about your feet. As you leave you start sneezing and spend the rest of the day scratching your newly acquired flea bites. If you are a gardener, cats will love your newly tilled soil and you will often find them digging in your flower beds, preparing to plant a little something of their own.

All her Christmas cards support cat charities and it's easy to buy presents for her because she is delighted with anything that has a cat on it. In return she presents you with a scarf knitted from cat fur collected from their beds and her clothes, or from the aftermath of a cat fight. When a favourite cat dies, she eats some of its fur as she believes that, in this way, they are absorbed into her DNA. The waste collectors dread her bins as they are heavy with used kitty litter.

She loves to talk about her furry friends and enthrals any listener with how many times they have projectile vomited this week. She is a happy soul but worries what will happen to Trixie, Fluffypants and the rest when she can no longer care for them. She swears that she gets a better standard of conversation from her fur babies than from people, and that stroking them keeps her blood pressure low. And please don't call them child substitutes. To her they are much more important than that.

So if you hear a voice in the bushes on a dark night muttering, "Puss, Puss, Puss, here Kitty, Kitty. Come to Mummy", you know who it is. Be compassionate and go and help her look for the monstrous black animal you caught earlier dismembering a mouse in your garden and squirted the hose at. Just don't ever tell her.

7. The Pessimistic Neighbour
: Amber Flag

"Someone said, 'Cheer up, things could be worse.' So I cheered up and, sure enough, things got worse." James C Hagerty

Occasional griping is perfectly normal and we all do it, but the pessimist has turned it into a way of life. This neighbour is permanently expecting difficulties and worries constantly about something – her job, her partner, her kids, other people's kids, the state of the country, the weather, the price of fish, whatever. She sees every day as a worst-case scenario. What will happen if her kids don't get into the right school? Supposing the new teacher is a paedophile? If she lets her kids play in the park, will they be abducted by aliens?

Talking to her for any length of time, with all her negativity and pessimism, can be stressful and leave you feeling tired and depressed. If she is otherwise a good friend and neighbour, then try to reassure her and help her put it all into perspective, maybe over a bottle of wine or two. She may just be having a bad day and all mothers worry about their children. It's part of the job description, after all. Then again, if she has a glass in her hand she will probably complain that it's always half empty.

However, if she's the sort of person who can suck the fun out of your life as well as their own, it's time to think again. Too much exposure to a true pessimist can be a real downer as they count their troubles rather than their blessings. Typical remarks start with something good that has happened to them, immediately qualified with a 'but'. They use the word 'but' a lot.

"I tried that diet but it didn't work for me."

"I went to an interview yesterday but I don't expect to get the job."

"We're planning a BBQ on Saturday but it will probably rain."

"We're going on holiday to Majorca but the hotel won't be as nice as it looks in the brochure."

"I've ordered some clothes online but they won't fit and I'll have to return them."

"I was going to buy one of those items advertised on the TV but I suppose they'll have run out by the time I get there."

They're a martyr to their health and if you say how well they're looking, they reply that there's a virus doing the rounds and they're bound to get it. If you comment on how quickly they sold their car, they'll counter with "Yes, but I had to let it go at a loss". It feels like if it wasn't for bad luck they wouldn't have any luck at all. They don't feel in control of events and believe positive outcomes are outside their control. It's a waste of time to try and persuade them that things will be all right. Be sympathetic when they see so much darkness in the world but refuse to share their view. They have chosen to see life in the negative. Continually expecting misfortune means that they are never disappointed and may even be pleasantly surprised when they have a bit of good luck or something works out well. But of course they will tell you that it won't last.

8. The Optimistic Neighbour
: Green Flag

"OPTIMIST: SOMEONE WHO FIGURES THAT TAKING A STEP BACKWARD AFTER TAKING A STEP FORWARD IS NOT A DISASTER, MORE LIKE A CHA-CHA." ROBERT BRAULT

A rare species this one and on the endangered list. They don't just look for the light at the end of the tunnel – they're the ones with the smile, shining a torch to light the way forward and bringing sustenance and warmth that just might save you from yourself and all that is out to get you. They will tell you that life is full of choices, that brooding is a waste of time and that you can make a positive decision to be happy rather than miserable.

They are genuinely pleased when told of someone's success, talk about their neighbours positively, and won't judge or criticise. If you make a disparaging remark about a neighbour, they will gently remind you of a good quality they have or a generous deed they have done. They put into practice the belief that doing a good deed makes you feel good about yourself. There is a magic about them that you wish you could bottle and sell and hope that just a bit of it will rub off on you.

Are they too good to be true? No matter what happens to them they are perennially looking on the bright side, and make the best of the situation, when the rest of us would be howling, gnashing our teeth and cursing our luck. He's the one who has Reinhold Niebuhr's quote framed and hanging prominently where he can see and read it every day. It goes like this: "God grant me the serenity to accept the things I cannot change, the courage to change the things I can, and the wisdom to know the difference." As a philosophy of life it takes some beating. Believing that everything will work out in the end stops him sweating the small stuff and let's face it, it's all small stuff. Naïve? Maybe. Some would say that he has adopted this approach as a coping strategy to deal with life's problems, but it has its merits. If it works, don't knock it.

Other neighbours can find this attitude irritating. Certainly the constant tuneless rendition of 'Whistle while you work' from *Snow White and the Seven Dwarfs*, 'The Optimist Song' by Gene Hamm, 'A Cockeyed Optimist' from *South Pacific* and 'Always look on the bright side of life' from *Monty Python* can be a bit trying.

The strange thing is that when you get to know them better, you discover that invariably life has been incredibly unfair to them and they have weathered disappointments and setbacks that would have destroyed many others, you included. But they treat it all as part of 'life's rich tapestry'. They regard negative events as not their fault and as isolated flukes that they have no influence over, whatever may happen in the future. They call themselves survivors not victims. They recite positive affirmations to themselves every day. Failure is considered to be an opportunity to start again with the benefit of hindsight. They will tell you that the past has gone and the future is unknowable and today is called the present because it's a gift. They have made a positive decision to be optimistic and consequently their glass is not half-full, it's full to the point of brimming over. They are not an obvious Pollyanna, but take a pragmatic approach to life. We can all learn a lot from watching them and welcoming them into our lives as friends, if we are lucky enough to have them as neighbours.

So, if you want to handle stressful situations better and have a healthier heart and lower the risk of having a stroke, start practising positive thinking today. Be grateful for the good stuff, make peace with the past, forgive, smile often, take responsibility for yourself, stop blaming others and channel envy and jealousy into action.

9. The Loved-Up Neighbours
: Green Flag

"LOVE THY NEIGHBOUR — AND IF HE HAPPENS TO BE TALL, DEBONAIR AND DEVASTATING, IT WILL BE THAT MUCH EASIER." MAE WEST

Now you probably think that I am talking about the young couple who are soooo much in love and lust that they can't take their eyes and hands off each other and who phone and text one another constantly. Face it — you're just jealous! And who wouldn't be? Broad shoulders, slim hips, sexy smile, all his own teeth. Well, just because you're a teeny bit older than she is, give or take a decade (or two), doesn't mean you can't look, does it? You just have to envy their youth and freshness, innocence and trust, childlessness and the freedom to jet off to Florence for the weekend on impulse.

But what you see may be an illusion. Once the thrill of the wedding has worn off, the honeymoon tan faded and the photo album put away, the reality of everyday living together bites. Long working hours, the stresses of life, managing the expectations of each other, parents and in-laws, not to mention the accumulated student and wedding debts, mean that the probability of separation are highest in the first few years of marriage. Those little traits that were once so cute become irritating habits. Gradually one starts to nag, criticise and demand change and the other progressively withdraws to avoid confrontation. Issues remain unresolved and fester as the relationship deteriorates. Then the 'For sale' sign goes up.

And then there's the neighbour who starts off as the Lonely Widower. He's the one who books a singles cruise and comes back not just with a few snaps, a tan and a new taste for some vile and unpronounceable drink, but with a new partner. As holiday souvenirs go this one is a corker. Described as 'bubbly' or 'a real goer', you can see the avaricious look she gives the house, car and neighbourhood as he valiantly struggles to carry her over the threshold. Yup, she's a gold digger, only he just can't see it.

As time goes on she sets about getting the house 'how she wants it', spending vast quantities of his money. You've seen the way she eyes up the workmen, and shows altogether too much cleavage. Strangely, she never seems to have any of her family over and is evasive about them when asked. However, his children start coming round much more often now they see their inheritance morphing into new sofas, a hot tub and a 60" plasma TV, and the staid family run-around is traded in for something sleek, noisy and expensive. He confides in you that she phones him twenty times a day just to say

"Hi". You know she's checking up on her investment. When she's with him she's clingy and never leaves his side in case someone else moves in on him. With the windows open or through the paper-thin walls you can hear them at it like rabbits, but when you mention it, they just laugh.

Be patient – it's unlikely to last. While over-60s marriages are on the up, second marriages last considerably less time than first ones. Once she gets tired of waiting on him, washing his less-than-savoury underwear, nights disturbed by snoring, fidgeting and farting and the endless Viagra-induced sex, she'll be off back to her book club and sleeping alone. By that time he'll be bored of salad, showering every day and not being allowed to watch the cricket on TV, and will be relieved to see the back of her. And could that possibly have been him you saw sneaking into the STD clinic?

10. The Needy Neighbour
: RED FLAG

"IF YOU ALLOW PEOPLE TO MAKE MORE
WITHDRAWALS THAN DEPOSITS IN YOUR LIFE, YOU
WILL BE OUT OF BALANCE AND IN THE NEGATIVE.
KNOW WHEN TO CLOSE THE ACCOUNT."
CHRISTIE WILLIAMS

They phone, they call round, they interrupt you when you're gardening, and they stop you when you're going out. Any time they see you, you know that you're in for a session of having to listen to a long litany of them whining that they are bored, tired and other meaningless rubbish. They will ask for favours, request help with a job that doesn't take two, require bucketloads of praise for everything they do, however trivial, and be very demanding of your time. They may even ask for money. They are uninterested in you and yours, wanting only to talk about themselves (an increasingly common and very irritating problem generally these days, don't you find?). If you try to excuse yourself on the basis of lack of time, an urgent appointment, a desperate need for the toilet or that you do not have what they want (they will have already established that you do), they use a clever device in order to prolong the conversation – they keep asking you questions. They know you are too polite to ignore them and they turn the conversation back to their favourite topic: themselves. They just can't be alone. And they have an uncanny ability to know when you are lying and will manipulate you to make you feel guilty and give them what they want – your time. And they seem to expect you to do every little job for them. "As you're putting out your bins, would you do mine, to save me doing it?", "If you're already going to take that stuff to the tip, you won't mind taking some of mine, will you?", "You can cut my lawn as well; it won't take you long", they wheedle. If they try to flatter you by saying, "You're so much better at wallpapering than I am", counter it with the riposte "Well then, you obviously need more practice!" which should put them neatly back in their box. Don't be conned by their appeal to show them "just one more time" how to put those stripes in the grass, or change a lightbulb, or you'll find you've finished the job for them – again.

At first you will put on a polite smile and wave a greeting whenever you see them coming, but all too soon you find that your heart sinks at the sight of them. Compassion fatigue has set in. Your expression quickly becomes a fixed grimace and you start changing your behaviour to avoid them. A symptom that you have a Needy Neighbour is when you find yourself gardening in the dark and checking that the coast is clear before sprinting to your car, pretending deafness to their calls for attention, and do a Le Mans-style start in your urgency to get away from them.

Trying to solve their problems by giving them advice gleaned from your years of experience and knowledge is so not what they want. They don't want to solve anything. All they want is your sympathy and attention – lots of it. But you will not be wasting your time in giving them advice in an earnest and cheerful way as they will eventually realise that you are not playing their game. At this point they can become quite affronted and may tell you in a haughty tone that they've heard enough and you may go. Take it as your permission to leave, and make a run for it! They will drop you if they can find someone more attuned to their particular brand of self-pity.

These neighbours are selfish in not valuing other people's time and commitments. You can never satisfy them no matter what you do. It will never be enough. If you allow it, they will become dependent on you. They have given countless other neighbours the same treatment but they have managed to escape their clutches and are delighted to see that their Needy Neighbour has latched on to someone else – you. Tolerating them is not the answer as they will eventually feel like an emotional ball and chain. Recognise the problem and learn to say "No". Don't feel sorry for them – they will see it as an act of weakness. Get caller identification on your phone, plug their name and number into it and don't pick up when they call. If you accidentally pick up and it's them, say, "You're breaking up", "My battery is running out" or "I'm just going into a tunnel" and hang up. Remember, the last excuse will not work if they have rung you at home, unless you live on a narrow boat. Programme your phone for a 'rescue ring' so that you can slyly slip your hand in your pocket and activate it. Explain that the call is urgent and you have to go. Install a spyhole in your entrance doors, front and back. Lock the gate to the back garden. Put blinds up at the windows so they can't see you're at home. Clear the junk out of the garage and shut the car in there when you're home or hide it round the corner. If they know your number plate, get a false set made up to cover them.

It'll probably get worse before it gets better, but you can be sure that they will eventually take the hint, although they can be notoriously thick-skinned. The relief and feeling of freedom will be well worth the effort.

11. The Lonely Neighbour
: Green/Amber Flag

> "PEOPLE ARE LONELY BECAUSE THEY
> BUILD WALLS INSTEAD OF BRIDGES."
> JOSEPH FORT NEWTON

There are many reasons why these neighbours have become lonely. It may be through bereavement of a partner, being housebound because of poor health or even losing the daily routine due to redundancy or retirement. In winter there are fewer opportunities to get out and socialise or have a chat over the fence. They once had a busy and fulfilling life and now, mostly for reasons outside their control, feel useless and sidelined. Most are proud of their independence – they just feel a bit isolated sometimes. Do not confuse them with the Needy Neighbour. They can be alone and indeed spend most of their time on their own and they don't want to intrude or be a nuisance.

You can subdivide them into the Sad Lonely (green flag) and the more Devious Lonely (amber flag). The Sad Lonely will use pretexts to engage you in conversation.

They'll take in your parcels when you're out and then hold them hostage so that you have to go round and collect them. When you get there it will not be in immediate evidence. "Come in," they say cheerily, "I know I put it somewhere," and keep you talking until eventually you manage to persuade them to go off and find it. They use the subterfuge of being nice and helpful because they are desperate to be liked and are pathetically grateful for any crumbs of companionship that are offered. They are adept at bartering for your time, be it with a 'spare' chocolate cake they have baked or by flattery in asking for your opinion on what colour they should paint the bathroom. An invitation to join your family for Christmas lunch will send them into paroxysms of handwringing and genuflection. They won't be the last to leave – after all they don't want to outstay their welcome and they fervently hope that they will be invited again next year. They want to leave you with a feeling that you have done a good deed so you'll ask them again. Including them in large gatherings introduces them to others and dilutes the onus on you.

You may think that you have nothing in common with them and they only want to talk about the old days. But wait. Get them onto a subject such as their experiences in the war, their working life as an auctioneer or their favourite hobby and you might find yourself enjoying their company. Set boundaries of time by saying that you will come back soon to hear the next episode (and mean it) and they will be satisfied.

The second type is the Devious Lonely and they are

much more cunning. Apparent acts of kindness mask an agenda of their own. This character doesn't give a fig about your time and couldn't care less about your busy life – they just want your company, when they want it, for as long as they want it and will stoop to lies if necessary to get it. For example, they might ask your partner to pop over as they are on their own and can't get the boiler to light. They might then offer him a drink, as a reward for his kindness, and go on to suggest that he inspect her husband's new car or some state of the art gadget – anything to get him to stay and keep her company. They decide that you must come over right now and use the pool for a swim as it is such a lovely day, which you accept with alacrity. When you get there, you find that this is not the quick dip that you were looking forward to. Before you can get anywhere near the water you are expected to drink copious amounts of alcohol and entertain them. Some people may find this neighbourly, but others will realise that the lure of cooling off was just an excuse to assuage their loneliness. Next time, politely refuse on the pretext that you're busy washing the dog. Or start digging your own pool.

For many, it is possible to feel lonelier in a room full of people than they have ever felt on their own.

12. The Borrower Neighbour
: RED FLAG

> "MY NEIGHBOUR ASKED IF HE COULD USE MY
> LAWNMOWER AND I TOLD HIM HE COULD, SO LONG
> AS HE DIDN'T TAKE IT OUT OF MY GARDEN."
> ERIC MORECAMBE

Feel you're being used by this neighbour? You're not alone.

There are some neighbours who treat your stuff as communal property and your place as the local hire shop with one exception – they don't have to pay. Hedge trimmers, chain saws, pressure washers, trailers, roof racks, ladders, drills – you name it, they want it. And always at the same time you need it. How do they manage it?

At first, in the spirit of neighbourliness, and because they caught you off guard, you reluctantly hand over your pristine piece of property, telling yourself it is good to help out others. When it comes back, months later and after repeated requests for its return, it's dirty, chipped, dented or broken. If you point this out they will say it was like that when they got it, shrug their shoulders or dismiss your pernicketiness with a laugh and tell you not to be so anal, that tools are meant to be used. And you just have been.

How can you stop yourself being taken advantage of? Well, now forewarned, you can arm yourself with a number of excuses so that you are ready for them. Finding a way of saying "No" without causing offence is tricky. Unless you couldn't care less, and are not bothered about reprisals, in which case just tell them to "F★★★ off." Tell them that you have borrowed the item from someone else. This can be ineffective if the loan is for a job that will only take a minute or two. To avoid bad feeling with a neighbour who is otherwise pleasant enough, you could offer to do it for them. But be careful that you are not making a rod for your own back. Not only have they got the job done, but someone else has done it for them!

You could tell them that it doesn't seem to be working properly, and they wouldn't want to have their fingers cut off due to a faulty guard now, would they? Turn down any overtures to help repair it – say it's under guarantee and has to go back to the manufacturer in Finland and the post takes for ever. They will either buy their own or hit on someone else. If you feel that you can't or don't want to refuse, set a deadline, for example by saying that you have plans to use it tomorrow. Make sure your stuff is indelibly labelled with your name so they can't palm you off with some inferior version. Borrow something of theirs (preferably worth more than yours), hold it to ransom against your own stuff and insist on a joint handover. Tell them you've just loaned the item they want to someone else (difficult if you have it in your hands at that moment but not impossible if you're brazen about it). For regular borrowers of the same item, say that yours is getting older and you don't want to put any additional wear and tear on it, and tactfully suggest that perhaps it's time they bought their own.

You can sanctimoniously remind them of the old adage 'Neither a borrower nor a lender be' and there is a good chance that they will go off in a huff, plotting vengeance. Sure enough, a month later there they are with the most expensive super-duper gizmo for which you have a desperate need. Hoist by your own petard, you are prevented from asking to borrow it for fear of being quoted the selfsame saying, accompanied by a supercilious smirk. Solution: stomp off to the nearest hire shop. They have the latest professional quality models at affordable prices and there's no maintenance. Even better, when another neighbour spots it and asks to borrow it, you can genuinely say that it isn't yours to lend. Or, if it is, lie.

13. The Hypochondriac Neighbour
: Amber Flag

"I Told You I Was Ill."
Spike Milligan's Headstone

Do you know a neighbour who fits this description? Someone who worries excessively about being ill? Who wipes the rim of a mug the instant you've finished? Who cleans obsessively? Who won't let their children play in the garden in case they contract some germ or other? Have hysterics if the kids come home with dirty hands or clothes? They may take their blood pressure several times a day, and find that the more they take it the higher it gets. They see normal variations in bowel movements as signs of cancer, mild skin infections as necrotising fasciitis and indigestion as heart failure. They have their GP on speed dial.

They snivel their way through the winter convinced they are dying. It's no good telling them that they can't possibly have swine flu, foot and mouth disease or Rocky Mountain spotted fever. To them the symptoms match precisely (they've looked them up on the internet) and the problem is very real and upsetting. Dealing with them can be frustrating but the best approach, if you are not a medical person, is to be patient and listen to their concerns, giving them your support to stop them getting panicky or depressed. Sometimes just saying, "You'll be OK," in a concerned and sympathetic way, rather than being dismissive, will calm them. However, even reassurance from a doctor may not fully convince them that they are not ill. "Doctors make mistakes. They miss things," they bleat. They know because they read about misdiagnoses in the papers every day.

Diverting their attention may work, but they may feel that you are not taking them seriously and are sceptical about their afflictions, which can increase their feelings of isolation. What they need is help to get to the bottom of their issues, be they real or displaced. A good neighbour goes with them to the doctor, waits while tests are done, enquires as to when the results are due, goes with them to hear the outcome and tells them what good news it is when they come back normal. Please resist the impulse to say, "I told you so."

This should suffice for a while unless the negative results of diagnostic evaluations send them off seeking a 2nd or 3rd opinion. Or they come rushing in, gabbling about a news item on TV reporting that a rare strain of influenza has undergone an antigenic shift, no one is immune and a pandemic is imminent. Guess who has all the symptoms? And it starts all over again.

If you suggest that they can help themselves get healthier by walking, taking up hobbies and practising meditation rather than medication, they won't listen. It's far easier for them to pop a few pills every day – they have great faith in the medical efficacy of prescription-only drugs. After all, if the doctor says you have to take them then you must be ill, mustn't you? Mention the well-known side effects of their tablets and they'll develop those too, even if they didn't have them before you alluded to them. And if they get diagnosed as a hypochondriac and prescribed medication, they'll worry about the side effects of that. Forgetting to go to a Hypochondriacs Anonymous meeting must mean they are in the early stages of dementia.

Whatever happens there are things you should not say to a hypochondriac. "That sounds serious," is one. "It's all in your head," is another because they'll think they've got a brain tumour. Saying, "My cousin had the same thing and had to have a very big operation," should be avoided, unless you want them to have an apoplectic fit or a panic attack. Make sure you have a paper bag to hand if you deliberately cause them to start hyperventilating.

And never, ever say, "It sounds like you might be a hypochondriac," even if they are.

14. The Medical Expert Neighbour
: Amber/Red Flag

"I could have gone to medical school, I said.
Except for the math and stuff."
Maryjanice Davidson

If you happen to mention a mild symptom you have that doesn't seem to be clearing up, their eyes go into ocular overdrive. He's had it, knows someone with it, his best friend's aunt's hairdresser's dog died from it and he is the fount of all knowledge about it. He then takes great delight in telling you the cause, treatment and prognosis. No matter how minor your problem is, he will diagnose some rare and incurable disease that he has read about in his library of medical textbooks which are fifty years old, picked up from the charity shop and hopelessly out of date. He will quiz you on other common symptoms that may or may not be related, nodding sagely as you confirm or deny their presence. There follows a lecture and a sharp intake of breath, a pause and "That can be nasty, that" while shaking his head, thereby writing you off.

Attempting to avoid any mention of ailments won't work either, as he'll scrutinise you as soon as he sees you and then comment on a small mark on your hand (you just had toast and Marmite), or the dark circles under your eyes (you simply have a hangover) or the fact that you are limping (your new shoes rub). Take control of the situation. If you can't prove him wrong (by taking off your shoe and showing him the blister), say you've had it looked at and it's quite normal, even if you haven't and have lain awake all night worrying about it (hence the dark circles) and are on your way to the doctor in a complete panic right this minute. If you dismiss his fears of your imminent demise, he will shrug and mutter about it being your funeral and how he was only trying to be helpful. Just be aware that he will gossip about it to another neighbour, the jungle drums will relay it round the neighbourhood and before you know it your best friend is ringing up and asking how long you've got.

Even worse are the well-meaning comments from neighbours when they discover that you are genuinely seriously ill. You're already in shock from the news, feeling depressed and frightened as to what the future holds. They'll bombard you with contradictory advice and stories about a friend who had the same thing, drank nettle juice for a month and was completely cured without any medical intervention whatsoever. You can explain that, while a lot of people think the same way as they do, it's not appropriate in your case, that you and your doctor have a treatment plan and you are happy with it. You could say that you'll mention their suggestions at your next appointment, which should mollify them somewhat if they think their ideas are being taken up with the medical fraternity. Don't be too hard on them – kind neighbours want to say something because they feel so helpless in the situation, and proffer their experiences and anecdotes with the intention of giving you some comfort, not realising that it doesn't. Those who've been through something similar will listen and propose some practical assistance – picking the kids up from school, looking after them to give you a break, walking the dog, cleaning the house (she'll love you for this one!). They ask, "How can I help?" rather than the throw away "If you need help you know where I am" however well-meant. They give you a hug without saying anything. They declare that you're going to be all right, that they'll be there for you, and how sorry they are that you have to go through all this. Then they produce cake and alcohol at 10am and help you consume it, all the while berating the unfairness of life.

Staving off the vultures who feed on bad news can be done with a bright smile and the information that you are "getting better every day", even if you feel like s*** and can't even keep water down. These lowlife neighbours are insecure and suffering from low self-esteem. Hearing about other people's adversity makes them feel better about their unhappy lives. Alerting others to your plight draws attention to themselves, and the more melodramatic they can make the situation sound, the better. Secretly they may even feel that you deserve your bad luck or it serves you right for some reason. Don't put up with those who take pleasure in your misfortune. You don't need these people in your life, especially now. Avoid. Instead, you could introduce them to your Hypochondriac Neighbour – they should have some interesting conversations.

15. The Free-Range Parenting Neighbours
: Green Flag

> "A LOT OF PARENTS WILL DO ANYTHING FOR
> THEIR KIDS EXCEPT LET THEM BE THEMSELVES."
> BANKSY

They believe in a hands-off approach to parenting, allowing their children to learn by experience without boundaries. Few activities are organised, there is no TV in the house and the brood is encouraged to have fun and discover things for themselves. Unfortunately, this means that they have plenty of time to get into mischief – and they do. They roam unsupervised, climb (and fall out of) trees, cut their own hair, attempt to dye the cat with Loo Bloo, eat every different type of plant to see if it's poisonous and generally run wild. They'll dismantle your washing line to make a zip wire from their bedroom window, see how long they can scream at full volume and camp in the garden in a thunderstorm. Their youngest asks if you've got any baking soda. Thinking he wants to do some cooking, you innocently ask what he is going to make. "A volcano," he replies. His latest project is a treehouse made from anything he can find, hammered together with 6" nails, and he wants a chemistry set for Christmas.

Now depending on your view of this method of child rearing, you might see this as either liberating or irresponsible. You broach Every Parent's Nightmare Scenario in an attempt to get them to rein their unruly progeny in – "Suppose he didn't come home?" – but these neighbours stick to their philosophy and counter your attempt at provoking guilt by stating sanctimoniously that their job might be to protect their children, but their career is to teach them how to protect themselves. They've read the statistics and think that overprotectiveness is dangerous and tantamount to child abuse, and the risk of abduction is vastly over stated. Touché. At this point their son arrives in floods of tears and blood, waving the knife he was attempting to sharpen. Now he'll be more careful they exclaim, because if you teach him knives are dangerous, he'll be timid and afraid. You think he'll be scarred for life.

They're interesting children when in their own home but keep them out of yours or else they'll climb inside the grandfather clock to see how it works, pull the dog's tail to see if it comes off and decapitate the roses to make perfume.

Those who micromanage their children's lives 24/7 just don't get it. They wouldn't allow their children to walk to school (shock-horror!) or play at other children's homes for fear of them being fed something to which they might be allergic or catch a glimpse of something unsuitable on a laptop. But they're the ones who end up with risk-averse children who need intensive support as adults, and you'll find them still living in the parental home in their 30s. Years of intervening to help their children so they never know failure has resulted in bubble-wrapped wimps who grow up timid and unable to handle difficult scenarios. Meanwhile, those free-range kids have familiarised themselves with disappointment, can deal with being let down, have learnt from their mistakes, can think through the problems, can come up with solutions and, even if they fail, can regroup and try again. They will persevere until they succeed and have gained confidence through the experiences along the way. If they survive long enough, that is.

Secretly, you're envious. Their children are smart and happy, independent and empowered. How wonderful your childhood would have been if your paranoid and unadventurous parents had let you be more independent instead of trying to wrap you in cotton wool because they were so scared to let you go and find your wings. These kids certainly have more fun than you ever had. If you believe it shouldn't be allowed, you could make an anonymous tip-off to social services. Alternatively, it's never too late: there's a whole world out there, kid. Go find!

16. The Downsizing Neighbours
: Green Flag

"In the end, three things matter: how much you loved, how gently you lived and how gracefully you let go of things not meant for you." Buddha

Pity them. They've sold their enormous country pile with the swimming pool, tennis court and secluded acres with the intention of downsizing and giving each of their offspring money for a deposit on a flat. Those same offspring who have been whinging for years about how lucky their baby boomer parents were to have had it so easy (forgetting about the recessions and inflation at 25%, no mobile phones or Sky movies). Who dropped frequent heavy hints about how they would never manage to own their own place, and who left newspapers open at advertisements for the new retirement villages. Who wandered about on their infrequent visits, covetously eyeing up their childhood home and silently speculating about how much equity there was in the place. Faced with the unpalatable alternative of multi-generation living and horrified at the mere thought of accommodating their offspring, partners and assorted children, step-children, dogs, trampolines and furniture, the parents finally succumb and sell to an up-and-coming young footballer and his wannabe wife, who have informed them of their plans to "modernise" their charming old home. Now they have downsized to your neighbourhood.

At first they relish their new found freedom and the resultant reduction in house work and maintenance. They go on cruises to the Galapagos Islands and spend three months touring Australasia. But the novelty wears off. Their oversized furniture doesn't fit the smaller and fewer rooms in their new abode, and the feel is dark and cluttered. It's like watching a size 18 woman trying to squeeze into a size 10 pair of jeans – you just know it isn't going to look pretty. They miss their wonderful old place with its character and space. The offspring don't come and stay because there aren't enough spare bedrooms, so the only time they can all be together is at Christmas and only if they rent a huge house at their expense. They become nostalgic for the good old days, but there is no going back. There's nothing to do. They realise that they were too young to downsize. They have lost their views, status, friends, lovely old neighbours, staff and sense of community. They stare into each other's eyes and trip over each other in the restricted square footage. They are bored.

Now that they have their inheritance in cash, the offspring have decided that, instead of putting a deposit on a flat and settling down to domestic bliss and wage slavery, they have packed in their day jobs and become beach bums in Goa, or ski bunnies in Courchevel or, if they're feeling altruistic, rehabilitating cute, furry animals in one of the more salubrious places in South America – nothing too taxing, you understand, and definitely no slumming it – with no plans to return until the money runs out. And guess where they'll pitch up at the end of it – broke, homeless, jobless and devoid of any intention of actually working for a living. Yep, you guessed it – your neighbour's tiny downsize. "It won't be for long," they promise, "Just until I can get something more suited to me." Unfortunately, they have neither the talent nor the qualifications for their dream job of TV presenter, top model, sports journalist, reality star, full time blogger or pop idol and rail against the world and their parents for forcing them to do that degree in law or accountancy. When the downsizers eventually kick them and their slothful friend out of their home (oh, yes, they'll bring an even more idle mate back with them) they'll find a squat and get a job in a call centre.

Let this be a salutary lesson to anyone thinking of downsizing.

17. The Organiser Neighbour
: AMBER FLAG

"WHEN STRANGERS START ACTING LIKE NEIGHBOURS, COMMUNITIES ARE REINVIGORATED."
RALPH NADER

Love 'em or hate 'em, every neighbourhood needs one of these! They mean well and the villages, towns and suburbs of the country, with their amateur dramatic productions, their jumble sales, street parties and summer fêtes, would be lost if it were not for this person. She is always busybusybusy, but is the first one to organise a petition, get a protest group started, or set up a fundraising effort for some local worthy cause. If somewhere is threatened with closure, a community project needs funds, the church roof needs replacing, a petition requires 10,000 signatures… she's yer man, so to speak.

If someone voices a concern about parking near schools, overgrown ponds, litter or toads being run over on their way back to said pond to breed, she will spring into action. When she gets going there is no stopping her. She is just bristling with ideas. The woman's mind feels like a browser with ninety-nine pages open – all at the same time. Her mind jumps about all over the place as she keeps all the plates in the air and spinning energetically.

She quickly assumes responsibility for the cause, elects herself chief spokesperson and equips herself with a clipboard, name badge ('Hi! I'm your leader!') and a list. She likes lists and has lots of them, and you will find your name already on several of them. She smiles a lot and is friendly, outgoing and chatty. But beware, because once she gets her teeth into you she is the proverbial Rottweiler.

She has the ability to charm, bully, manipulate or barter – whatever is necessary – to get what she wants. You will find yourself being nagged, bribed or sweet-talked, as appropriate, into helping at the garden open day, baking a dozen cakes, writing a letter to your MP to voice your opinion on the planned development on green belt land or being an ugly sister in the Christmas production. She will catch you at a weak moment (or drunk, or both) and cajole you in a wheedling voice, quite unlike her usual far from dulcet tones, how she is sure you would just love to knock up some banners for the 'Save the whale' march. When she greets you with "I'm so glad I've caught you" you know you're in trouble. And she is not above playing one person off against another. "Well, of course, so-and-so has already said they'd do such-and-such," she'll proclaim, which you suspect is a whopping fib but don't want to be outdone by so-and-so who is a neighbour you can't stand.

She wears you down with flattery, "It just wouldn't be the same without you. You were SO good as the dead body in the last production!" She will interrupt your weak protestations and your meek objections of, "But, but, but…" and ride roughshod over any feeble excuses such as, "I'm having an operation that day." Watching her work a room is an object lesson in not letting anything get in the way. There is an unstoppable momentum about her that is admirable. You could try the "Which part of the word 'No' do you not understand?" retort but it won't work. She just won't take "No" for an answer. She'll just make you feel guilty by looking at you in the same way a puppy would if you kicked it. You'll capitulate anyway so what's the point? The downcast look of deep hurt will immediately be replaced by a beaming smile, and a confident "Marvellous! I knew you would" and another tick is added to the clipboard with a flourish. Face it; you've been well and truly bested as usual. Bow to the inevitable. You know you'll enjoy the experience, even if it does turn out to be the back end of the pantomime cow.

18. The Aspiring Author Neighbour
: Amber Flag

"A BOOK MAY BE COMPARED TO YOUR NEIGHBOUR:
IF IT BE TOO GOOD, IT CANNOT LAST TOO LONG;
IF BAD, YOU CANNOT GET RID OF IT TOO EARLY."
RUPERT BROOKE

Her lavatory is papered with rejection slips from every publishing house and agent in the country. Most of them are wonderfully pithy and abominably rude: "…devoid of interest…", "…absurd and unbelievable fantasy…", "…not enough talent to compel me to read as far as the second paragraph…", "…a waste of the recycled paper it is written on…" and so on and so on. The words "mediocre", "dull", "rambling" and "clumsy" abound. One suggests, "If you dream of being a writer, dream on."

She scribbles into the wee small hours, consoling herself that 'Zen and the Art of Motorcycle Maintenance' was rejected 121 times. When she introduces herself, she hands you a business card with her name, website address and a description of herself as 'Author'. She's on all the social media sites and spends far too much time twitter-tattling away. She denies that she is procrastinating in order to evade having to actually write something. Once in the distant past she pulled strings to get a novel published with a newly established indie publisher who confused her name with that of a popular writer and whom she never corrected. It languished at number 6,967,319 on Amazon, never troubling the bestseller lists, and you picked up a copy for 1p just to see what it was like. The single review is spot on. "How does this rubbish get published?" it queries. Then adds, "Must have been written on the back of an envelope in ten minutes. No, I'm wrong – make that five."

'Never give up' is her motto and she has the skin of a rhinoceros. She needs it. Convinced the next one is going to be her entrée into the literary glitterati, she practises her acceptance speech for the Man Booker and Baileys Women's prizes (amongst others) and what she will say to the gushing interviewers on breakfast television when she is famous. She regularly practises her signature which she dreams of one day using at book signings, where queues of devoted fans will wait to get an autographed copy of her latest bestseller.

Whenever she is speaking to you she suddenly whips out a notebook and mutters, "I can use that," or "That's a good idea!" If she is listening to a conversation you are having with someone else, you will see her eyes go glassy as she works out how to use some snippet in her latest project, as her heroine battles against the odds. And never, ever tell her your great original idea for a novel or she'll steal it and present it as her own. If she ever does get into print, even a short story in the local church newsletter, you will find yourself or something you told her used unashamedly and without acknowledgement or with your name minimally altered. If you don't want a thinly disguised version of yourself appearing in one of her books, avoid her, otherwise all the neighbours will quickly identify you as the protagonist and you will be the butt of some gossip. After all, if it's in print it must be true, mustn't it?

If you don't want to hurt their feelings, there are a number of things you should never say, such as, "How many have you sold?" or "Have you won any prizes?" or "How big was the advance?" or "Is your publisher one of the big five?"

If you happen to be a well-known published author who writes under a pseudonym, don't let on or she'll be grilling you for ideas on how to get into print and begging you to introduce her to your agent or read her manuscript and give her your feedback. If you're not, use her as inspiration. She would make such a good central character in a comic novel, so go and buy yourself a notebook and prime your laptop in readiness to write that masterpiece you've always meant to. Oh, and don't forget to order some of those business cards with your name and 'Author' proudly printed on them.

19. The Entrepreneurial Neighbour
: Amber Flag

> "Entrepreneurs are simply those who understand that there is little difference between obstacle and opportunity and are able to turn both to their advantage."
> Niccolo Machiavelli

The Entrepreneurial Neighbour ranges on a continuum that includes Spivs, Inventors and Wannabe Big Shots. The Spiv avoids anything remotely like honest work, lives by his wits and has his phone surgically attached to his ear. The Inventor beavers away in his shed in his spare time looking for perfect solutions to all those tedious little problems. He tells you he's working on a self-cleaning plughole, a car that teaches you to drive, a pencil sharpener that removes the wood evenly, a microwave fridge, an unhackable password and a computer that tells you what's wrong with it, in words that you can understand. The Wannabe Big Shot has never had a good idea in his life but knows one when he hears it, promptly steals it from its originator and markets it under his own name.

The Spiv knows just where to get that new laptop or Rolex watch you want or a pirate DVD of the latest must-see film at a knockdown price, because that's probably what it is – knocked off. You can hear him in the garden wheeling and dealing on his mobile. He has no visible means of financial support yet drives a top of the range beamer and has a holiday home in Malaga. His other vehicle is a non-descript van which he backs up to his garage so you can't see what he is loading or unloading. And he does this a lot, mostly in the dark, with help from some very dubious looking characters. He calls himself a businessman and can be quite charming, but is not the sort of person to cross. He is very generous to you at Christmas, which you are aware is a bribe but can't resist, and he knows you won't shop him because you are now in receipt of stolen goods, and an accessory after the fact.

Your Inventor has applied numerous times to Dragons' Den to show off his weird and wonderful gadgets, but always fails to prove that they work or that anyone would need it or buy it. He was particularly proud of his ideas for duster boots for dogs and cats, umbrellas for chickens and a tie that doubled as a hand warmer. He couldn't understand why there were no takers.

And then there's your Wannabe Big Shot who is desperate to be rich and famous. He'll come up with some obscure idea, and with some clever PR and plenty of spin he'll convince those with money that it is a goer. He'll take any and all opportunities to promote himself and extract dosh from anyone gullible enough to buy into the business supposedly to 'invest' and 'grow the market', despite the accounts showing that he has never turned a profit and the venture is an unsustainable business model. Closer analysis of his sales pitch, some research on the internet and a bit of common sense of the 'If it sounds too good to be true it almost certainly is' variety, will lead you to the conclusion that he is building a pyramid scheme, possibly even a Ponzi scheme, and that it is likely to come crashing down in the not too distant future. By then he will have absconded with the proceeds to Panama (chosen for its lack of any successful extraditions to Britain) leaving hordes of angry creditors banging on his door. Or your door if he has fraudulently used your address instead of his own. The business will collapse owing squillions, the investors will never recoup their losses, and your ex-neighbour has succeeded in his ambitions, by achieving wealth at other people's expense.

The moral of this tale is don't buy or invest in your Entrepreneurial Neighbour if you can't tell your Richard Bransons from your Bernie Madoffs. And don't tell anybody about your brilliant idea if you haven't patented it, registered its domain name on every continent, are launching next day, or have got a watertight, signed contract with distributors.

20. The Teaser Neighbour
: Red Flag

> "Thou shalt not covet thy neighbour's wife,
> for there are plenty of others."
> Otto Rank

Got one of these neighbours? You'll know if you have. She's young, has long, lustrous come-to-bed hair which she flicks provocatively, is size zero with 38DD boobs which she flaunts at every opportunity, dresses like an expensive whore, looks at your partner from under her perfectly groomed eyelashes in a suggestive way, but barely acknowledges you. In short, she's hot and she knows it. Meanwhile your partner is mesmerised with lust, and spends the next half-hour incoherent because he's drooling so much.

If she's talking to you (which means there isn't a man in the vicinity) she can seem quite normal, except that her eyes immediately dart to any sign of movement that might mean a man has walked into her field of view. Then you're dispensed with. Her eyes lock onto her target like a missile and you watch incredulous as this woman turns all coy and silly. It's a fascinating transformation to observe – rather like a cobra that has swallowed a chameleon. She will have cultivated a laugh that sounds sexy to the male ear but irritating to everyone else, accompanied by the Lady Di lowering of the head and looking up (a submissive gesture that appeals to men), and knows exactly the effect sucking on an ice cube has on the average guy.

Summer is her favourite time, when her skin turns golden and she can wear shorts that show off her endless legs. Funny that at this time of the year she suffers from so much clumsiness and often drops things in front of your partner and, before he can gallantly pick it up for her, bends down so she can expose her bum cheeks or cleavage to him. It reminds you of one of those monkeys on heat.

She likes to sunbathe topless even though the garden is overlooked on all sides or she has workmen in, and has the most interesting array of washing on the line, mostly skimpy in red and black with apertures in unusual places.

In the evenings she usually pulls the blind in her bedroom but leaves the light on so your teenage son can have his own private strip show in silhouette. You have tactfully pointed out that you and half the street can see into her bathroom, which means that anyone who wants to can see her having a shower. "Oh, really?" she giggles. Your son thinks telling her is spoiling his fun. What he doesn't tell you is that he has discovered how often he can orgasm in a day. You could say she's given him a neighborgasm.

The only book she has read is 'Fifty Shades of Grey' which she ostentatiously carries around with her. If your partner remarks on this at all, it is to wonder why she wants to paint anything grey and moans about all these different tones where once there would only have been one – grey – and it was undercoat.

By the time she has got to forty there will have been three husbands and the looks are starting to fade. I say fade, but the tan is as vibrant as ever, although now of the spray variety. The skin on her arms is taking on the same texture as distressed leather – flabby with lots of wrinkles. She might look like a teenager from behind and dresses like one too, but definitely looks the wrong side of fifty from the front. Her makeup is heavier and the Botox appointments are more frequent. The ability to laugh or even smile has become restricted and she now looks like a hyena in rictus. You can hear her coming with her jingling jewellery, tippy-tappy heels (not so often these days as the bunions are getting very painful) and girly giggle so unbecoming in the middle aged.

If she's young you've got nothing to worry about – your guy is much too old and not rich enough for her. As she gets older, she's less fussy, but by now he's probably past it or has his eye on younger totty anyway.

21. The Mysterious Neighbour
: Green Flag

"LOVE IS BLIND – BUT NOT THE NEIGHBOURS."
MEXICAN PROVERB

There is a house in most neighbourhoods where nothing ever happens. The house doesn't stand out from its neighbours. Everything is neutral, grey, drab. There's no house name and no number proudly displayed on a pretty plaque brought back from a family holiday in Spain. There are nets at every window and at night the curtains are so tightly drawn, not a chink of light escapes. No brightly painted front door or exuberant window boxes in summer. No tree lights merrily twinkling in the window at Christmas. It's almost as if everything about the house is done so that it fades into the background and goes unnoticed and unremarked upon. No dogs barking, no children running about, no doors slamming, or raised voices – nothing. It's as if no one lives there or it is empty for long periods. But there is sometimes a car in the driveway and you can see the occasional light on, so someone lives there, but who?

The house is not posh enough for it to be a celebrity, and the car disappears during the day so you suppose that someone goes to work. If you're the sort of person who shrugs and gets on with their own life then the house and its occupants will quickly be forgotten and ignored. After all, you've got enough to do and worry about, and if they want to be mysterious and private, then so be it. But for some neighbours, mostly those with too much time on their hands, their curiosity will be aroused and their eyes, ears and imagination will be working overtime for the slightest hint of information as to who the Mysterious Neighbours are. But they are doomed to disappointment for no more clues are apparent and they finally have to admit defeat.

The evidence is indeed slim. No one has seen any visitors and the postman confirms that he has never delivered any mail to the house. Not even the curtain-twitching neighbour, who misses nothing, knows who they are or what they do or where they go or even how many people live there. The front garden is tidy but no one can recall seeing anyone mowing the lawn or trimming the hedge. Rumours abound that they are vampires who only go out in the dark. Or ghosts.

Eventually some neighbour plucks up the courage or the cheek to call on a pretext. They have to call round nine times before they find anyone in residence. They report back their findings. A man answered the door. Medium height, medium build, no distinguishing features. He declined to buy any raffle tickets (their idea to find out their name) and didn't seem to know the area when told it was for a local community project. He turned down a request from another intrepid neighbour to witness a signature on an application form on the grounds that his writing was illegible and he hadn't got a pen and was late for an appointment. All done politely so no one could take offence but the rebuff was clear.

In the end, even the most inquisitive give up when faced with a mystery that cannot be solved, and the house and its occupants remain a puzzle and an enigma. The subject comes up from time to time at the school gate or over the garden fence or when a new neighbour moves in and asks, "Who lives in that house?" and you all look at each other and shrug and then someone moves the conversation on to something more interesting.

22. The Secretive Neighbour
: Amber Flag

"How much time he saves who does not look to
see what his neighbour says or does or thinks."
MARCUS AURELIUS

The Secretive Neighbour is different from the Mysterious Neighbour, if only because you see the Secretive Neighbour around a lot and everyone knows who they are and what they do. Or at least they think they do. It's their behaviour that differentiates them.

When you knock on their door, you have to wait while bolts are drawn back and keys turned in multiple locks. A chain prevents the door from opening fully, and they peer out at you through the crack. Talking to them is hard work as they can be taciturn to the point of rudeness and getting basic information of any kind out of them is like trying to nail a jelly to a wall. Questions are often ignored and any answers elicited are vague and unsatisfactory.

Seeing them in town you might attract their attention with a cheery wave, but they don't respond or seem confused and shifty when you stop them to check that it isn't a case of mistaken identity. They don't seem to want to chat and make an excuse to end the conversation. They walk off and then disappear down a side alley or quickly melt into the crowd.

Secretive Neighbours are overly guarded about what they tell you and won't disclose details of their life, their likes and dislikes or a funny story that you would normally share with friends, and this prevents a relationship with these neighbours from being established. It's as if they don't understand the rules of how relationships develop – if I tell you something about me, you have to tell me something about you. Normally, if you reveal something personal about yourself to someone and they don't respond in kind then you can feel unfairly exposed or snubbed. Telling a self-deprecating tale about yourself shows that you are comfortable with having flaws, that it is OK not being perfect and that you are unlikely to criticise them for not being perfect either. But they give nothing away.

Maybe they're just shy and they feel uncomfortable talking about themselves. Perhaps they feel vulnerable opening up to other people and revealing their true selves because they're worried that you will find them wanting. So rather than being rejected, they reject you. Maybe they have a history that they don't want you to know about in case you judge them or spread gossip about them, and possibly past events with previous neighbours have reinforced this view.

Many of your other neighbours think they're just

paranoid and weird. The irony is that their policy can be self-defeating because secretiveness attracts curiosity and heightens interest. Just what is it that they're so secretive about? What are they hiding? Then the rumour mill gets to work. Every sighting becomes charged with significance. Someone discloses that they caught them peering under all the cars in the road and claimed they were just searching for their cat when no one had ever seen a cat in their garden. What were they really looking for? Even the most minor sighting gets magnified out of proportion, and is repeated, embellished and analysed way beyond its real, and probably innocent, meaning. When they vanish overnight, the story on the bush telegraph is that they were in the witness protection scheme. But is it true or is this just more rumour mongering or misinformation?

23. The Lowering-the-Tone Neighbour : Amber/Red Flag

"KEEPING UP WITH THE JONESES WAS A FULL TIME JOB WITH MY MOTHER AND FATHER. IT WAS NOT UNTIL MANY YEARS LATER WHEN I LIVED ALONE THAT I REALISED HOW MUCH CHEAPER IT WAS TO DRAG THE JONESES DOWN TO MY LEVEL."

QUENTIN CRISP

We all dread finding ourselves living next door to this blot on the landscape and there's usually one in every street. This is not a neighbour, this is a neighsore – the eyesore of the street. The house sticks out from its neighbours with their tidy gardens and co-ordinated colour schemes. The weeds are growing through the paving and the seeds are blowing towards your garden. The hedge is so huge that it has encroached on your territory and you scratch your legs trying to squeeze past it down your driveway. As you were doing this a tile slithered off their roof and narrowly missed your car. Any trees have reached 30' and have become light sinks, blocking out the sun and making your rooms dark even in the summer. Their drainpipes have come away from the walls and, if you live in a semi, there are ominous damp patches starting to appear on your ceilings. When others put out their wheelie bins on the correct day, and obediently take them in after the rubbish has been collected, this lot leave their bins out all the time and they seem to be permanently overflowing with takeaway cartons and used nappies. The neighbourhood foxes see it as foodie central and tip them over to get at the contents, making even more of a mess. It's difficult to tell the occupants apart as they all have bellies that protrude further than their boobs/moobs, barely covered by stained T-shirts with rude words printed on them. The males in the household, however, can be identified by the belches and the necessity to scratch their arses and adjust their genitals in full public view. The inside is every bit as bad as the outside and it's the sort of place where, on the rare occasions you have been brave enough to venture inside, you have to wash the soap, if you can find any, before using it.

Something must be done. You've already chained your wheelie bins to the fence to stop your neighbours claiming they were theirs and hijacking them when theirs are full, and to prevent them stealing yours and leaving you with their broken one. They strenuously denied theft when you went and reclaimed it, even though you pointed out that you had painted your house number on it in very large numerals. The trouble is, if you report them to the council, they'll know it was you. Taking matters into your own hands seems to be the only answer. Now you could be neighbourly and offer to repair the downpipes at your expense. After all it is in your own interests: the valley between your roofs is full of rotten leaves, you've noticed a musty smell in your house, there's a nasty water stain spreading on the party wall, you have a peculiar cough which you can't get rid of and you have spotted mushrooms growing out of your bedroom ceiling. As for the garden, you could invest in a gallon of Glyphosate and a sprayer or a flame-thrower. The latter can be extremely effective, if a trifle indiscriminate. And remember that spewing fire may make you rather conspicuous whereas the former option can be carried out under cover of darkness and is as effective, if a tad slower.

A variation on this neighbour is the Occasional-Lowering-the-Tone Neighbour who appears quite normal for most of the year until it comes to special occasions such as Christmas, the World Cup or a royal wedding. Then decorum is thrown out of the window. Otherwise normally sane people do some very odd things at these times and none of it is in any way, shape or form, in good taste. England flags appear on the front of the building, which wouldn't be so bad if they were of the usual size and material – after all, it's nice to show that you are patriotic. But no – they're 20' high and done in indelible red and white paint directly onto the brickwork. Face ditto. T-shirt ditto. Car ditto. Dog ditto. Definitely verging on jingoism. Then there's Christmas. From November onward, your neighbour spends hours each day fine-tuning the annual display. Santa emerges from the chimney, eight reindeer in all their glory and jingle bells cavort across the roof plus sleigh, and penguins, igloos, snowmen and assorted seasonal paraphernalia form a tableau in the garden, liberally sprinkled with sticky white goo from a snow blowing machine. Illuminated icicles drip ominously from the gutters. People come from miles around to ogle at it and secretly to pity the neighbours, of which you, of course, are one. Hordes of spectators gather each evening for the big festive switch on, causing a major traffic hazard for miles around, and other neighbour's lights to flicker portentously. There are reports in the local paper that the astronauts in the International Space Station can see it. It feels like you are in some kind of zoo. The illuminated star you put up over your front door, which you thought rather tasteful and subtle, is dwarfed into insignificance by this extravaganza next door. Furthermore, the perpetrators insist on dressing up as elves and ho ho ho-ing amongst the visitors, encouraging them to donate to some dubious charity no one has ever heard of. They get very upset if anyone calls it tawdry. "All we're trying to do is make people happy and give something back to the community," they say, as they carefully step over the spaghetti of wires and cables disgorging from the house. However, in the murky rain of a December day it looks like they're having a garage sale on behalf of the costume department of the local amateur dramatic society, and there are rumours that the postman is going to sue them after he was knocked unconscious by an antler that fell on him from one of the reindeer.

What to do? If you complain then you appear to be a Scrooge, especially as they're collecting money for charity from the gawpers oohing and aahing at Rudolph's nose flashing on and off to Paul McCartney singing 'Simply Having a Wonderful Christmas Time'. Christmas is meant to spread good will to all men and women, after all.

You've heard a rumour that next year they're planning a big screen showing the film *White Christmas* on a continuous loop. Wait until the rest of the neighbours hear. Best idea is to go away for Christmas – Las Vegas can be nice at this time of year.

24. The Sporting Neighbour
: Green Flag

"For what do we live, but to make sport for our neighbours, and laugh at them in our turn?" Jane Austen

You know the ones – looking all bright eyed and bushy tailed at 7.30am on a Sunday and off for a run en famille, while you're bleary eyed and slopping around in your old washed-out dressing gown. It's seen better days and was once pristine white but you accidentally put it in the washing machine with your son's rugby kit including the jockstrap. You meant to get rid of it but it has sentimental value as you bought it to have your first baby, who is now a strapping 15-year-old. Just looking at their immaculate white Lycra and brand new top-of-the-range running shoes reminds you yet again that the only place for it is the bin. You watch them jogging off down the road in his and hers matching outfits, pedometers strapped to legs, heart monitors beeping and calorie counters whizzing away. They carry bottles of organic, spring-fed water and look slim, tanned and fit. You resolve to go back to the gym even though everyone else there makes it all look effortless while you're sweating and breathless just trying to get on the machines. On their return from their 10-mile warm-up, they regale you with the details of their heart rate, calories burnt, and number of steps taken, all recorded on their sleek, hypoallergenic, water-resistant wristband trackers, which they tell you are essential on their path to health and fitness. They've completed nine London marathons, bettering their time on each occasion.

Holiday time sees them loading the car with every conceivable aid to exertion including surfboards, bikes, canoes and ski carriers. On their return they entertain you with hair-raising tales of climbing, potholing and coasteering.

They are the only parents to positively look forward to school sports day and are very competitive in the Mums' and Dads' races. They do not believe in the old adage that "it's the taking part that counts, not the winning". If they don't win, they sulk for days and up the training regime for next year.

Their sitting room boasts a cabinet full of naff looking trophies of figures swinging clubs (prize for most seals?), bats with nets (fly swatting?), and balls of every size and shape (no comment!). They gleefully tell you about the parachute jump they are doing for charity and ask if you would like to join them. You decline with a quickly improvised and garbled story about some old sporting injury preventing you from launching yourself out of a plane for fun, much as you would like to, while simultaneously putting your hand on your back and dramatically wincing to emphasise the point. The truth of it is that you are terrified at the thought of it and nothing on Earth would get you up in that plane. Even if it was on fire they would have to prise your fingers off whatever you grabbed to prevent falling thousands of feet into terrifying nothingness.

While these Sporting Neighbours are keen to participate, there's another neighbour in this category who doesn't take part, but lives to watch sport and is obsessed about it. He is of course The Sports Fan. It is no coincidence that the word fan is short for fanatic. He is sometimes selective in his choice – usually football – and even more selective as to whom he supports. He wanted to be a footballer when he was younger but gave up when it was pointed out that he was too slow, lacked skills, had no talent, smoked and weighed too much. Apart from that he thought he was the next Ronaldo. He always buys the latest strip to wear to show his allegiance, even if his team comes out with a new one every week or two, and goes to every match, home, away, friendly or not so friendly. He can tell you what the score was, the scorer and who they were playing on any match day, and where the team finished in the league every year since it started in 1892. Naturally, he is a season ticket holder and has been sitting in the same seat since he was 5 years old, when his dad used to take him as his dad did before that, and collects every team programme ever printed. He is fiercely loyal even when his team are relegated, which is most seasons. He cried for a week when they were knocked out of the FA cup in the first round. His social life revolves around them and he talks about nothing else. When they finally drop out of the leagues altogether, the club goes bankrupt and the ground is sold to developers, he is devastated and is reduced to watching the likes of Arsenal and Man Utd on TV. But it just isn't the same and nor is he.

25. The Lecherous Neighbour
: Red Flag

"DIRTY OLD MAN: NOUN, INFORMAL. A MATURE OR ELDERLY MAN WITH LEWD OR OBSCENE PREOCCUPATIONS." ORIGINS 1930S.

The first thing you do when you go to a neighbour's party is scan the room surreptitiously for this character. Sure enough, there he is talking to a woman and standing close to her so that he can look down her cleavage. You'd go over and rescue her if she were a friend, but she's your Pain in the Arse Neighbour, so you smile smugly and head for the kitchen. But you have to stay vigilant or else you'll suddenly feel heavy breathing on your neck and there he is leering over your shoulder so he can look down *your* cleavage. This time it's your Pain in the Arse Neighbour's turn to smile smugly. Dressing so that your embonpoint is not visibly on display does not discourage him. Quite the opposite. He'll sidle up to you at the buffet table or bar and reach across you so that he 'accidentally' brushes your boobs. He is very good at violating your personal space so avoid narrow corridors without checking where he is. He is liable to use the restricted space to make a rude joke and pat you on the derrière to reinforce the double entendre. Make sure you lock the toilet door if you need to use it, especially if he's hovering in the vicinity. If it doesn't have a lock, find a dark corner at the bottom of the garden and make sure you're not followed. Don't accept his offer to get you a drink just to get rid of him. He's liable to find you and hand you what looks like an innocuous glass of Diet Pepsi but chances are he's spiked it with vodka. Or Rohypnol.

When you reject his clumsy and totally unwanted advances, be prepared to hear the word "Frigid" sotto voce. Don't bother dignifying it with a reply, however snappy, it'll only give him some encouragement which you certainly don't need. Sticks and stones after all. Let him believe it and he'll move on. His wife, however, is convinced that you are after him and will give you filthy glances all evening as if it is all your fault and you are trying to steal him away. This is probably some bizarre sex game they play between them. Married couples of this type go in for things like that, especially at parties.

He's invited you to use his swimming pool any time you want, but hints that it is skinny dipping only. Mutter "In your dreams" and decline by saying that you're allergic to the chemicals. He'll be disappointed and you'll be off the hook. Unfortunately, he likes to go skinny dipping himself, especially when you're cleaning the upstairs windows. He has a habit of wandering round the house naked and you have witnessed the unpleasant sight of him standing at the window fondling his bollocks just as you were walking past. Funny coincidence, that. Make sure you take a good look and laugh. He ogles your 13-year-old daughter who is 5'8" and looks 25, but don't worry. She's likely to be more streetwise than you are, and quite capable of giving him the finger and ignoring him. They are often just looking for a reaction, so don't show you're angry or frightened. Try to appear bored or unconcerned, even if you can feel your heart hammering, and they may lose interest and leave you alone.

Once, the postman delivered to your house a hardcore porn magazine in a plain brown envelope addressed to him and you opened it by mistake without looking at the addressee. Your instincts told you he's a pervert and a creep and now you have the evidence. If bits of your washing start disappearing from the line, especially underwear, and you find him standing outside your window staring in, check him out on the Sex Offenders Register. An anonymous tip-off to the Neighbourhood Watch committee may also be in order. With a bit of luck, you'll hear the wailing of sirens at 5.30 one morning as police cars screech to a stop outside his house, officers batter the door down and come out a few hours later carrying several heavy black bin bags, followed by your neighbour with a blanket over his head to hide his identity from the press photographers. Now who tipped them off, I wonder? One thing you can be sure of is that they're not there to help him with his recycling.

And if he tells you he's bought a camera drone for Christmas, you can be confident that he'll ignore the laws that state they cannot be used close to people other than the person in charge. Collecting pictures of people who can be identified from them is contrary to the Data Protection Act. Get yourself an air rifle and start practising.

26. The Hunting, Shooting, Fishing Neighbour
: Amber Flag

> "Until he extends the circle of his compassion to all living things, man will not himself find peace." Albert Schweitzer

If you live in the countryside, you may have one of these as a neighbour. They believe that only lesser beings have to work for a living, and treat the staff like dirt, even though the cleaner has a PhD in astrophysics. They don't value education because no one in the family has ever been bright enough to be accepted at any university. Their son only scraped a pass in GCSE woodwork because the game keeper helped them carve a pigeon. Why would they need further education when they were brought up to take over the estate and someone else is paid to manage it while they enjoy life? They are too thick to realise that the estate manager has been ripping them off for years.

In times past they had servants living in, but they

can't get anyone these days, at least not for what they are prepared to pay or the way they treat them and order them around. They baulk at shelling out the minimum wage, believing that domestics should consider themselves lucky to be scrubbing their floors and be grateful. They make them eat their lunch outside (which the staff has to bring it with them as nothing is provided) even in the harshest of winters, begrudging them time off the job. No cuppa, homemade soup or generous slice of cake and a friendly chat in a kitchen warmed by a vast AGA. Let them drink from the horse trough.

Their type is ruddy faced and grossly overweight and they like eating large roasts of red meat, preferably cooked to the point of cremation with vegetables boiled for hours until they are mush, and nursery puddings, such as spotted dick and custard. The meat is likely to be something they have killed themselves, as they think murdering birds and animals for pleasure is great fun, and are incapable of thinking through the ethics. Get a dozen of them together and you have a new definition of 12-bore. They teach their children and grandchildren to shoot from an early age and are then surprised when they grow up to be sadists and wife beaters.

They stomp about looking as if they are going to a fancy dress party, wearing old fashioned tweed jackets, flat caps and baggy knickerbockers tucked into long, thick woollen socks. If they're genuine old money, these will be tattered and limp, smell of wet dogs and mothballs and be patched and worn since they have been handed down through the generations. If they're nouveau riche, desperately trying to look the part and be accepted by the country set, their apparel will be new, clean and stiff and they'll look distinctly uncomfortable, constantly fidgeting and scratching. The women favour fur and feathers, and other bits of dismembered beasts such as hunt saboteurs, which is why they haven't been invited to open the village fête since the year they were pelted with tomatoes by the vegans manning the 'Rehoming Battery Hens' stall.

They are accompanied on walks by hordes of dopey, drooling Labradors and yappy, uncontrollable terriers and if you stray off the footpath or stop for a picnic on their land, they'll tick you off in a loud pompous voice. As they have a shotgun tucked under their arm, you are inclined to defer. They'll tell you it's broken, but it looks like it works. He remembers a time when drinking and driving were acceptable, the village bobby turned a blind eye to the local squire and he could sneak back from a lock-in at the pub in his 4x4. He's been caught and banned from driving twice but it doesn't stop him. As soon as he goes out in the car, you can quite clearly see that he has a mobile phone in his hand and he is shouting into it while steering an erratic course down the road. If you feel inclined, you could always shop him to Crimestoppers, and you might even get a financial reward for performing a civic duty.

27. The Vegan Neighbour
: Green Flag

"MY BODY WILL NOT BE A TOMB FOR OTHER CREATURES." LEONARDO DA VINCI

'All meat is murder' is their philosophy and they like to preach it to anyone who'll listen. As the joke goes, "What do you call a militant vegan? Lactose intolerant." They believe that they exist to spread love and compassion for animals into all areas of life. Consequently, they feed their menagerie of pets on meat-free food, which means that they are always sneaking in through your cat flap and stealing your pet's food. You haven't got the heart to tell them when they go on about how healthy their pets are on a vegan diet. Tiddles isn't letting on either, as he sits in the sun insouciantly washing his fur with essence of chicken. How they stop them catching and eating mice and birds is anyone's guess or maybe the cats have learnt not to bring their presents home. Neither have you confessed that the trifle you gave them when they came round for dinner had gelatine in it as you forgot to get the meat-free alternative.

Vegan women get very hacked off when told that they'll have to change their diet when they get pregnant. First, they hate it when you assume that they would want children. Not everyone has the same yearning to procreate and increase the number of screaming kids on an already overcrowded planet. Second, they can lecture you on the facts that a vegan diet can be just as healthy as a non-vegan one and it is not necessary to become a meat-eater just because you're expecting. They're likely to be a lot more clued up about what makes a balanced diet than you are. People think eating meat makes them as strong as an ox. They're forgetting that the ox got there by eating grass.

They don't buy or use products made from or tested on animals, such as the contraceptive pill (they will extoll the virtues of vegan condoms) and have a sign saying 'Meat-Free Zone' in the front window. Their leisure time is spent protesting against fast food chains and abattoirs, and you can't help but notice, as they openly flaunt it, that they have '269' branded (not tattooed) on their arm. Ouch! This shows their solidarity with a calf rescued from slaughter whose ear tag was the number 269. They like to spread the vegan word so can be found at festivals and fairs. They're the ones who pelted the Hunting, Shooting, Fishing Neighbour with tomatoes at the village fête.

When you go round, check your attire. No leather shoes or belts which might offend. Please don't say the same tired old lines such as, "This would be great with meat balls!" They've heard it all before and the joke has worn thin. And check out their washing line – the sheets will be made of pulped and spun wood fibre from trees specially grown in Scandinavia.

Not all vegans go about telling everyone that they are vegans. Most just get on with their lives. So if they do happen to mention it, save the smart remarks and the jokes about plants being living things too. There is a whole world of difference between picking an apple and killing a living creature. Never offer them a bacon sandwich and only have a BBQ when the wind isn't blowing in their direction.

Those who don't eat meat will have the last laugh because it has been shown that they have a lower mortality rate. And if they finally tire of chick peas and tofu and revert to being carnivorous, you could always tease them by telling them that they have lost their veginity.

28. The Whinger Neighbour
: Red Flag

"If you keep telling the same sad, small story, you will keep living the same sad, small life." Jean Houston

You get home from work tired and stressed and the doorbell goes before you have even taken off your coat. They have heard you come home and have rushed straight round (they were probably listening and lying in wait for your return) because they have something to complain about and they want an audience for their diatribe. It could be something totally trivial or it might be a bigger issue, but, rest assured, it will be about them. Everything is seen as a threat, an inconvenience or a nuisance, and they take it as a personal affront. It may or may not involve you directly. If the electricity goes off, they come around in a flap complaining that they have a freezer full of food and it's all going to spoil and they won't be able to cook dinner. For some obscure reason this seems to be partly your fault and you must phone the electricity company immediately and get them reconnected. You patiently point out that you are also cut off, gasping for a cuppa, have the family coming home for supper shortly and it's just one of those things – there's always the chippie. As they have already reported the problem to the electricity company, there is nothing you can do and you patiently tell them that you expect it is being repaired as you speak. While it is flattering to believe you have some influence, you doubt whether a phone call from you will make any difference. Hopefully they'll go off placated and the power will come back on, just as you predicted. Not that you'll get any credit or, perish the thought, thanks.

Next time it will be because a visitor to your house has parked their car an inch too far across their access. Not that it has blocked them in or inconvenienced them in any way, but it has trespassed onto their property and violated their rights. Then, a van delivering a parcel to your house accelerates away far too fast and goes through a puddle splashing their car. This is patently your fault again and you must bring the delivery company to task. "Did you get the registration number?" you enquire, not that you have any intention of doing anything about it but are simply trying to appease them. "No," they reply. Your patience is wearing a bit thin by this time so you point out with exaggerated patience that the parcel was delivered by a distribution company, not the manufacturers, and as the problem is theirs they should make the complaint. Off they go in a huff, with mutterings about not taking them seriously.

They complain when you have a gathering and that

you're making too much noise. Sitting in your own garden, during normal daylight hours and talking and laughing with friends is clearly a crime.

When you speak to them, they can't simply comment on something, make small talk or exchange pleasantries about the weather as most neighbours do. You get a monologue about their health, their other half, Government policies, how expensive food is… and always in the negative. They whinge and whine about their favourite topics (a very limited list), and bring the same subjects up again and again whenever they see you. It is so depressing, not to say mind-numbingly tedious. You can always try saying, "Well, anyway must be going," or make an effort to distract them by changing the subject, but make sure you have a good selection of topics ready because they are adept at bringing the conversation back to what they want to talk about.

A neighbour of yours frequently wastes half an hour of your time complaining about how much work they have to do, how busy they are and that there just isn't enough time to do everything, his boss is crap and he just doesn't know how to get his work done. You have exhausted all the usual suggestions like "Why don't you…", "Have you tried…" and he has given you a dozen superfluous and usually irrelevant reasons why it wouldn't work for him. He catches you yet again when you are having a bad day. You are long past feeling any sympathy with his situation, compassion fatigue having set in a long time ago. When you can get a word in to interrupt his tirade against the world, suggest he spends less time whinging and simply gets on with it. "You can either have the problem or you can work out the solution. Think how much time you'll save," you can tell him in no uncertain terms. Be prepared for the shocked silence which will follow. Needless to say, he will never speak to you again, which is fine with you as you won't have to listen to him going on and on and on and not being prepared to do anything about it. But you will notice that he simply starts all over again with another neighbour, and it will amuse you to watch her body language as she fidgets and shuffles her feet, glancing round for an excuse to escape, just as you once did.

Want to know how to have as little to do with Whinger Neighbours as possible? Get a spyhole for your door and check who it is before opening it. Make sure you get caller ID on your landline and program their numbers into your mobile so you can cut them off. Learn their routine and make sure you don't cross paths. If you have to have them round, make sure it's only to larger gatherings, and ply them with alcohol. With a bit of luck they'll pass out on the sofa. A trick that might work in some cases is to listen to the usual litany of grievances for a while (preferably without yawning) and then (and this is the tricky bit) say with as much genuine sympathy as you can muster, "Goodness me, that sounds dreadful for you. I just can't imagine how you cope with all those problems." The moaner is supposed to say something along the lines of "Well, I suppose it isn't all bad," or words to that effect. Basically, you're acknowledging that it is a big problem for them and you appear to be taking their suffering seriously. But if you don't get the tone of voice right so that it is sincere (and let's face it, this is a tall order), it will just sound sarcastic and may make matters worse if they think you are making fun of them. But do you care?

29. The Brand Label Neighbour
: Amber Flag

> "I push every day against forces that say
> you have to go faster, be more effective,
> be more productive, you have to constantly
> outdo yourself, you have to constantly
> outdo your neighbour – all of the stuff
> that creates an incredibly productive
> society, but also a very neurotic one."
> ELIZABETH GILBERT

Mildly irritating, they want to know exactly what you have bought when you come home with any shopping. Everything is scrutinised and pronounced upon. If it doesn't pass muster, she tells you what you should have bought. If you tell your Brand Label Neighbour about your new watch, she'll become terribly excited. "Is it a Gucci? Is it a Rolex?" she'll squeak. Her disappointment will be apparent when you show her the offending article. If it isn't hideously expensive, she doesn't want to know. She will wave her own overpriced, top-of-the-range timepiece at you and, with a completely straight face, tell you that a portion of the proceeds from that particular model has gone towards saving Tasmanian Tigers from extinction. You don't like to point out that Tasmanian Tigers became extinct in 1936 when the last surviving specimen died of hypothermia after being locked out of its sleeping quarters in a zoo.

You have no idea how she keeps up with the latest trends which extend to every area of her life. She is a fashion victim, seriously high maintenance and a sucker for that horrible expression, 'this year's must-have accessory'. She's quick to identify what is going to be the next consumer craze. She's gone through pilates and Zumba and Insanity and is now into something even more extreme. Even her car has to be the swankiest colour. As long as yours starts and goes, you couldn't care less what colour it is. She is into status decorating and each time you go round to her place she has the colour charts out and tells you that they are revamping but won't describe it in any colour you can recognise and relate to. She'll talk bafflingly about some bizarre and uninformative names of colours such as Silent Air or Sculpture or Mosquito Bite or Cracked or something that sounds more like a cocktail – Frozen Fire – or a nasty disease – Fustanella (a modern Greek man's kilt, do keep up), so you have no idea whether it could be light or dark, bright or subtle. If she asks your advice (unlikely, I know), just tell her that her taste is so much more imaginative than yours, and she'll nod in agreement and buy another dozen sample pots of some barely indistinguishable shade of white. Of course, the colour she especially wanted was Obselete but when she tried to order it, they told her that the company didn't make it anymore, which she told them was a pity because it went with everything.

When you tell her how pretty her outfit is she'll tell you in hushed tones, with furtive glances around to ensure she is not overheard, that it's the oldest thing in her wardrobe and it is two years old. Two years old! You'd better not mention that you have stuff going back twenty years which you wear regularly, and that when she complimented you on your vintage look, it was just what you have always worn. Jeans have to be the latest designer label and on trend with the right cut, style and finish, the correct shade of blue, black or grey and she'll examine the stitches with an eagle eye, to see if they are long or short and whether there are enough or too many of them. Apparently pockets should be diagonally angled flap button without too much moustache (nope, me neither). To have patchwork or not? Who knows? High waist or low? The rips and frays have to be in the right place and of the right length and amount of wear. Tired and worn out looking? Tick. Stonewashed? OK. Flared or baggy? Who cares? Well, you can always try to bluff it out and say you have heard on the grapevine that these are next season's must-haves, even if they are your old 1980s 501s that you found down the back of the wardrobe and are amazed you can still get into.

Her nails used to be long, square and sport exotic

nail art but she quickly realised that this was considered tacky. (In her world there's a fine line between trendy and tacky. A lot depends on which celebrity started the look, probably by accident when it was the first thing they found on the floor after a one-night stand and with a hangover, but got caught by the paparazzi on the way out.) Holidays are taken in the tourist fleshpots of Puerto Banus, Barbados, Dubai or Florida with the other philistines – aesthetes and bohemians like you go to Puglia, the Aeolian Islands or one of the pueblos blancos such as Gaucin, which she's never heard of.

She can tell her Stella McCartney's from her Phoebe Philo's and knows what a fashion faux pas is. (You tried to get one, but no one seemed to know what you were talking about and gave you some very funny looks.) She has to be seen at all the 'right' places – Henley, Ascot, Glyndebourne, Cowdray and Chelsea (the flower show not the football ground) although she is blissfully unaware of the dress codes and can't understand why she was denied access to the Royal Enclosure for showing a bare midriff. She was thrown out of the Steward's Enclosure at Henley and told, "The intention is to maintain the atmosphere of an English garden party, not a club night on Ibiza" and ruined a very expensive pair of Manolos treading-in at the polo. Christmas is a real nightmare for her as she chases all over trying to get her spoiled brats the latest absolutely essential Disney toy, because they must be the first to have it and there is an expectation that Santa will bring it for them. She knows what tantrums will follow if she isn't successful and usually ends up buying it from the touts on eBay, who were astute enough to hoover up the entire stock in September. She ends up paying three times the recommended retail price, but considers it well worth it.

But there are some tricks which can even fool her. If it's fashionable then the chances are that someone, somewhere has copied it. Fakes can be acquired for all sorts of merchandise and nothing will impress her more than a (fake) Rolex. Just make sure you get more than one as the gold tends to wear off the fakes rather quickly and she'll want to examine it frequently to check. If she knows her onions, she'll be aware that the magnification of the date is smaller on a fake than on the genuine article, a real Rolex has no misspellings and the engraving is always perfect. If she insists that she can hear it ticking, you have been caught out because she knows that the real McCoy is virtually silent.

If you can't be arsed to keep abreast of all the latest whims, she'll write you off as an old fogey which will save you ducking behind the hedge in embarrassment when you see her coming while wearing your usual attire of baggy leggings and granny slippers, with chipped nails and your roots showing.

30. The Noisy Neighbour
: Red Flag

"Nothing makes you more tolerant of a neighbour's noisy party than being there."
FRANKLIN P JONES

These are the ones we all dread and are the most common cause of complaints between neighbours. My guess is that some of you, dear readers, will have turned to this page before any other! Type 'Noisy Neighbours' into a search engine – and you may already have had the need to do this – and you'll get thousands of hits. Noisy Neighbours cause sleep deprivation and they have been known to drive people to murder.

There are three sorts of noise: occasional, frequent and constant. If you're a curmudgeonly old sod who hasn't been invited to the one party that the neighbours have had in 10 years and the guests are laughing and slamming car doors as they are leaving at midnight on a Saturday, get over it as it's unlikely to be repeated on a regular basis. And if the next door neighbour whistles 'When the Saints go marching in' every time

Southampton play, try to distract him if it bothers you, especially if they beat your team yet again, causing them to be relegated. Strimmers, lawn mowers, chain saws, leaf blowers, DIY and building work have all come in for criticism, but most are short lived, happen during daylight or within reasonable working hours and just have to be tolerated in a close community.

Noises you are most likely to be bothered by include:

1. Shouting, swearing and rowing – who has the energy for this at 2am?
2. Dogs barking – the owners are probably out, which is why the dogs are barking. Your neighbour will vehemently deny that they do it because when they are at home, the dogs don't bark.
3. Children screaming/kicking balls against someone's wall – kids will be kids.
4. Noisy sex – do they want half the street knowing what they do, how often and for how long?
5. Parties/radio/TV/music practice – hopefully little Araminta will improve on her violin but why does any sane parent buy their offspring a drum kit?
6. Shoes tapping on wooden or tiled floors – the trend for removing carpets has exacerbated this problem.
7. Revving cars/motorbikes – anti-social, guys. And stop removing the silencer: it's illegal.

You get the picture. These can be of particular disturbance to those who work night shifts, and who are trying to sleep during the day. Alternatively, it may be workers coming home late or leaving early to do shift work who are causing the noise, albeit inadvertently. But let's face it, Noisy Neighbours are not known for their consideration towards others or they wouldn't be the nuisance that they are in the first place. If you recognise yourself here, please have some thought for the neighbours!

Supposing a new neighbour moves into the flat next to yours. Unfortunately, he likes clocks, especially those of the chiming and cuckoo variety, and hangs several on your party wall. He swears he never hears them when they strike on the hour (and sometimes the half-hour and the quarter and three-quarter) but he must be stone deaf as the cacophony is ear-splitting. It gets so that you become very agitated as the chiming times approach. After some negotiation and, finally, a tactfully worded letter from your solicitor, he agrees to take them off the party wall and silence them all overnight, which saves your sanity and quite possibly criminal damage or an assassination.

There are good earplugs and noise-cancelling headphones on the market, or you could look into insulating your house if the noise is persistent. Sleeping pills are an option, if you can dissolve them in something so they don't notice. Are they breaking the law? Yes, it's a good bet that they are. But before you go round there with your baseball bat, stop and assess the situation. Your neighbour may be unaware that there is a problem so be polite, explain the situation while sticking to the facts and suggest a resolution or a compromise. If you are told to

"F★★★ off" and are considering all the best ways of doing away with them, ponder the thought "Are they worth my spending the next ten years in jail?" Start plotting as to how you'll get your own back instead. You'll find the end result sooooo much more satisfying. Report them to the council and rest assured that the authorities are not allowed to say who reported them, although if you have been the one knocking on the door at 1am in your jim-jams they are going to have a fair idea.

31. The Hoarder Neighbour
: Red Flag

"THE MORE THINGS YOU OWN, THE MORE THEY OWN YOU." ORIGIN UNKNOWN

Excessive hoarding is the compulsion to collect stuff along with the inability to get rid of anything. We all collect things that should have been consigned to the bin years ago – your 'Progress Prize' from nursery school, the dress you wore to your prom that you can't get into anymore, a lucky pair of socks, pebbles from the beach in Ibiza where you got off with the holiday rep in 1996 – that sort of thing. But this is hoarding on a grand scale, stockpiling of useless, broken rubbish including old newspapers, clothes, egg boxes, plastic bags, books and junk of all kinds. Although it may be of no use to anyone, nothing is thrown away, because to hoarders, none of the stuff is trash. They may even hoard rotting food.

Is it that he (and it is more usually a he) is too lazy to clean up? No, not at all. He can be such a perfectionist that he believes that, if he started to sort it all out, he might miss something or do it incorrectly. Discarding triggers anxiety so he doesn't throw anything away in order to avoid the stress. When it gets to the stage that he can't sit down for all the piles, he simply moves the stuff into the bath. When there isn't room in the house anymore, and he is shuffling about in narrow corridors between the stacks, he piles it up in the garden. It's more about the fear of throwing something away than about hoarding per se. Eventually hoarders become isolated because they're too embarrassed to have people come round, and there is no room for them to sit down if they did. The conditions in which they live become unsanitary as they can't wash due to all the treasures amassed in the shower. The kitchen is virtually inaccessible and bills remain unopened amongst years of accumulated mail.

If you have a hoarder as a neighbour and the situation has deteriorated to the extent that there is a risk of fire or the spread of disease from rodents or vermin, then someone has to step in to help. Often reality programmes on TV depict hoarders as prisoners, trapped in their own homes, with irate neighbours frightened of the effect it is having on their property values. But wading in and offering to clear the lot will only increase this neighbour's feelings that everyone is against him, that he is going to lose everything and be left with nothing. He feels safe surrounded by his possessions and has intense emotional attachment to them. He may even give human characteristics to some of the inanimate objects. He would suffer considerable grief at the prospect of them being taken away and disposed of and could feel so threatened that he turns violent, so be careful.

The first step might be to contact the hoarder's close relatives because he is never going to seek help himself. Hoarders simply don't recognise that there is a problem, which is part of the disorder. But if all they do is take some of the stuff away, the hoarder may feel an intolerable emptiness as the root cause has not been dealt with and they will simply begin collecting all over again. Failing that, the only solution is to get in touch with mental health services. The clutter is just a symptom of a much more serious psychological problem, and professional help is called for.

Cognitive behaviour therapy focuses on looking at the causes of compulsive hoarding and then slowly goes about changing the behaviour. It is not easy and it may take many years for a hoarder to let go, especially if the condition is long standing. If you recognise this neighbour, don't turn away. The earlier it is caught, the better the outcome. Be a good neighbour. Do it today.

32. The Nosy Neighbour
: RED FLAG

"WHAT IS THE MEANING OF 'GOSSIP'? DOESN'T IT
ORIGINATE WITH SYMPATHY, AN INTEREST IN ONE'S
NEIGHBOUR, DEGENERATING INTO IDLE CURIOSITY
AND LOVE OF TATTLING? WHICH IS WORSE, THIS
HABIT, OR KEEPING ONE'S SELF SO ABSORBED
INTELLECTUALLY AS TO FORGET THE SUFFERINGS
AND CARES OF OTHERS, TO LOSE SYMPATHY
THROUGH HAVING TOO MUCH TO THINK ABOUT?"
LUCY LARCOM

The other neighbours will warn you about this one if you're a newcomer to the street, but if they don't, you'll soon come across them. They'll welcome you to the area in person and then the questions – or should I say interrogation? – will start. They'll want to know where you've come from, what you do, how many children you have and all the other perfectly reasonable things that people ask on first acquaintance. Then they'll want to know how much you paid for the house, your car, even your clothes. Every time you go out they seem to be there and the conversation always begins with a question. Where are you going? Who with? What was in that parcel that was delivered yesterday? The questions are beyond the mere polite and become increasingly intrusive. Who was the visitor you had staying? What were you rowing about with your partner? How are you going to stop your daughter seeing that dreadful friend of hers? In the interests of neighbourliness you don't want to tell her to mind her own business (or do you?), so how do you deal with it? Even their children peer over the fence while bouncing on their trampoline, and you've seen them open their windows when you're in the garden with friends and skulking behind the curtains so that they can hear what you're talking about.

They will take great delight in telling you all the gossip about every neighbour. Who is having an affair with whom. Who has just lost their job. Who has a gambling habit. Whose child has been suspended from school for biting another child. Who has been caught shoplifting. Surely you can't be living in such a den of iniquity? You have no way of knowing whether what they are saying has any basis in truth. These are nasty allegations that it would be difficult and awkward to casually bring up with another neighbour so that you can clarify the situation. And then the penny drops. If they are telling you things about other people that make you feel uncomfortable, rest assured they are telling similar tales about you behind your back.

As much as you would like to tell this person what you think of them, however politely, there might be consequences. Attempting to befriend them so they get to know you in the hope of stopping them gossiping about you is unlikely to succeed and may just give them more ammunition. After all, this is their raison d'être. Neither will doing outrageous stunts like running round the garden in the nude or being seen talking to the plants, gurning or even mooning at them, in the hope of making them feel uncomfortable about watching you. It won't. On the contrary, it'll just give them some wonderful titbits to share with other neighbours, who may be more interested than you in what they have to say, and it will only get you a reputation for being weird. Or weirder. The only solution is to keep your business private, smile and wave when you go out so they know that you have spotted them, even if you haven't. They won't like you to know they are watching or eavesdropping in the hope of picking up some juicy snippet of information. If they try to engage you in conversation, keep going and say you're busy and can't stop.

In some cases, it may be possible to erect a barrier such as a fence, trellis or shrubs between your property and theirs, to prevent them spying on you. I'm sure leylandii was specifically invented just for the purpose by someone who had a problem with a Nosy Neighbour. Make sure you close your blinds or curtains in the evenings. While nets at the windows cut down the light coming in and obscure any nice views you might have, they do sometimes have their uses. The

Nosy Neighbour will not have net curtains because they might miss something going on outside. Remember, it is very easy to look into a lighted room from outside when it is dark, but impossible to see someone looking in from outside. Now, of course, we know you are not the nosy type, but you might start to take more of an interest in their comings and goings. If you can discover that they are doing something that is illegal, immoral or just plain embarrassing, you could use it to blackmail them into leaving you alone. If after all that, they continue, you've probably got yourself your very own stalker.

If you have particularly Nosy Neighbours, dig a big hole in your garden, preferably in the dark and when you know they are in. They will hear the noise and spy on you to see what you are up to. Then drag a body-sized black bin bag full of manure out of the garage, glancing round furtively all the time, drop it in the hole and, maintaining the shifty performance, quickly fill it in. You will have very good runner beans next year and the Nosy Neighbour will forever after avoid eye contact with you.

33. The Artist Neighbour
: Green Flag

"ALL COLOURS ARE THE FRIENDS OF THEIR NEIGHBOURS AND THE LOVERS OF THEIR OPPOSITES."

MARC CHAGALL

When people talk about artist stereotypes, it conjures up a picture of men with beards and moustaches, wearing berets, and striped Breton jumpers. You can't be a 'proper artist' without these attributes. Which excludes all the women. Well, most of them. Another popular stereotype is that of the starving artist living in a garret, which, considering the rent on attic rooms these days isn't surprising. A creative genius, frustrated with his art, misunderstood due to the ignorance of a fickle public, he obsessively produces stuff which doesn't sell, but won't compromise his artistic integrity to paint or make art that he hates but which someone might actually buy. He lives outside reality and believes he will only be famous when he's dead. He gets very disillusioned by people who say they are looking for something large, blue and cheap to match their décor and fill a certain space.

Most professional artists today, like writers, do not make a living from their art alone. They prostitute themselves by teaching in order to keep a roof over their heads and eat, making art in their spare time, answering the 'calls for entries' to various galleries and societies, putting on exhibitions, and entering competitions in the hope of getting selected from the thousands of other equally talented hopefuls. They are usually hard working, organised, dedicated and committed individuals, whose angst about deadlines is the same as that for anyone in an office or business. They do, however, look at life in a different way from most of us mortals and for that we should thank them as they bring originality and inventiveness into our lives. That's why they have knitted coats for the trees outside your house, invented mind-blowing installations and have extraordinary semi-abstract sculptures in their gardens. And it's why their idea of interior design is painting their walls in wonderful complementary colours that you wouldn't dare use, which is why your home and just about everyone else's are painted in shades of Bland and Boring. Every room is cluttered with treasures from their travels to India and their residences in Morocco, with shabby chic sofas covered in textiles from Peru. They wear jewellery of their own making from beads, twigs and shells all artfully tied together with raffia, and dress in costumes rather than clothes. The overall impression is charming and eclectic and looks like it was thrown together casually, but it works.

But there is another, more opaque arty-farty type

who loiters in the so-called higher echelons of Art (with a capital A) and who impress (baffle) the sycophants who inhabit their world with a language deliberately obfuscating. Their work is considered 'edgy', which usually involves bodily fluids and lots of empty space. They tip out the contents of their bin and call it an installation. If you get a much sought after invite to their private view, darling, and an introduction to the artist, they will be constantly looking over your shoulder and scanning the room for someone more important and/or rich to talk to. And Art at this level has a language all of its own. To listen to these artists explaining their work (it has to be explained because no one has a clue what it's meant to be) is like knowing a second language well but not fluently. They baffle you with art speak to elevate the mediocrity of their work, using words such as 'gravity' and 'resilience' and 'gestural' in the catalogue or gallery wall captions, which usually end with the author stating that the work 'raises questions'. 'Challenging' excuses a work for being repulsive. 'Ahead of the Market' means it is unsaleable. You recognise the words but the context is difficult to fathom, and you are left with the feeling that you haven't understood a word of it. But, of course, you can't say so for fear of ridicule.

Artists as neighbours bring colour and imagination into your life. They invite you to their Open Studios and Private Views where you might find yourself rubbing shoulders with someone famous. If you're lucky enough to have one for a neighbour, cherish them.

34. The Mega Rich Neighbours
: Green Flag

"The envious man grows lean at the success of his neighbour." Horace

Unlikely as it sounds, isn't there one of these in your street? Fancy new cars with personalised number plates, most up-to-date TVs and phones, kids at private schools, weekends spent at their second home in Cornwall, skiing in Klosters or Jackson Hole during the season, summers in Sardinia or Tuscany, a racehorse in training in Newmarket which they watch from the Royal Enclosure when it runs at Ascot and Epsom. And they have no trouble getting tickets for top bands, Wimbledon and the Cup Final. Their garden is designed by a Chelsea Gold Medal winner and the lawn is manicured by horticultural professionals. Their windows are cleaned once a week and the interior paintwork is touched up once a month. It makes your place look shabby, even though you clean your windows regularly – once a year. Face it, you're green with envy.

How do they do it? Why do they need more cars

than there are drivers in the house? They'll be evasive when asked what they do – import and export, most probably, which covers a multitude of nefarious activities or CEO of a multinational company (more legit but equally disreputable), or something in finance in the City (definitely dodgy). It all looks suspiciously idyllic and effortless. Try not to feel inferior. You can't keep up with them so better not to attempt it on your wages, or you'll end up bankrupt. And don't be tempted into get-rich-quick schemes in an attempt to obtain the dosh to compete. They are probably thinly disguised scams tantamount to gambling, and you will lose it all and be worse off than you were before.

By ingratiating yourself with them they might toss you a few crumbs such as a free week at that West Country seaside bolthole, or offer you their last season items that they consider out of date, like their kitchen units complete with granite only hewn at sunrise from the south side of the mountains in a remote valley in Brazil. Rummaging through their bins might also prove profitable and don't forget to find out which charity shop they take their discarded clothes to, so you can nip down there and grab yourself a designer label for next to nothing.

Why do you want to keep up with them anyway? Money is a poor substitute for real satisfaction and fulfilment. If your behaviour has got to the point of obsession then stand back and take a long, hard look at your life. Being honest with yourself, you may find that it's not about the money at all. Have you forgotten or shelved some dream or goal that you can take out, dust down and give it another go? Often we use others as an excuse and a way of taking out our frustrations that things are not going the way we want them to. Think about what it is that you are envious about and decide to do something about it. Every journey starts with one small step and if you feel that what you want is too difficult, break it down into smaller bites that you can achieve. Use them as a spur to galvanise you into action. Get counselling if that is what is required, set up that online business, find a course that interests you and leads to that qualification, buy a notebook and start to write that novel. Find someone you admire and ask them to mentor you. Update your CV and enrol with a recruitment agency. Join that gym. Be brave! And do it now, today, right this very minute. Stop reading and just do it! Don't wait for motivation – motivation comes with the doing.

You may not be able to change your situation, but you can change the way you feel about it. Stop looking at the new car, stop endlessly thinking about them, don't compare, concentrate on what you are doing, keep busy, be happy. Console yourself with the possibility that they are probably in hock up to their eyeballs, maxed out on the credit cards, have continually borrowed against the equity in their property to fund the school fees and now owe more than it's worth. They may be worried sick that their kids are on drugs and that they themselves are heading for the divorce lawyers and the food bank.

Who knows? One day they may tell you that they are envious of you.

35. The Note Writing Neighbour
: Amber Flag

"Don't throw stones at your neighbours if your own windows are glass."
Benjamin Franklin

Apparently overnight, little notes appear. Someone has waited until it's dark to post a letter to you or pin one up (or lots of them) in your communal hallway or on every telegraph pole and wall space they can find. They may be polite, with a please and a thank you. They may be informative. But usually, if they are anonymous, they are unpleasant and rude. They may be neatly handwritten or they may be printed in large font and in capitals WHICH MEANS THEY ARE VERY ANGRY!!! A well written note to the neighbours should be funny to have the desired effect, and here are some examples.

"I think you should know that there is a poltergeist in your apartment that moves the furniture about in the night and drops bowling balls down the stairs. Please have it exorcised."

"Your piano playing is excellent and worthy of the

professional stage but we would prefer not to listen to it at 7.30am on a Sunday morning."

"Those who live in glass houses should not wander about in the nude."

"Someone has taken a parcel that was left in my porch, addressed to me. It contained chocolate from a joke shop. The joke is that it was really laxatives. Enjoy!"

"Listening to your love life is better than all those porn channels! We especially like the names you call each other! Just in case you ever want to go pro, I have recorded it on the enclosed CD. PS. We've discussed it with the neighbours and we all think she's faking it."

"Many thanks to whoever watered my hanging baskets while I was away. I never liked petunias much anyway."

"As you have forgotten to pick up after your dog, I did it for you and thought you'd like it back as a memento. I put it through your letter box for your convenience."

"Grass grows by inches. It is killed by feet."

"We don't mind you living off the fruits of love but please don't throw the skins out of the window."

Perhaps you're going to work in the morning and find an anonymous note under your windscreen complaining that you took up too much room when you parked your car last night, so someone else – the aggrieved author of the note – had to park 200m away. Truth is you were tired, it was late and you were busting for a pee. It was careless and lazy and you know it. It drives you mad when you are on the receiving end of similar selfish parking. But would you ever stoop to leaving an anonymous note chastising the perpetrator for such a heinous crime? The Note Writer has the moral high ground, but they've made you feel like a child being reprimanded. If they'd had the decency to sign it, you would apologise, wouldn't you? Wouldn't you? Instead you spend the entire journey to work hypothesising about who it might be and what you'd like to do to them. When you get home, you ensure that you have parked very precisely in the middle of your allotted space. After all, the next request might be written on your car in acid.

The writer Marcel Proust (1871–1922) had problems with his upstairs neighbours who ran a dental surgery in the room above his bedroom. The dentist's drill prevented Proust from concentrating on writing his lengthy masterpiece 'A la Recherché du Temps Perdu', translated as 'In Search of Lost Time' or more elegantly as 'Remembrance of Time Past'. His book 'Letters to His Neighbour' is a collection of those written to them and reveals how delicately and exquisitely a request for peace can be made. They raise the usual scribbled foul-mouthed note to an art form with their wit and grace.

So, if you're thinking of penning a little billet-doux to an obnoxious neighbour, remember that humiliating people into changing their behaviour is unlikely to be effective, but humour and charm can defuse the situation, make the recipient smile and most reasonable neighbours will comply with the request, especially if they know it has upset you. It's up to you to decide whether to sign it.

36. The Copycat Neighbour
: Amber Flag

"Luckier than one's neighbour, but still not happy." Euripides

They say that imitation is the sincerest form of flattery but Copycat Neighbouring is not just mildly irritating, it's downright creepy. The underlying motive is, of course, not simple envy but jealousy. Envious people tell you to your face that they just love your new kitchen and that they are now going home to paint their cupboards or buy a makeover magazine or start ripping theirs out. Not so the jealous copycat. Their eyes are on swivels when they come round, looking at what you've done or bought but never uttering a single comment or compliment. In their eyes, it gives you status and they think it will do the same for them. They never ask you where you found it but as soon as they get home, they're on the internet trawling through hundreds of sites to find out. The next time you happen to go round to theirs, there it is. But not quite. The copycat never quite gets it right either because they've done it on the cheap, or simply because what they've done doesn't suit the rest of their décor. The thought that comes into your head is "What's that doing there?" and then you realise that it's a poor facsimile of what you have. You can't say anything but they get their satisfaction from knowing you've seen it, and they'll know you've seen it because you can't tear your eyes away from this travesty of interior design. They watch you with a smug expression on their face. They'll proudly tell you that it cost so much less than yours. You mutter something along the lines of "Yes. Um. Very nice" because you're a polite neighbour. Try not to laugh, although you're probably so stunned and horrified that laughing would be impossible. And do remember to close your dropped jaw and lower your involuntarily raised eyebrows. If it makes them happy, then fine. It just means that they haven't got enough imagination to think for themselves. But does it satisfy them? If they recognise that it is inferior, that having the same as you doesn't solve their problems or give them the desired status or you subsequently get something else that they are jealous of, it can turn into something a whole lot darker. A sort of object-centred stalking.

It can be both hilarious and sad to watch the neighbours competing. If the Copycat Neighbour hears that another neighbour has purchased a fancy set of taps for the bathroom, they'll go out and replace theirs. Unfortunately they purchase an inferior brand and 6 months later they realise there's been a leak, the timbers have rotted and the whole bathroom has to be stripped out so a new floor can be fitted, all at vast expense. If someone on the street puts some ornate troughs under their windows and fills them with flowering plants in the summer, they'll rush out and buy shallow plastic reproductions in a garish orange, which crack under the weight of the contents, and the plants wither and die. As they heave them to the bin, a heavy piece falls onto their foot breaking a toe. If you finally manage to buy the new car you have always wanted from the main dealer, by saving for years and taking out a large loan, they will buy an identical model cheaply from a dubious source, which turns out to be stolen or a cut and shut. If you tell them you are going on holiday to an exotic location for a special anniversary, they will book the economy version and catch some horrible bug and be hospitalised for a week. Building a conservatory? You can be sure that within a short time a conservatory in kit form will appear in their garden but never get completed because there will be bits missing.

Eventually, when you decide to move on, make a point of not leaving them a forwarding address just in case they decide to follow you.

37. The Party Loving Neighbour
: RED FLAG

"I THINK IT WAS MUCH BETTER WHEN YOU GOT ON YOUR HORSE AND RODE TWO MILES TO TALK TO YOUR NEIGHBOUR." LAURA SCHLESSINGER

Who hasn't come across one of these at some time? There are various categories of these neighbours. There are the inconsiderate ones who belt out hard rock all hours of the day and night at maximum decibels with the windows open. Their houses have strange looking people wandering in and out, up and down the stairs, in the garden or street with glazed expressions and dilated pupils, wafting clouds of interesting smelling substances behind them and leaving used syringes about. Every night. These are more like mini-festivals than parties. They have those pop-up gazebos in the garden as well as chimeneas or fire pits. The noise is ear-splitting, and there's such a queue for the single toilet, many of them expose themselves en plein air instead. The food consists of falafels, burgers and cupcakes. The drinks are cocktails. Not a good combination to be sick on.

The other extreme is those seemingly innocuous little get-togethers for drinkies and nibbles, where everyone arrives dignified and sober and leaves dishevelled and paralytic. Even in elite neighbourhoods there are those who love having lots of parties, but naturally they only invite those with money and influence who they want to impress. So not you, then. They chose to buy this particular house because it was described in the estate agent's details as "good entertaining space". This is estate agents' doublespeak for a huge open area which is impossible to heat the rest of the time, and that echoes like Jonah in the whale when you are in it without fifty other people.

Then there is the social minefield known as 'party etiquette'. A good rule is that you should be seen before being heard to arrive – you don't want to enter a room to total silence and everyone staring at you, or they'll assume you're on some sort of illegal high. Introducing yourself right at the start of a conversation is unacceptable. No, I don't know either. It's just not done. Resist the urge to liven up a dull conversation by talking about your achievements. No one wants to know that you just got promoted to account manager in a company no one has ever heard of. Or, worse, that you just won the lottery. Likewise, keep quiet about any stories where you come out the hero of the hour, especially if they're about work. You might be proud of the fact that you saved the day when the photocopier broke down, but spare the rest of us. And no one likes a smart-arse. However, self-deprecating anecdotes, provided they are not smutty (judge your audience), are usually acceptable and help break the ice. Eat before you go – it may say nibbles, canapés, buffet or finger food but this is not an open invitation to pile up your plate and stuff yourself at your host's expense. Remember that alcohol loosens the tongue – if you think you might regret telling some neighbour what you think of them when you're inebriated, go into the kitchen, chuck the contents of the glass you were given on arrival down the sink and fill it with water. It was probably spiked anyway – some party givers do this to their guests for 'fun'. The fun isn't meant for you.

Parties – you either love 'em or loathe 'em. If the latter, then you'll detest making small talk to people you don't know ("Let me introduce you to Marcy. She's a Taurus too. I know you're going to be great friends! You have so much in common!"), and will never see again (well, not if you see them first). There's nowhere to sit and your legs ache because you're not used to wearing your new shoes and can feel a blister starting to form on your bunions. You've spent hours getting ready, spent a fortune on a new dress that you'll probably never wear again and have spent half the day at the hairdressers having your hair cut, coloured and primped at extortionate rates. You must be the world's worst applier of makeup and have ended up looking like a startled owl. You find parties so excruciatingly boring that you will fake almost anything to get out of going. "Oh, such a shame," you say blithely and lying through your teeth, "I have to have root canal treatment that day." "It's a Sunday," they counter. "Well I have a very obliging dentist who works weekends," you flounder, quickly changing the subject.

So when you go to your next social gathering, look out for the party hater. They'll be sitting in a corner reading a book they brought with them, drinking tap water and scowling. Unless you're Brad Pitt or Rihanna, don't disturb them.

38. The Snooping Neighbour
: Red Flag

"Every man is surrounded by a neighbourhood of voluntary spies."
Jane Austen

We're all so busy these days that it's a relief when a neighbour tells you not to worry, because she can let the delivery driver in when they come with your new sofa or an engineer comes to repair the washing machine. She just needs a key. Since it saves you taking time off work, she has presented you with an easy solution. You've known her for some time and consider her harmless and in any case, you have nothing worth stealing. Problem solved! Or have you just opened a can of worms? Although you may think that this person is being kind and neighbourly and offering to do you a good turn, after reading this story you will be much less trusting and more suspicious when someone offers to do you a favour. Believe me, you have good reason.

You're busy and under pressure so will be genuinely

grateful when this particular neighbour offers to help. Perhaps, it is the middle of a cold winter, and the boiler is playing up and needs servicing. You naively hand over the key to your house and think nothing more about it. The engineer comes and, when you get home, the house is lovely and warm. You thank your neighbour profusely and give her a big bunch of flowers, but you forget to collect the key and she doesn't mention it again. You mean to go round and get it but it slips your mind. After all, it is handy for her to have one if you lose your keys or something else happens and you had to ask for her help again.

A few weeks later you come home from a long day at work and are just about to collapse in front of the TV when you notice that a pen on the side table is not quite where you thought you left it. It is on top of the little notepad by the phone. It's there to note down messages and remind yourself to collect a prescription or worm the dog. Anyway, you always place the pen at the side of the notepad and always on the right, as you are right handed and this is logical. But there it is – on top of the notepad. You stare at this little picture of still life for a long time, puzzled as to how the pen came to be on the top of the notepad and not at the side. Had you inadvertently put the pen on top of the notepad when you last used it? You can't recall and shrug it off as another senior moment. Perhaps someone else in the household has moved it. But it leaves a little question mark in your head, and every time you come home you find yourself looking around, although uncertain of exactly what it is that you are looking for. Then it happens again. A letter from the bank that you had opened that morning and left on the hall table to be dealt with later is definitely not where you left it. No one else in the family has been in while you were out and the kitchen door has been closed so the cats couldn't have got in. You know instantly that someone has been in and moved it, and you know who it is.

So you set a trap. Remembering a trick from a spy movie you sneakily wedge a tiny folded piece of paper low down in the front door when you next go out, so you can just see it from outside. When you return some time later, you check that it is still there before opening the door. For several days it remains as you left it. Then one day when you come back you notice that it isn't visible, and when you open the door it is lying on the mat. You feel sick. This person has been through all your private papers and possessions. Don't bother asking her for the key. Take the next day off work and ring every locksmith until you find someone who can come out that day as an emergency to change the locks. She'll know that you've sussed her when you blank her.

39. The Boring Neighbour
: Red Flag

> *"A bore is someone who deprives you of solitude without providing you with company."*
> Oscar Wilde

Sometimes you find yourself in the middle of a conversation and are suddenly aware that you haven't taken in a word that is being said. You've switched off whatever the subject was and are thinking of something else entirely. The reason you are conscious of this moment is that the person doing the talking is staring at you quizzically and clearly waiting for an answer. You're bored. You've listened to a diatribe of self-absorbed, opinionated trivia about something you have absolutely no interest in. However fascinating they find their collection of match boxes or tin soldiers, you do not share it. And hearing it lovingly described in minute detail using far too many words when a few would have done has brought you to the point where you are losing the will to live. So you drifted off into your own thoughts and were just making a mental note to remind yourself to buy a new nit comb.

The place you usually encounter boring people is at parties and other social gatherings such as weddings and funerals. Before you know it, other people have drifted away and you're left in a one-to-one conversation with them. Except that it isn't one-to-one. It's all one way. They talk in a monotonous tone and v-e-r-y s-l-o-w-l-y which reflects the speed of their thought processes. Their repertoire of conversation topics is limited to stuff such as the life and times of the inventor of the pneumatic drill (definitely boring!) or riding the same rollercoaster 5000 times. If they're competitive, they talk about their latest modular origami or O'Ekaki puzzle or how they like to file lawsuits as a hobby. They'll tell you that they are thinking about suing Nostradamus. Then there's the Boring Neighbour who has a fascination with axolotls and goes into paroxysms describing them and their life cycle. Fortunately, you can spot him as he wears a T-shirt with a picture of a grinning axolotl and 'No axident' on it. He regales anyone who will listen with a recital of his poetry about them and the difficulty of finding something to rhyme with axolotl. You suggest some. Bottle? Wattle? Ah, yes – throttle! He is not amused.

Bores have no sense of humour, often look at life's rich tapestry in a negative way and are completely oblivious to your increasingly desperate attempts to disengage from their invective. They can bore for England. In fact, they are quite probably Olympic standard.

If you are very unlucky, they may be recently separated or divorced in which case you will be treated to a tirade of what he said and what she said, and then what he did and what she did. They either slag off their ex in a bitter outpouring of resentment and self-pity or bombard you with long rambling reminiscences of places they'd been and things they did in the good years, and how wonderful it all was and how they wish they'd done this or said that. You are not expected to contribute to these monologues. On the contrary, if you try to suggest letting go and moving on as the healthy way forward, they will glare at you and, with a pious expression, tell you that you don't understand. Victim mentality is written all over them. Nothing is their fault and they fail to understand how their partner could have left them for someone so ugly and with a less secure and well paid job. If someone threw lemons at them, they'd claim they were too depressed to make lemonade. They'd suck them, which probably accounts for their expression.

After a while (it feels like hours but is only ten minutes) you start to glance about, hoping to catch the eye of someone who will appreciate your predicament and who will come over and rescue you. However, everyone else is chatting, laughing, eating, drinking, pretending to be deeply engrossed and totally ignoring you, probably deliberately. As long as you are occupying the Boring Neighbour, they are spared from getting stuck with them. Thanks, guys. Not. So next time you find yourself at a function, give the room a quick appraisal and identify the Boring Neighbour. They're the one with the defeated aura slumped in a corner, with grey clothes, grey hair, grey face. Look at the shoes. Boring people wear boring shoes, it's a scientific fact. Avoid eye contact, otherwise they'll inevitably make a beeline for you and you'll have to suffer exactly the same conversation you endured last time, even if you have successfully managed to avoid them for years.

40. The DIY Neighbour
: Amber Flag

> "Failures are divided into two classes:
> those who thought and never did
> and those who did and never thought."
> John Charles Salak

His motto is 'Why waste money getting someone in to do a job you can do yourself?' Although he may be convinced he can do anything, he has never had any training or served an apprenticeship. He's picked it up as he's gone along. I mean, how hard can plastering be? Or changing a tap washer? Or building your own house? Often he finds out the hard way and is a regular at A&E.

Large skips sit like land-locked boats on the road outside and fill up with other neighbours' cast-offs which then mysteriously disappear overnight as yet other neighbours forage in the dark and remove anything they fancy. Sheets of plywood and lengths of timber are piled up in the front garden and bags of cement lurk underneath a tarpaulin. Roof tiles lie in a drunken stack and rotten window frames lean forlornly against rusty, discarded wheelbarrows. A permanent bonfire of treated wood, plastic and containers of dubious substances glows menacingly and spews noxious fumes into the atmosphere, likely causing a new fissure in the ozone layer directly overhead. The inside of the house is no different. There's a hole in the ceiling where he put his foot through while boarding out the loft. Electrical cables hang limply and end ominously in bare wires.

He has a veritable arsenal of tools, but his favourite is the lump hammer, which he considers to be multipurpose. He is extremely unrealistic about his skills but undaunted by the task ahead; being a considerate neighbour he never starts before 8am during the week and stops the noisy stuff before the kids go to bed. At weekends and bank holidays he waits until 10am and then the neighbours are treated to a constant throb of noise, which he swears are well below permitted levels. He'll tell all his neighbours what he's going to be doing and how long the job will last. Unfortunately, he grossly underestimates the time he will take to finish the work. He certainly won't tell you that a huge crane is required to lift materials over your roof and into the rear of his property, blocking the whole road for the best part of a day and dripping mud and sand all over your car.

It wouldn't be so bad if he confined the damage to his own property, but this character has a habit of upsetting his neighbours. Party wall agreement? What would he want one of those for? According to research by

Abbey Home Insurance, over half a million households across Britain have suffered damage as a result of their neighbour's handiwork. A common bone of contention is sawn-off branches falling on greenhouses and cars. He means well and is very apologetic, but he is inclined to be accident prone along with his bodged DIY. If you live in a flat underneath him, watch out for damp patches on your ceilings after he has replaced the toilet and forgotten to tighten the seal.

He decided to weld the exhaust underneath his car. It would have been OK if the bodywork hadn't been made of fibre-glass. He managed to set fire not only to the car but also to the garage where he was working and destroyed the lot. He considers himself a bit of a dab hand when it comes to motors and on another occasion he managed to fit brake pads the wrong way round (not advisable) and rebuilt a gearbox so that there are three reverse gears and only one forward.

Another time he decided to remove the paint from a small table in the kitchen. He decanted the paint stripper from the bottle into a plastic container so that he could dip a brush into it easily. Leaving it overnight on a laminate floor, he came back next morning to find that the paint stripper had eaten through both the plastic container and a large circle of the flooring. The moral of this is that there is a reason why paint stripper is sold in glass bottles. Nowadays you can purchase a little gadget very cheaply that tells you where pipes run behind walls. Very useful. Yes, you've guessed it. The DIY Neighbour failed to check and proceeded to drill straight through a water pipe. The first he knew about it was when he realised that he was standing in a growing puddle of water.

If he offers to install your new kitchen for a fraction of the price that fancy place in the high street charges, don't hesitate. Refuse. Point. Blank.

41. The Problem Solving Neighbour
: Amber Flag

> "THE WORLD IS FULL OF PEOPLE THAT HAVE STOPPED LISTENING TO THEMSELVES OR HAVE LISTENED ONLY TO THEIR NEIGHBOURS TO LEARN WHAT THEY OUGHT TO DO, HOW THEY OUGHT TO BEHAVE AND WHAT THE VALUES ARE THAT THEY SHOULD BE LIVING FOR." JOSEPH CAMPBELL

This neighbour has the solution to every problem and eventuality. His favourite phrase is "Do you know what I'd do?" and without waiting for you to reply he launches into a lecture on the precise steps you must take to remedy the conundrum that he perceives you are grappling with. There is nothing he can't give his opinion on. This can be quite useful if you are truly undecided about whether to paint the shed blue or green, or you don't know where to find something obscure locally, although the internet has taken care of most sourcing problems. A couple of clicks and you can acquire the original 1960s manual to go with an obsolete piece of machinery, handily uploaded onto a CD to save postage. You could spend years searching second-hand book shops and auctions and never find it.

His speciality is dilemmas. He likes a good dilemma where you are being forced to choose between alternatives, both unfavourable, or both having positive and negative aspects. Supposing you have a very important decision to make, say, about whether to stay in a stressful job that is well paid, has prospects and could ultimately lead to your dream job but the hours are long, or change to a lower paid, less stressful occupation with shorter hours? You oscillate between the two, knowing that whichever path you take, it will have a huge impact on your life. Or you have a pet with a serious medical problem, and can't decide between options that the vet has given you. If you genuinely need help in resolving a dilemma, most people would be flattered to think they could help. If you trust this neighbour and know that he will look at it from all angles, carefully and calmly analysing the pros and cons, be objective and bring a new perspective that you might not have thought of, then go ahead and present him with the facts. As a neutral party he will have more of an unbiased view than friends or family might have.

A good listener will let you talk, only occasional prompting or asking a pertinent question to elicit as much information as possible. They'll steer you through consideration of the risks and consequences associated with each outcome. It may be that you are indecisive because you don't have enough information, and the discussion will help discover the omission so that you can go off and find out more about it. In the end, a good Problem Solving Neighbour won't make the decision. They will help you work it through for yourself. They've just been the facilitator. However, be very wary of people who dismiss your feelings, who are ultra-negative about your concerns, or try to force you into making a decision based on what they would do. They are not you and may not have your best interests at heart. Everyone has their own agenda.

If, on the other hand, you only wanted someone to listen to you whinging and make sympathetic noises and now he expects you to take his advice and will be deeply insulted if you don't, you've just created another dilemma and this time, because he's part of the problem, he can't help you solve it.

Or you could just toss a coin. Notice how you feel when you see the decision that has been chosen for you by chance. Are you disappointed or did it actually come out the way you secretly wanted? Life is too short to spend a lot of your working life being miserable. Just remember, no one on their death bed ever said, "I wish I'd spent more time in the office."

42. The Know-It-All Neighbour
: Amber Flag

> "The old believe everything, the middle aged suspect everything and the young know everything." Oscar Wilde

He may not know absolutely everything, but he sure as hell knows an awful lot more than you do, which can be very annoying. He has a positively encyclopaedic knowledge of the most extraordinary subjects, ranging from the prosaic to the useless. As you get older you find you have to let some memories go to make room for all the new stuff. Your brain's storage capacity is full and you have reached information overload. At least that's your excuse for the odd senior moment here and there. You used to know it all, but now you just can't remember it all at once. Sometimes it's like rummaging around in a very dark and dusty cellar for something you can't recall whether you kept or threw away, with a torch whose light is dimming.

Fond of starting a conversation with "Did you know...?", this neighbour ambushes you when you least expect it. He may have attended some erudite seat of learning in the distant past and been an intellectual heavyweight at one of the Oxbridge colleges, have written learnéd papers, given lectures at seminars and have an alphabet of letters after his name – bachelor of this, doctor of that, fellow of the other. Now retired, there is no one he can converse with who shares his interest in limnology or can debate the conflict between relativity and quantum mechanics or the merits of NPV over IRR[1] in corporate finance. Be patient. Listen to him and learn – you never know, the topic might just come up at the next pub quiz, and you'll be able to impress your fellow team members with your knowledge of the name of the hill in Athens where the highest judicial court sat[2] or what a ratoon is[3] or what you call the hollow between your nose and top lip[4]. OK, so I'm showing off, and so is he. Fact based dominance is a form of bullying. He can't resist interrupting you in full flow to correct your tense or grammar.

Being knowledgeable is not the same as being intelligent. Some people are sponges when it comes to facts and like to use their superior memory to make others feel inferior. They will not listen to you and will dismiss anyone else's opinions. They miss the point of a joke because they're obsessed with the detail. Sometimes it can be a façade they use to hide behind because they are ashamed of their lack of education.

If you want to get one over on him, it might be tricky. After all, his entire life is spent learning new facts. He loves Trivial Pursuit (all versions) and is a stalwart of the local pub quiz teams. For a short time, he was the question setter until the organisers sacked him because no one could answer any of the questions and everyone refused to turn up again unless he went. As a hobby, he pores over atlases and books of quotations and reads the dictionary for fun. He knows his sizes of Champagne bottles, the colour of Thunderbird 4 and the meaning of all signal flags and pennants. Heaven help you if you fly the Union Jack upside down. But he won't apply to Eggheads in case he gets shown up by Dave or Judith. You have to find that Achilles heel, the one topic on which he is weak. Proving a Know-It-All wrong may be all it takes to stop him being so annoying, but he'll never talk to you again.

And remember – he might have knowledge but not self-knowledge otherwise he'd know the answer to the question, "If you're a Know-It-All, how come you don't know how irritating you are?"

[1] Net Present Value and Internal Rate of Return.

[2] Areopagus

[3] new shoot sent up from sugar cane after cropping

[4] philtrum

43. The Multi-Generation Neighbours : Amber Flag

"EVERY ONE OF US PREYS UPON HIS NEIGHBOUR, AND YET WE HERD TOGETHER." JOHN GAY

It seemed like a good idea six months ago and so on trend. Now the novelty is wearing thin.

Worn down by mortgages and credit card debt, bills and children who demand all the latest gadgets and who will only wear designer clothes and trainers, Generation X is finding life tough. They always thought that they'd have the perfect house, a good job with a fantastic salary, a gold plated pension, and at least two foreign holidays a year. Now in their 40s, shoehorned into a tiny house with no prospect of affording the next step on the ladder (mostly due to their profligate lifestyle and inability to economise) and with the possibility of redundancy on the horizon, they have had a reality check. So they whinge and whine to their parents about how expensive school trips are, how the children have grown out of their shoes and how they can only afford a week's holiday in a caravan in Skegness. They drop hints about how jolly it is when they are all together, how Mummy and Daddy are getting older and how they won't want to be lonely, rattling round in this great big house when one of them 'goes', and what fun it is spending quality time together as a family.

Secretly they seethe about how lucky the older generation were to be able to buy a big house on only one income with cheap rates of interest. They conveniently forget inflation at 25%, the winter of discontent, strikes and various recessions that their parents had to survive. The younger generation only see a lifestyle with any mortgage long since paid off and the benefits of a final salary pension scheme to cushion their parents for the rest of their lives. They see themselves having to work until they are in their 70s and retiring on meagre state pensions, stuck in their rabbit hutch of a house and with no prospect of moving to something more spacious. So they cajole and bribe and promise they'll look after them if they can move in. They go on about how their parents will never have to sell the beloved family home they grew up in, and give no thought to the eventuality of nursing someone 24/7 who has dementia and is doubly incontinent. If they have given it any thought, it has passed through their mind to dump them at A&E – after all the old folk will no longer know who they are or remember where they lived. They can tell everyone that their parents have gone into residential care and their inheritance will be safe from the greedy tax man.

And so the cuckoo kids come home to roost. And what do the parents think about all this? Privately they are horrified at the prospect of three generations living under the same roof. Living cheek by jowl and doubling the chores. The bills for food, heating and water will triple at least and they are timid about raising the possibility of asking their offspring to contribute, as needless to say, they have never offered any financial help towards the increased costs, expecting to live rent and expenses free. It just wasn't something they had ever considered. They would never have crawled back to Mummy and Daddy in their forties, considering it shameful and a sign of incompetence. They would have cut back and made do. Their children claim that multi-generation living is the latest trend but their parents see it as a social stigma on those moving back to the childhood home and reflects a bigger failure than someone over forty on a bus. But the threat hangs in the air that if they refuse, the offspring might have to move a long way away in order to be able to afford to eat and the grandchildren will be forced to live in so-called poverty and get bullied for going to school without the latest phone. They might be prevented from seeing their grandchildren ever again. Some might think this a blessing. Instead they bite their tongue and pretend to welcome them back into the fold.

Now their lives have changed for the worse. They were just about to retire to a cottage by the sea and spend some time travelling the world. Instead, there is a queue for the bathroom, children and grandchildren taking priority as they have to go to work and school. They are expected to be a taxi service, taking grandchildren to and from school as they live in the country and there is only one bus a week. There are rows just because they don't follow the absurd rules to the letter and allow the grandchildren to watch TV for more than their allotted time, and feed them unhealthy snacks, such as – shock horror! – anything with white sugar in it, and aren't constantly cleaning every surface with anti-bacterial wipes. They are forced to cook stuff they don't like. To accommodate work routines, they eat much later than they would if they were on their own, which gives them indigestion. The oldies can't understand why they don't all sit down to eat together en famille but their grandchildren aren't hungry because they've grazed all day and then head off to social activities or retire sullenly to their rooms to play music loud enough to wake the dead. Working parents get home at different times and forget to mention that they had a four-course business lunch and only want a snack, which they will expect to have put in front of them. Then their children want to watch reality TV, soaps and game shows, when they would rather see a documentary on the life of the sisserou parrot of Dominica. Both the grandchildren and their parents never turn the lights out when they exit a room, leave gadgets on charge or stand-by and forget to lock the doors last thing at night. The grandkids kick footballs into the flower beds and have reduced the lawn to a mud bath. When they finally fall into bed, frazzled and exhausted, the grandparents have to listen to their daughter and son-in-law having vigorous sex. The offspring question why they should help out by cleaning the windows or putting out the garbage when their parents have always done those chores for themselves and they don't see why they should. This pathetic whinge can be roughly translated as wanting to keep more of their time and money for themselves and letting the incumbent 'staff' do a lot of the tiresome, time-consuming and demeaning housework for them, and being grateful for the extra company to boot.

Golf and lunches out for the grandparents fall by the wayside, and they lose contact with their friends because they are too tired tidying up after their family and babysitting to go out and the house is in too much of a mess to invite friends round. And now there are mutterings about elbowing the oldies into a self-contained annexe (for this read: convert the garage into a bedsit), getting rid of their parents' old brown furniture (heirloom antiques) and all the clutter of pictures and ornaments, then taking over the house as their own and modernising it. After all, it's their birthright – they just don't fancy waiting for the oldies to finally pop their clogs at the age of 103 when they'll be too old to enjoy their inheritance or it's all been spent on mobility scooters, stair lifts, fancy hearing aids and private hip replacements. The entitled want-it-now generation, wants it NOW and stuff what anyone else wants.

Before you go down this route, think carefully. If you didn't get on as a family before or even if you did, living in a Multi-Generation household is generally a recipe for disaster. The motive is almost always money, and the cuckoo kids will just get ever more demanding, and will eventually turf you out of your own nest.

44. The Organic Neighbour:
Green Flag (well, what other colour could it be!?)

> "TRY ORGANIC FOOD... OR, AS YOUR
> GRANDPARENTS CALLED IT, 'FOOD.'"
> ORGANIC FOOD ADVERTISEMENT

Not only have they chosen to live a healthy lifestyle, they want to leave as light a footprint as possible on the environment too. They use phrases like 'back to basics' and 'reducing the toxic load' and try to use only pure, natural and chemical-free products as part of their responsible existence.

So bear with them when they say how hard it is living in a non-organic world. This can be an expensive way to live. You can only be fully signed up to the organic movement if you are a rich pop star, because organic stuff is not cheap. Organic chickens at £12 each as opposed to battery farm cast-offs at four for a tenner, for example. And the price of organic veggie boxes delivered to the door and organic pet food…! Any waste food is fed to their chickens or goes into the compost bin and is returned to the soil so that they can grow their own.

The baby is fed on 100% organic fare from top brand names that have sanctimonious mission statements on their websites promising healthier, more beautiful children with IQs that will secure them entry into Mensa and Russell Group or Ivy League Universities. The manufacturers (or co-founders as they like to call themselves) used to be financial traders or lawyers in the city, and have cleverly packaged the pap in unique and attractively designed pods that all mothers will be able to recognise instantly amongst the plethora of advertising on TV and in yummy mummy magazines. This means that they must rush out and buy them in order not to feel that they are letting their baby down by buying inferior products. What they don't know is that the baby food in both the upmarket ranges and their competitors comes from exactly the same factory, and that it's just a marketing ploy to make them feel guilty if they don't buy the most expensive. After five years, the whizz kid inventors have an exit strategy to sell to the highest bidder and retire to Gloucestershire.

Their kids are not allowed to go to school mates' parties because they might consume e-numbers that they're not used to and come home so hyperactive that they are still awake and climbing the walls at 4am. But when they finally drop off to sleep, it's on bedding made of nettle fibre which is, of course, 100% hypoallergenic and guaranteed to be formaldehyde and antimony free. Even the carpets are natural sisal and there is organic hemp or flax insulation in the loft.

Clothes, bought at lifestyle boutiques situated in

trendy London post codes, are all made from organic fabrics ethically sourced from South America with labels hinting at clean, healthy, outdoor lifestyles, imported by non-organic cynics based in Neasden. Jewellery consists of amber and agate, snowflake obsidian and sea glass, jet and jade strung on bamboo cord. Shoes are made of hemp and cardboard, with recycled rubber soles, hand stitched with no toxic glues, and are eco-friendly and sustainable to give that feel-good, guilt-free factor the Organic Neighbour likes to have, worn with socks made from organic cotton or mohair.

Cosmetics have to conform to the COSMOS standard. Cleaning products must leave no chemical residues and feature basic components such as vinegar, salt and baking soda. Even their personal hygiene products must be made with pure and natural ingredients such as jojoba and coconut, all organic of course. They avoid unnecessary car journeys, walking or cycling wherever possible, never set foot on a plane and drive an electric or hybrid car, which they bought second-hand to avoid the new car smell which they know to be the carcinogenic off-gassing of PVC. They only read books printed on sustainably sourced paper and decorate their houses in organic, water based, solvent-free, herbicide-free, pesticide-free, mercury-free, toxin-free paint. Their furniture is organic wood (sustainably farmed), and stuffed with wool from sheep fed an organic diet.

So until you win the lottery, the dog will have to survive on bog standard tinned food and you'll pick up the organic stuff at the supermarket when it's past its sell by date and marked down below the price of their usual stuff.

However, you have read in the newspapers that all this is just so last year, darling: artisan is the new organic.

45. The Social Climber Neighbour
: Red Flag

> "Too many people spend money they haven't earned, to buy things they don't want, to impress people they don't like."
>
> Will Smith

You've just moved in and the next door neighbour can't do enough for you, ingratiating themselves into your life and seemingly interested in knowing everything about you – where you've come from, where you work and what your job title is. They give your car, furniture, jewellery and clothes the once over. A year later they are going skiing with the high-flying, socially well-connected friends you introduced them to and you haven't been invited. Now they don't bother to acknowledge you at all. They have discovered that you are of no more use to them and they have moved on – and up. Sound familiar? You've just been used by the Social Climber Neighbour.

To start with they seemed normal enough, if a little 'in your face'. It quickly became clear that status is extremely important to them. You know this because they keep saying that their current house is only a stopgap and they will be moving to something bigger or better located before long. They drop names of important people and try to find out who you know, inveigling you into having a party so that they can meet your friends, and pick those that could be useful to them. Then they insinuate themselves into your friends' social circles for ulterior motives, so they can move up a social notch or two.

A title has them positively swooning. Always looking for those who are better connected and more popular, they cultivate people for who, not what, they are. They smarmy up to people who have something they want and then repeat the behaviour to meet their friends, dropping you in the process, and all the time conscious of their move up the social ladder. Think of the friends you have who won't commit to meeting up or cancel arrangements at the last minute. They hold off while they wait for a better offer, and if it materialises, you and your plans fall by the wayside. The Social Climber is someone who believes that rich and powerful people are better than other people, and they won't let you stand in the way of their social mobility. Sadly, they don't realise that they are looked on with hilarity and distain by those they wish to ape.

Scratch the surface and you will find them self-centred and completely lacking in empathy. Question them carefully and you will discover they are economic with the details of their past life. They avoid naming precisely which school they went to, hold their knife and fork in a way the Queen would never dream of, have handbags with 'Channel' instead of 'Chanel' on them and inform you that their luggage was made by Lewis Vuitton. They claim they went to Cambridge but someone who knew them in their youth tells you they attended a college of further education there just so that they could brag about it. Don't you just hate it when people imply something knowing full well that you will infer something else?

So how do you deal with a neighbour who is a Social Climber? Well, you probably won't have to. They will drop you like a stone when they realise that you have nothing they can use to further their own ambitions, so just be quietly grateful. They are very class conscious and snobby. You can tell the status of any guests they are expecting by the amount of work to the house and garden carried out in advance of the visit. For perceived royalty the grass has an application of weed killer, the edges are cut with scissors while on their hands and knees, the windows are polished inside and out and the front door gets a new coat of paint. They'll irritate you by making frequent, irrelevant and derogatory references to what they call your 'regional accent'. In fact, they are originally from Liverpool, but they have deliberately cultivated received pronunciation. Well, until they are tipsy. That is when the nasal tones of the delightful Scouse accent resurface, once described by Fritz Spiel as one third Irish, one third Welsh and one third catarrh, and immortalised by Lily Savage and The Beatles.

The Social Climber knows the price of everything and the value of nothing, as they say. You finally see the light when they announce that they like to choose their friends. You have always found that friends just happen, usually when you least expect it, but you decide, on this occasion that you will take a leaf out of their book. You choose to unfriend them.

46. The Frenemy Neighbour
: Red Flag

"KEEP YOUR FRIENDS CLOSE BUT YOUR ENEMIES CLOSER." ATTRIBUTED TO THE CHINESE GENERAL SUN TZU BUT MADE FAMOUS BY MICHAEL CORLEONE IN THE GODFATHER PART II (1974)

A combination of the words 'friend' and 'enemy', the term 'frenemy' came into popular usage in 1977, although it is claimed to have been around as 'frienemies' since 1953 as a description of the American and Russian relationship. If you find yourself puzzling about a remark someone makes to you that leaves you feeling uncomfortable and wondering what they meant, then you might just have encountered a frenemy.

An enemy disguised as a friend, it's difficult to spot them at first because they're sneaky. They say something nasty in public or give you a backhanded compliment and then hug you and say they didn't mean it. But you know they did. You know the type: after you say you've lost a few pounds they confide, "I don't care what they say about you, you're hardly fat at all." They know precisely what they are doing and they are aware that what they are saying will hurt you but they go right ahead and do it anyway. They're too cowardly to confront you as an enemy so they belittle, undermine and stab you in the back, in between being sweetness and light. Unlike a true enemy, frenemies don't hate you. They hate themselves for not being more like you. They want to destroy you because you make them feel inadequate without even trying. Don't apologise for being you. Often found in the work place too, they are pernicious, fake friends who cannot be happy for any good fortune you have, deserved or otherwise. They just have to spoil something good with a deliberately chosen poisonous remark.

If you take a neighbour into your confidence and tell them that you are writing a novel, you might find it annoying when they say something like, "Of course, I could write a book if I had the time." If you let them read some of it, you might be told grudgingly that "It's not too bad, considering." Considering what, you have no idea, but you will know that you have chosen the wrong person and that they're a frenemy. Another time, your so-called friend and neighbour forgets your birthday. You wouldn't mind but, when you mention what your partner gave you, she tells you in no uncertain terms that "It's a stupid time to have a birthday", as if you had any choice in the matter. When you think about it, she was always bringing round cakes when you were on a diet and when she cancelled plans you used to feel relieved rather than disappointed. You once overheard her talking to another neighbour who had just had her first pregnancy scan and was proudly, but shyly, showing you both the picture of the baby. "How sweet," your frenemy says, "Was it a mistake?" When she finds out that someone has a degree in psychology she announces in front of them that "Psychology just tells you what you already know in words that you can't understand." Everybody laughs, but you are left in no doubt that it was meant to be a put-down. Another time she tells you that she likes your dress and she gave one exactly like it to the charity shop last year. She is filled with jealousy and her friendship is toxic, negative and draining. Don't bother confronting her about her behaviour and how it makes you feel. She just isn't worth it and you won't want to give her the satisfaction of knowing it upset you. Let the relationship go. Frenemies do not have your best interests at heart, but they do have their uses – they show you precisely the sort of friend you do not want to be. And frenemy is a great Scrabble word!

47. The "Isn't it terrible?" Neighbour : Red Flag

> "WELCOME THY NEIGHBOUR INTO THY FALLOUT SHELTER. HE'LL COME IN HANDY IF YOU RUN OUT OF FOOD." DEAN MCLAUGHLIN

Life is hard for this neighbour and it becomes hard for you too – to listen to a constant stream of issues which are troubling and upsetting them, ranging from global warming to the housing crisis, accompanied by the constant lament of "Isn't it terrible? Oh, isn't it TERRIBLE?" They watch the news and read the papers and just don't acquire the compassion fatigue that inflicts us all when faced with wars and famines on a daily basis. They seem to have the weight of the world on their shoulders, feeling distraught by whatever the latest situation is but feeling totally powerless to do anything about it. They may even believe it is all or partly their fault, because they haven't changed the light bulbs to low energy, or they turned the thermostat up 1 degree when it snowed, or forgot to gift aid the stuff they dumped at Oxfam, or didn't buy a Big Issue from the seller outside the supermarket.

They find it difficult to keep things in proportion and feel any problem, even on a personal level, to be intractable and insoluble. You can offer advice, suggest places to get help, be a good listener but all efforts will be rebuffed for one reason or another. And they are very good at coming up with reasons why they can't fix things. "Oh, I couldn't do that," they whimper pitifully, avoiding your steely gaze and wringing their hands, while sitting in a dejected heap. You continue to reassure them and try to cheer them up, feeling increasingly drained and frustrated by their lack of enthusiasm and refusal to want to improve their lot. But it's a vicious circle, because the more they feel how terrible a situation is, the more likely it is that they will be rejected and then the situation will feel even worse, which gives them more reasons to protest that no one understands them.

Although they may ask for advice, what they want is for someone to acknowledge how they feel and help them manage those emotions of sadness, anger and guilt. Empathising with them and agreeing that there is nothing you can do about the situation on the other side of the world or even round the corner will help. You can follow this up with some physical comfort. This can take the form of a hug, if you know them well, or a brief touch on the hand or a ruffle of the hair if that's what is appropriate. You alone cannot give them the absolution they need, because only they can do that for themselves.

For your own sanity, there has to be a limit on how long you let them witter, so when you get to a point where you sense you can move on without them falling apart or appearing to dismiss their concerns, do so. Ask them about something you know they like or are looking forward to. Don't let them go back to the same subject. Tell them about a visitor you are expecting, or the funny story of what happened when you put your groceries in the wrong trolley, or find a positive slant for them about the situation that so bothers them. Depart on a good note and you leave them less negative than you found them, which can only be a good thing to help them develop resilience to life's inequalities and emotional experiences.

Listening to complainers is bad for your health: it's official. According to neuroscientists, being exposed to long periods of non-stop griping, including watching it on TV, makes you more likely to do the same thing yourself. Furthermore, it results in the death of brain cells in the hippocampus. I always suspected that watching EastEnders rotted your brain.

They are their own worst enemy. If they were a stick of rock, they'd have 'victim' or 'martyr' written right through them. Even therapists, whose job it is to listen to this self-pity with kindness and understanding, have been known to get rid of them as clients because they are so irritating. So when you feel you have had enough of being nice and sympathetic to them there is only one thing left to say:

FOR PITY'S SAKE, GET OFF YOUR ARSE AND DO SOMETHING ABOUT IT!

48. The Flashy Neighbour
: Green Flag

"My neighbour doesn't want to be loved as much as he wants to be envied."

IRVING LAYTON

The Flashy Neighbour is often pitied and laughed about behind his back as a figure of fun and ridicule rather than attracting the envy and attention that he thinks he deserves. He loves to show off and always has the latest gadgets and gizmos. He leaves his brand new sports car outside on the drive for the neighbours to see, and proudly tells you the price he paid for it. This character is always telling you how much he pays for everything. He doesn't haggle because that would be too demeaning (also he doesn't have the balls) and he wants you to know that he can afford top whack. He never has a personalised number plate on his vehicle because then no one would know how new it was. He drives off with a screech of tyres, scattering leaves and dust, and arrives back in similar vein so that anyone in earshot looks up and notices him. He chose the one with the twin exhausts because it has a rich, deep-throated burble, like the Merlin engine on a Spitfire, so you can hear him coming for miles. He likes unusual models that stand out from the crowd, and always in bright red. This is definitely not faithful Mondeo man.

Sadly, he suffers from a condition known as Peacock Syndrome. When not in his flash car, he struts about with a flat-footed swagger just like the peacock displaying his gaudy feathers to an unresponsive female audience. He likes to brag about his possessions and takes every opportunity to let others know how well off he is with the sole intention of impressing them. Little does he know that all this does is send out the wrong message. Fat, ugly and the wrong side of fifty, he looks at his reflection in the mirror and sees a toned, tanned, full-blooded male with movie star looks that any female should find fascinating. And he's not fussy – anything in a frock between the ages of fifteen and forty will do, especially if they're as fanatical about fellatio as he is. He is of a type that flock together, preening their feathers and flaunting their affluence. Only a fool would take him at face value – the fables he tells are far-fetched and fanciful, the Ferrari is a replica and the trust fund fortune is a figment of his imagination.

He values exclusivity as he thinks it puts him above the plebs so can be found at the local golf club that has a very long waiting list, where he attends all the functions. Not that you will ever find him on the fairways, you understand. He just wants to be able to drop into the conversation that he is a member so that you will be impressed, and he likes to use the jargon, especially those with double meanings such as 'the full-finger grip', 'foursomes', 'following-through', 'the forward press' and 'the finishing position'. He likes to get himself elected to committees so that he can flaunt the title of Vice President (President is better) or Commodore or Chairman (never Chair or Chairperson) and attracts fulsome praise for his fustian speeches. He writes flamboyantly with an antique Faber-Castell or Parker Falcon writing implement and likes to celebrate World Fountain Pen Day on the first Friday of November each year. He thinks of himself as a fine fellow, when you know he has the moral fibre and fortitude of a flea.

Other hobbies include keeping koi carp and he can tell you exactly which fish are worth the most and their current value. He has his initials picked out on the overwrought iron gates so everyone knows where he lives. Books adorn his coffee table; they are in pristine, unread condition and bought by the pound (that's weight, not money), chosen to supposedly reflect his intellect – but we all know that no one has actually read 'A Brief History of Time' (let alone understood it) and he's clearly a feeble featherbrain. His dogs have to be large and preferably foreign – Fila Brasileiro, Finnish Hound or French Mastiff – no poodles or lap dogs for this guy, although he might allow his current trophy girlfriend a handbag dog or anything else that is fashionable and draws attention to him when he's with her.

Sadly, the peacock is simply trying to compensate for having no personality. Living a flashy life must mean you are successful, right? Wrong. Deep down he knows that his fiscally frivolous short-term focused behaviour is flawed, and he's a failure. But if you like flashy, fair-weather, fallible fraudsters in flamboyant, f***-me cars and you're fancy free, not too fastidious and aren't looking for faithfulness, knowing it will quickly fizzle out, well, you know what they say – 'a ride for a ride'.

49. The Territorial Neighbour
: RED FLAG

"IF MAN ASKS FOR MANY LAWS, IT IS ONLY BECAUSE
HE IS SURE THAT HIS NEIGHBOUR NEEDS THEM;
PRIVATELY HE IS AN UNPHILOSOPHICAL ANARCHIST
AND THINKS LAWS IN HIS OWN CASE SUPERFLUOUS."
WILL DURANT

This neighbour's behaviour is most likely to become
apparent after you have either deliberately or accidentally
insulted them. Touchy and prone to throwing their toys
out of the pram, they quickly go into a huff. Having
taken offence at whatever crime they believe you have
committed against them, they react in the only way they
know how – they go into fortress mode. If they can't see
you they can pretend that you don't exist, and then you
won't have the opportunity to upset them again.

So they start to metaphorically circle the wagons,
and the battleground becomes the boundary with
your property. If there is already a tightly packed row
of leylandii between you and your neighbour, then the

chances are that they were planted by a previous occupant who was territorial. You may live in a house with such a hedge on your side of the fence that has become much too tall. So, thinking you are doing the neighbours a favour, you prune it drastically to a more amenable height. You naively think they'd be grateful because it means that more light will get in through their windows. The neighbours are incandescent with rage. "People will be able to look at us!" they cry. You are bemused. Why would anyone want to look at them? They tell you that they are about to sell the house but now no one will want to buy it, and it's your fault. They genuinely believe that they have more chance of finding a buyer if the house is hemmed in by vegetation, and they have to have the lights on during the day even in summer. Perhaps they are hoping for a family of troglodytes to buy it. Perhaps they are a family of troglodytes. So what do they do? They plant a new hedge of leylandii on their side of the fence, just to make the point. It grows rapidly and seriously encroaches upon their garden, which isn't particularly generous in the first place and nothing grows in its shade. They still can't sell their house and you hear through the neighbourhood grapevine that they believe you are to blame, and nothing to do with the fact that it is overpriced and poorly presented. In desperation they finally drop the price at the estate agent's suggestion and someone gets a bargain. The first thing the new owners do on moving in is uproot those dratted conifers, and you get along with them just fine!

You may find that your next door Territorial

Neighbour monitors the workmen who are putting up a new fence for you to ensure that they do not trespass by so much as one centimetre onto his land, constantly arguing the position of every post. Another tactic they use is to dump stuff such as spare roof tiles, bricks, old wheelbarrows and pieces of timber on the boundary between your properties, especially if there is no solid fence. Eventually it looks like something out of the Troubles and every time you are in the garden you find yourself humming 'Through the Barricades' by Spandau Ballet.

You may come across them where there are no allocated parking places for residents and spaces on the street are in short supply. He will leave a couple of rather scruffy traffic cones, with the initials of the local utility provider on them, in his favoured spot when he has driven away. Your delightful neighbour has stolen them to mark out his territory and woe betides you if he discovers that you have removed them and parked there. He may then morph into The Note Writing Neighbour.

Every neighbourhood has houses with boundaries that resemble the Great Wall of China, built for the sole purpose of security and privacy, complete with razor wire. You can't even see through the gate which is solid, imposing and bristling with entry phones and cameras. Anyone who has electric gates is a Territorial Neighbour. They create a physical and psychological barrier which reinforces the owner's sense of disconnection and isolation from the world. The occupants are so insecure that they need to have some visible obstacle to signify to the outside world that you are not welcome. It is amusing when you see them circling the area desperately searching for somewhere to park because the mechanism has broken down and the gates are firmly stuck in closed mode! The funny thing is that burglars are more likely to target their property because they think they are protecting something valuable.

Being territorial is simply a way of showing their disgust and how much you have hurt them. Frankly, are you bothered?

50. The Manipulative Neighbour
: Red Flag

"A real diplomat is one who can cut his neighbour's throat without having his neighbour notice it."
Trygve Lie

The Manipulative Neighbour is not necessarily as poisonous as you might imagine, although it is true that they are out to get what they want from you. Indeed, many are quite charming, flattering you by claiming that you are the only person who could do this and that you would do it so much better than anyone else. The Organiser Neighbour comes into this category. So you find yourself agreeing to doing the costumes for the local am dram panto or standing in the pouring rain outside the supermarket with a collection tin in your hand, despite swearing that you wouldn't do it again after the fiasco of last year. You have to admire their persistence and gall. Truth be known, we all do this occasionally.

Then there is the seriously obnoxious neighbour who

makes it their life's mission to manipulate and groom others. They may be difficult to spot at first as they often have a certain amount of charisma about them, subtly establishing your trust in them and appearing willing to help you out without apparently expecting anything in return. They will even do things spontaneously for you, without being asked, and at the beginning it seems like normal neighbourly behaviour. But when they begin doing things you didn't ask them to do and don't want done, you start feeling uncomfortable. They say things like, "I know you don't have time so I thought I'd trim those bushes for you." They've taken control away from you. If you tactfully try to object, they respond with a martyred air and tell you that they were only trying to be helpful, leaving you feeling guilty. Gradually you realise that you have been manipulated and are now obligated to them for all they have done for you, and the expectation follows that you will return the favour. If you don't, you will be reminded about all the times they have lent you this or that, looked after your pets while you were on holiday or invited you round. They might even be able to tell you exactly how many times you have accepted their hospitality and pointedly compare the paucity of invitations they have had from you.

Don't be fooled into thinking that this person has your best interests at heart. They are not like you. Their agenda is solely concerned with themselves. Their purpose is to make you feel remorseful so you do what they want, regardless of how you feel. The fact that you don't have time, are too busy or don't want to do something is completely irrelevant. You owe them and they want to collect, how and when they want. What you want simply doesn't come into it. They've boxed you into a corner. Eventually all you feel is resentment at being so callously used. You look back over your relationship and wonder just how you got to this point. The answer is that they planned it, right from the start. At this point, they play their trump card – they tell you about someone else who is grateful to them, *unlike you*. Whatever.

You may have to deal with this person carefully, considering that they are your neighbour and you are stuck with them until one of you moves. You must take back control and not let them do things off their own bat. If they continue, you will have to confront them and politely, but firmly, ask them to stop. When they want you to do something for them, just say that you're sorry but it isn't possible. You don't have to give a reason. Be friendly and say it with a smile, but be definite and never, ever capitulate under pressure from them.

Unfortunately, that isn't the end of the matter. They will tell anyone who will listen the story from their point of view, and paint themselves as the underdog. You will end up being the churlish neighbour who they were only trying to help. They have no respect for you but demand it from others. Don't worry – everyone knows what they are really like. In normal neighbour relationships, people help each other out and are genuinely humbled if their altruistic behaviour is reciprocated, but they don't expect it. They certainly don't keep score.

51. The Self-Sufficient Loner Neighbour : Green Flag

> "LONELINESS IS THE POVERTY OF THE SOUL.
> SOLITUDE IS THE RICHNESS OF THE SOUL."
> MAY SARTON

Now, if you are a naturally sociable person, this neighbour will have you totally confused. They seem to give out mixed messages and blow hot and cold, one day being friendly and chatty and the next day ignoring you completely. It baffles some people as to why their neighbours act like this. Their behaviour is interpreted as weird, deliberate, or arrogant, and that they only give you the time of day when they feel like it. You end up not knowing where you stand with them. Is it you? Have you upset them? Did you forget to wash this morning? But have you ever stopped to think that there might be a perfectly good explanation? They could be having an off day, be close to tears, about to explode with anger, be in an alcohol or medically induced haze, a hallucinogenic state, concentrating so much that they are oblivious to anything, deaf, in a trance or be listening to an unseen iPod. They might be in their own world, self-conscious, shy, depressed, sleep deprived, anxious, focused, don't recognise you out of context, be unobservant, have poor eyesight or hearing, be totally unaware of anything around them, in the zone or even all of the above!

Believe it or not, there are plenty of people who like to be alone. These lucky individuals are unabashed at walking into a pub on their own or asking for a table for one in a restaurant. In fact, they'll be enthusiastic about solo dining and extol the virtues of Eenmaal in Amsterdam, a pop-up venue for single diners, and be the first to try out London's new restaurant for lone customers. The most famous person who liked her own company was Greta Garbo, who was paradoxically a movie star who rejected fame and whose wish to be alone applied to both her public and private personae. She loathed publicity and lived a reclusive and solitary life, albeit while living in New York. The American poet and novelist May Sarton expressed it perfectly when she said that "Loneliness is the poverty of the soul. Solitude is the richness of the soul" and here lies the key to your Self-Sufficient Loner Neighbour. They are independent and self-reliant individuals who have absolutely no problem with being alone. Truth be known, they prefer it. They can do what they want, when they want, without answering to anyone else, and don't need the approval or comfort of others that so many of us crave. If you don't need others, there is no requirement to expend energy being friendly. Their perceived aloofness is just their way, and family, as well as neighbours, are not a hugely significant part of their life. They seldom give out their mobile number as it is for their use not yours, their excuse being that it is switched off all the time. They do this so they won't be disturbed. They shut their front door quietly, so they can sneak out without being accosted by their neighbours. They like to drive two-seaters so they can't take your kids to school when your car won't start, and would buy a one-seater car, if such existed, to give the ultimate excuse not to offer a lift to anyone at all. Their hobbies include reading and other solitary pastimes. Twister is not their idea of fun. They're the person at a party sitting in a corner reading a book. A holiday on a cruise ship, with 3000 other people, is their idea of hell. They would love to spend a blissful Christmas in a remote croft in the Highlands – alone except for the wildlife.

So when they retreat from you, remember – it's not about you. Don't take it personally. Give them the space they so clearly need and let them have the benefit of the doubt. If they are having a thoroughly unpleasant day, feeling like the world is closing over their heads, a cheery greeting from you may be just what they need. It will help them believe that someone cares, not everything is against them, and enables them to get things in perspective again. Never underestimate the impact that a simple kindness can make.

So just because they are private and reticent about getting involved in the messy lives of their neighbours, don't assume that they are emotionless or rude. They may exude an aura of capability, but if they ever ask for your help, it will mean that they are desperate, so please don't turn your back on them just because sometimes they are distant with you.

52. The Condescending Neighbour
: Red Flag

*"If you injure your neighbour,
better not do it by halves."*
George Bernard Shaw

It's all in the tone of the voice and That Look they give you along with the patronising remarks. They have this knack of making their neighbours feel stupid or inferior. Being rude is a deliberate ploy by them to undermine and belittle others, often in public because they think it looks clever in front of their equally obnoxious friends. Secretly they are insecure and jealous of you. If those present at your encounters laugh with them and you thought they were your friends, she is trying to separate them from you and it looks like she has succeeded. True friends do not like to watch someone they like being picked on. True friends are those who know you and still like you. If your Condescending Neighbour is talking about her upcoming party, she'll say, "I would invite you but I'm afraid you'd have nothing in common with the other guests." Another time you'll overhear her say, "Oh, yes it's lovely. Mind you, I would never wear something like that." You realise that you aren't the only one to be the butt of her snide comments so you canvass your nice neighbours for some other choice quotes from her and discover a goldmine of vicious asides which have left the recipient speechless. Then you all have a good laugh together which dispels the negative feelings she left you with. At some time or another you have heard her say:

"That colour was so very popular last year."

"Oh, you're a *vegetarian*…" said in the same tone as if you had told her you were an axe murderer.

In response to a neighbour who told her, "I've just come from the hairdressers," she responded with, "Was it shut?"

After asking how old a neighbour's child was she observed contemptuously, "He's very backward for his age."

On hearing which school a neighbour's children attended, she was reported to have said, "Well now that they have expelled that child at No 47, I'm sure it's reputation will improve."

Best advice is to ignore some remarks and confront others, but pick your fights with care. If you are confident enough, you could try playing them at their own game. If they happen to (intentionally) mention something you've never heard of, and you query it, they say something like "Let me see if I can explain it in terms simple enough for you to understand." Then they proceed to give you a lecture on the subject in a patronising tone, treating you like a complete dunce. By doing this they take on an air of superiority that most people find extremely irritating, intimating that they are so much more intelligent than you are. If you can bear to, pretend that you still don't understand and pursue the subject for further enlightenment, querying, "Do you mean this?" or "Do you mean that?" until you have tied them up in knots and exposed the narrow limits of their own knowledge and the penny finally drops that you are winding them up. You'll know you've got there when their expression changes to one that resembles a rat trap and they pause in full flow, draw themselves together, fix you with a suspicious glare and change the subject. Congratulations. They will be much more wary of you in future and are unlikely to try that particular game with you again now that you have made a fool of them.

When you have identified them as the Condescending Neighbour, the trick is never to ask their opinion. They regard this as feebleness on your part and they'll be in there with a cutting retort and laughing about you behind your back. And don't let them see you seething with discomfort or anger – they are watching for this reaction and it just encourages them. Resist the urge to punch them – they're not worth it. Anger is too strong an emotion to waste on someone you don't like. Develop a thick skin and trust your own judgement.

53. The Bully Neighbour
: RED FLAG

> "YOU MAY TALK OF THE TYRANNY OF NERO
> AND TIBERIUS; BUT THE REAL TYRANNY IS THE
> TYRANNY OF YOUR NEXT DOOR NEIGHBOUR."
> WALTER BAGEHOT

For some reason unbeknown to mankind, a lot of people have been unlucky enough to come into contact with bullies all their life, and most learn to deal with them at an early age. Maybe there are just a lot of them around! A bully takes many guises and their behaviour exists on a continuum from sly nudging to get what they want through to all-out intimidation, with shouting and threats. Not one of them knows the meaning of the word altruism, having absolutely no regard for others. If they had a coat of arms, their motto would be 'Sodomy omnibus altrui', roughly translated as 'Bugger everyone else'. Most people like to think that they have control of their own lives and loathe the idea that someone is grooming them to do what they want, without the slightest consideration for their time or what they might like to do or how they might feel.

You have to handle them judiciously as they often have a short fuse, so you have to know how far you can go so you don't cross them. In 2006, Charles Martin from Cincinnati, Ohio shot a 15-year-old boy and killed him, simply because he had the temerity to walk across his lawn. It is not unknown for bullies to come into your garden without so much as a by-your-leave, usually when they know you are out, trim the hedge between you and leave the clippings for you to clear up. Or they might decide that they don't like the smell from your bonfire of autumn leaves and come round, again when you're out, and pour a bucket of water over it. The fact that this neighbour regularly burns all sorts of dubious rubbish in his back garden, contrary to local regulations, is clearly different. He wants control and takes it. Next time, lock the gate so he can't get in, thereby taking back control of the situation. If he sticks a hose over the fence and points it in the direction of the offending blaze, chop it off with the shears.

There are a number of salient facts that pertain to all bullies.

1. They never ask for permission because they cannot deal with the possibility that they will be denied what they want.
2. They are very secretive.
3. They are unable to share or cooperate with others or discuss matters rationally.

4. Access is always refused or bartered for a favour in return.
5. They only socialise with people they consider useful to them.
6. They are totally focused on their own world and what they can get for themselves.
7. They tell lies about you to other neighbours, especially those you are friends with, in an effort to exclude and isolate you.
8. They never take responsibility for anything that goes wrong in their life, and will always find someone else to blame, however erroneously.
9. They may agree to do something for you but let you down at the last minute in a pathetic effort to exert control.
10. They like to make their feelings very clear – it's how they shore up their own identity.
11. They have the emotions of an ice cube.
12. They love to hear about any bad luck you have had.

Make sure you put a positive slant on anything negative that happens to you. Don't feed their schadenfreude – they get off on hearing about your troubles, failings and misfortunes. But be careful if you have some good news. Don't mention it to them directly because they won't like the fact that you have been lucky. On the other hand, you might enjoy witnessing their resentfulness when you tell them, ever so innocently, of your promotion, lottery win (you wish), new car, achievement or business success – just be on your guard for deprecating remarks or subsequent reprisals.

Good neighbours will stand up for you and take no notice of their tales of what you may or may not have done to upset them, and will repeat the bully's accusation to you so that you can refute it or have a good laugh about it.

Bullying tends to be a downward trend in that bullies only torment those they see as being subordinate, while ingratiating themselves with people they consider important to them. But they need to be careful, because what they don't appreciate is that one day, when they are on their way down, they will come across those same people that they have intimidated in the past. And when it becomes apparent that they are in a weak position, any supposed allies will quickly change sides or melt away at the first sign of trouble. People never forget a bully and will grab any opportunity to get their own back if the opportunity arises.

Psychologists have found that sometimes bullies cannot retaliate directly against the source of a provocation so they take their hostility out on someone they see as a vulnerable target. This is known as displaced aggression, in that they are shifting the frustration they feel about a totally different situation onto you, even though you are not the guilty party. You are not, however, a whipping boy for other people to blame for their own shortcomings, so if you don't understand what they are talking about, don't put up with it. If you stand your ground, they will back down. Yes, Bully Neighbours are often cowards when confronted head on. Generally, they only attempt it once. They will, however, brood on their loss of face and unfortunately bullies settle scores in spiteful ways, and will wait for a suitable opportunity to get back at you.

If the bullies believe that their tactics are working and they are getting their own way, they will think you are a wimp and then they will push the boundaries further and further to test what you are prepared to tolerate. If you are of the 'live and let live' type you will shrug your shoulders and let them get away with it just for a peaceful life, believing that if you ignore them it will stop. It won't. Appeasement merely rewards them and feeds their need for power. You will have shown that you can be controlled, so you become their main target and victim. There will come a day when they make one demand too many and you will have no choice but to take a stand. There is no alternative. You will have to face up to them and it will not be pretty. Prepare yourself for abuse, defiance and angry taunts. Be strong. They may come round to your house and shout at you for things you know you haven't done. Politely suggest they go home, calm down, and find out the facts. But don't expect an apology when they discover the truth. Bullies never apologise. They think that by apologising they lose face and are seen as weak, but psychologists agree that apologising when you are in the wrong is a sign of strength of character and shows courage. It doesn't have to be grovelling, just sincere. And there's that little extra frisson in knowing that an apology is the best way to get the last word!

In the end, when dealing with the Bully Neighbour, nothing fazes them more than showing them that you will not be intimidated. If possible, laugh at everything they say as they hate being humiliated or made to look stupid. Maintain eye contact, adopt a positive stance and stare them out. Exuding self-confidence, even if you are not 100% certain of the details, will always throw them off balance. They will forget what you said but not how you made them feel. Be prepared for the initial backlash, but ignore that too. These are not nice people and you do not need them in your life. If they are bullying you, they are trying it on with others too. These are people who wouldn't piss on you if you were on fire, unless there was something in it for them. If you think you are being bullied by your neighbour, nip it in the bud. It is easier to stop a bicycle than a juggernaut.

54. The Swinger Neighbours
: Amber Flag

> "SEX BETWEEN TWO PEOPLE IS A BEAUTIFUL THING – BETWEEN FIVE IT'S FANTASTIC."
> WOODY ALLEN

If you think your neighbours might be swingers, how can you be sure? Did you know that there are secret signs and symbols that swingers use to attract other swingers?

When talking to your neighbour, drop in the word 'vanilla' to describe something and wait for the reaction. Most people don't use this expression, unless in relation to ice cream, but it is a term that swingers allegedly use to describe non-swingers. If they use the phrase 'in the lifestyle', you know you're right. There are plenty of urban myths around to help you identify swingers, one of which is that they have pampas grass growing in their front garden. However, on its own this is no guarantee that your suspicions are correct. But if it's growing out of white landscaping rocks, you may be on to something. Do they have a flagpole? Do they fly a flag with a pineapple on it? Getting warmer. Alternatively, they may place a pineapple by their front door, which you probably thought nothing of, except that it was a strange place to put a pineapple when you tripped over it when returning a borrowed item. And you rapped on the door using their door knocker in the shape of a pineapple. If you're at the supermarket when you encounter your neighbour, surreptitiously glance into their trolley. Is there a pineapple in there? Is it upside down? Bingo!

So you're down at the gym and that guy or woman is just how you imagine a swinger looks. How can you tell? Are they wearing a ring tied to their shoe? Is that a yin-yang tattoo on their arm or shoulder? Ankle bracelets, thumb rings and toe rings are supposed to be swinger signs. If their jewellery has the word 'SLUT' on it, this is a sure indication. Wearing black rings on their right ring finger is another way of expressing their preferences, unless of course they're a Goth in which case it simply goes with the territory.

When you get home from work, look across and see if their overhead garage door is open. This may suggest that there is a swap party going on. It's another sign. Of course they may just have forgotten to close it, as we all do, or couldn't be bothered.

They tend to talk about people as couples, and guests at their parties are all in pairs and might be carrying overnight bags. When they go out socialising, they dress to get laid so a woman will be wearing a coat over her attire even on the hottest summer's evening. If you catch them in some interesting costume on their way out, they'll say they're going to a fancy dress party. Now, most people go to one of these perhaps once a year, but every week?

And if they invite you over for a drink and there's a fire pit in evidence and a hot tub steaming away in the back garden, prepare yourselves for an interesting evening. Their parties are frequent but never rowdy. On the contrary, they are suspiciously quiet as they don't want the police calling round, and all guests leave without making the usual goodbye greetings and hugs as they're exhausted and satiated and the clinches have all been done earlier. Oh, and they'll have a self-satisfied smirk on their faces and wink as they pass you when you're taking the dog out for a last pee.

We won't ask why you want to know if your neighbours are swingers. Curiosity, adventurer or voyeur perhaps? Just be aware that swingers won't have sex with just anyone. That's an urban myth too. They're just as picky as the next person as to who they'll get down and dirty with.

55. The Tiger Mother Neighbour
: Amber Flag

> "IT IS BETTER FOR A WOMAN TO COMPETE
> IMPERSONALLY IN SOCIETY, AS MEN DO, THAN TO
> COMPETE FOR DOMINANCE IN HER OWN HOME WITH
> HER HUSBAND, COMPETE WITH HER NEIGHBOURS
> FOR EMPTY STATUS, AND SO SMOTHER HER SON
> THAT HE CANNOT COMPETE AT ALL."
> BETTY FRIEDAN

Be afraid. Be very afraid. Tiger Mother has ambitions for her offspring that are way beyond the sharp-elbowed, pushy mother. She is fiercely competitive and has a cloying stranglehold on her children who are never allowed to be bored or have time off to entertain themselves. Every hour of the day is stuffed with activities to ensure that one day they are one of the privileged elite. By the age of three they are fluent bilingual readers. At five they can discuss the metaphysical poets, why they prefer George Herbert to Henry Vaughn and discuss the philosophical and spiritual aspects of each one's work. By six they know the difference between a simile and a metaphor. They know what zygapotheses are and the structure of deoxyribonucleic acid. The theory of relativity holds no fear for them. Only Latin is spoken at home.

When they get to twelve they don't play computer games, they design them. Television is banned, except for educational purposes. School holidays are spent with tutors, visiting museums, tennis coaching or taking part in an archaeological dig. Sleepovers and playdates are anathema and considered a waste of time if you want to raise a genius. Anyway, no other child is their intellectual equal.

You will hear them next door chanting their times tables by rote at the same time as doing their Suzuki violin practice. Even gap years are supervised activities and not the free-for-all adventure dossing on Thai beaches that is most young people's rite of passage prior to uni.

Pity those children – getting less than an A★ is unacceptable and they will be threatened with dire consequences and loss of their most prized possessions, even favourite teddies, if it happens again, and she is not bluffing. Her discipline verges on abuse. She does not understand why some parents want to be friends with their kids. She doesn't ask or negotiate: she orders and they obey.

Tiger Mothers will surround themselves with people who can be useful to them in their stratospheric upward mobility, and network ruthlessly to find internships that will look good on their children's CVs. She ignores most of the other mothers at the school gates as she considers that they are unworthy of her attention. She knows this because she has Googled them all and their partners to see if any of them merit her attention, which probably lets you off the hook. Be grateful – she has rude nicknames for any parents whose children could be considered to be competition, although there won't be many. She is not above being on the sidelines at her kids' football matches and yells and swears worse than their coach. Before sports day, she trains for months to ensure she wins the mother's race, which upsets your Sporting Neighbour, thereby setting her kids an example. She is the alpha female, with a significant other who achieved partner status at a precociously young age and is destined for great office. She identified him early on as being good genetic material for her children.

Criticise her progeny or their regime at your peril. This tiger has sharp claws and teeth and will not hesitate to use them. The children will probably grow up to be United Nations Secretary General or something in international development or manage some global project relating to security chains, solve the world's food problems, find a cure for Alzheimer's, or all of the above. Alternatively, they'll get to nineteen, rebel and drop out of life's aggressive and perpetual struggle, which they now see as dehumanising and futile, spending the rest of their lives as a beach bum/surf dude. If they last the pace until thirty, they'll burn out and live as a recluse in some antipodean paradise, carving trinkets for the tourists or saving dolphins.

Ponder for a moment what Tiger Mothers do after their young cubs have grown up and gone out into the big wide world. Do they mastermind their careers for them? Make finding them a suitable partner their next project? Their skills may be put into abeyance for a short time, but then there'll be grandchildren and she will start all over again.

56. The Highly Sensitive Neighbour : Green Flag

"I'VE BEEN ACCUSED MY WHOLE LIFE OF BEING TOO SENSITIVE. THIS ACTUALLY KIND OF PISSES ME OFF, BUT MAYBE THAT'S JUST BECAUSE I'M TOO SENSITIVE."
SOPHIA DEMBLING

Have you just had a discussion with a neighbour who complains about noise which you can't hear or that doesn't bother you? Who has tears in their eyes when talking about a piece of music they have heard, or a work of art they have seen recently or when you tell them that you had to have the guinea pig put down yesterday? Perhaps you know a neighbour who has just left another job claiming that nobody noticed how hard they worked and they just couldn't take the stress anymore? Who are so conscientious that even the simplest decisions make them anxious about making the wrong choice? Who notice the smallest details, such as the fact that another neighbour always wears green socks on Saturdays? You think that they wear their heart on their sleeve and take things very personally, but in reality they are a Highly Sensitive Person, or HSP. Dr Elaine Aron identified that 15–20% of the population can be described as Highly Sensitive, and that there are equal numbers of men and women, so there is bound to be at least one living near you.

They will leave your party early on some pretext, but the real reason is that they cannot be in a highly stimulating environment for long before they feel overwhelmed by too many sights and sounds, resulting in a sensation of suffocation or claustrophobia. An HSP can sense things that other people don't, and picking up on all those nuances, subtle undercurrents and atmospheres is exhausting. They are acutely aware of all those non-verbal cues in people's faces, their posture and tone of voice, which convey so much information to them, and may conflict with what is actually being said. To them, ambiance is a physical thing, having shape and colour. As if by magic they know when you are upset (or lying) even though you thought you were covering your feelings well, and putting on a brave face. And they're good listeners, although it is a little disconcerting to find that they are constantly dabbing their eyes as you tell them your woes and seem to be feeling your pain more than you are. They genuinely experience your angst so please don't dump on them too often.

They cannot bear to hear people shouting, dogs barking, engines revving or be with those exuding negative vibes. Tragic events on the news, with all the associated emotional scenes, can seriously upset them.

They never go to films with extreme violence and aggression. Being in stressful situations for a long period results in tension and can lead to lower back problems and digestive disorders. Multi-tasking is a word they dread and they hate being in a situation where they have lots of plates in the air simultaneously, which makes them irritable, so don't put time pressures on them, if possible. Consequently, they structure their lives to avoid rushing – they allow plenty of time to do a job and they are rarely late for a meeting. Their homes are tidy and uncluttered. If they commit to arranging an event, it is well planned in advance to avoid the last minute panic that many people relish. To avoid crowds and noise they are the first into the supermarket when it opens and suss out the quietest times to use the gym. They travel off-peak and make long distance journeys by car in the small hours to prevent getting stuck in rush hour traffic.

They may seem anti-social, and are frequently misunderstood by the rest of us, but life drains them and to recharge and protect themselves they need a lot of time alone, with peace and quiet. Respect this.

And if you recognise these symptoms in yourself, stop believing there's something wrong with you.

57. The Second Homer Neighbour
: Amber Flag

"IF YOU BURN YOUR NEIGHBOUR'S HOUSE DOWN, IT DOESN'T MAKE YOUR HOUSE LOOK ANY BETTER."
LOU HOLTZ (AMERICAN FOOTBALL PLAYER, COACH AND ANALYST)

If you have Second Homers as neighbours then you live somewhere desirable for its views, weather, vibes or bijou cottages and shops. Lucky you! Most of us dream about escaping from the drudgery of the working week to a second home, with the idea of perhaps one day living there full time.

The typical stereotype of the Second Homer is someone from London who buys a lock-up-and-leave fisherman's cottage in Cornwall. They arrive late on a Friday night, disgorging children from an immaculate and brand new four-wheel-drive Chelsea tractor, harassed and stressed from a long working week in the city. If they talk to their neighbours, it is to complain about the lack of parking in the narrow streets which were only ever designed for pedestrians and carts, not vehicular traffic belching carbon monoxide. They bring their own food and shun the village shops because they're not organic, and eat out at the most expensive seafood restaurant that the locals can't afford. They have an idyllic view of the bay and believe that the sun always shines and the sea is always calm and blue. They rave to their London friends and neighbours about how de-stressing their second home is, how they keep the community buoyant in the summer by supporting jobs, not realising that these are only temporary and not given to locals but mostly done by itinerant foreign workers at less than minimum wage.

The reality is that, when they open the front door, there is a pile of junk mail and an overwhelming smell of damp due to lack of heating and ventilation and a dead mouse in the bath. On Christmas Eve, they arrive to find the pipes have frozen and split, water has escaped and the ceilings have collapsed. They can't understand why the plumber (whose family has lived in the village for generations and is still living with his parents as he can't afford to buy anywhere because he has been priced out by the so-called grockles) won't come out immediately and fix it. Or that romantic tinkling brook running past the front door has turned into a raging torrent and swept away half the garden and flooded the downstairs. For the affluent who could afford the old harbour master's cottage, they arrive to find that the winter storms have driven 15cm of water, sand and seaweed in on a storm surge at the spring tides or squatters have taken up residence. While they were absent, the neighbours have cut down the boundary trees and erected a fence, gaining several feet of territory in the process and someone has stolen the quaint lobster pot, anchor, driftwood seat, colourful floats, bunting and other seaside paraphernalia from the coastal-themed garden. Then they buzz off on Sunday afternoon and go back to their mansions, reducing the place to a ghost town. This means that there aren't enough local children at the village school and it has had to close, resulting in a two-hour round trip every day during term time. You can't really blame the locals for griping – most times of the year, except for what passes for a British summer, and maybe Easter, Christmas and half terms, the place is deserted. No wonder that places like St Ives and Padstow are using their neighbourhood plans to prevent any new builds going to people not working in the area or having lived locally for a number of years, as Second Homers suck the life out of communities.

Secretly the Second Homer is worried about the costs of council tax and maintenance, on top of the private school fees and hefty mortgages they are paying. The sea air is taking a toll on the property and it is a financial money pit. All that, combined with the treacherous travel over snowy moors at Christmas and the time taken to get there in the summer when the A303 is a car park, and it is no wonder they are weary. Not to mention the flocks of friends descending for a freebie holiday during which they don't lift a finger and expect to be waited on hand and foot. So they are thinking of selling up. The trouble is that it's now far too expensive for the local market, bonuses in London are being squeezed, people aren't buying second homes like they were and they will have to pay capital gains tax on any profits. And how would they explain selling up to their cronies?

58. The Perfect Neighbour
: HANG OUT ALL THE FLAGS AND LOTS OF BUNTING!

"A GOOD NEIGHBOUR IS A FELLOW WHO SMILES AT YOU OVER THE FENCE, BUT DOESN'T CLIMB OVER IT."
ARTHUR BAER

Does such a mythical creature exist? If you have a neighbour who fits this description then you are fortunate indeed!

Their house is not immaculate and housework does not take priority over anything more interesting (i.e. everything else). The children are polite and considerate. They are not young Einsteins and even their parents admit that. They offer to collect your kids from school when you're busy, tired, harassed or just fancy half an hour to yourself, without making you feel guilty. They even take your kids and watch them play football in the pouring rain when you have to work late. They notice when you're unwell and buy extra food so you don't have to go out. They bring a casserole over when you come out of hospital or a bottle of wine when your partner's left you. They offer a shoulder to cry on and listen patiently while you have a whinge, but are not judgemental. They know where to get information. They share your sadness. You laugh at the same things. They are genuinely pleased at any windfall you have and offer support for the tough decisions that have to be made. If they say they'll do something, they never let you down. They don't out stay their welcome.

Their clothes are not designer unless they got lucky at the jumble sale or charity shop. They lend you their posh clothes when you get a special invitation and have nothing to wear. They loan you their tools and don't make a fuss when you break something (and, of course, you apologise and promise to replace it). They borrow something and bring it back in better fettle than when you lent it to them. They water your plants when you're on holiday without drowning them or forgetting. They offer the right help at the right time without you having to ask.

They invite you to their BBQs and include you in their family gatherings which are always full of fun and laughter. They always say the right thing when you are feeling overwhelmed – how do they do that? When you're upset they put their arms around you and simply say "There, there. It'll be all right." You know it won't, but it gives you enormous comfort.

And it's not just about what they do. It's about what they don't do. They don't talk about you behind your back or spread gossip about you. They don't burn obnoxious rubbish on a sunny day when you're likely to be in the garden. They give you plenty of notice when something is happening that might inconvenience you, and go out of their way to ensure the minimum disruption when they have building work going on. They defend you when others are being nasty.

They do all this and more AND EXPECT NOTHING IN RETURN. And that's what makes them Perfect Neighbours.

And isn't that what we should all be doing?

Those Nicknames For The Neighbours We Love To Hate

"NICKNAMES STICK TO PEOPLE AND THE MOST
RIDICULOUS ARE THE MOST ADHESIVE."
THOMAS CHANDLER HALIBURTON

Come on, admit it. You have nicknames for the neighbours, just like the rest of us! It might seem spiteful and vindictive, but it is fun! The habit of bestowing a nickname on someone has been the subject of research by sociologists and offers some fascinating insights into neighbourly relations and how people behave towards each other. The word 'nickname' means 'extra name' and originates from the Middle English 'eke name'. In an age where 82% of Londoners don't know what their neighbours do for a living and 70% don't know their full names, it is inevitably that a moniker is given to them, so that they can be quickly identified when discussing them with someone else. How they are chosen depends on the circumstances, but the hallmark of a clever nickname is the ability to conjure up a picture of that person, or concentrate a defining event involving them or highlight a particular character trait or physical attribute in just one or two words. To differentiate between two neighbours both called Fred, one might be Just Fred and the other might be Fred-with-the-spaniel. The best names display dry wit, sarcasm or a well-observed peculiarity specific to that person. Nicknames create a secret language between those in the know, and reinforce a 'them and us' mentality, and usually indicate a lack of respect or deference. Usually the victim is unaware of the nickname, unless someone has the temerity to use it to their face in a moment of anger or frustration, or you have confided it in an unguarded, usually drunken, rant to another neighbour and they sneakily repeat what you have said to the neighbour in question, thereby getting you into (even more) trouble. As they are more often than not derisory, the neighbour is unlikely to find out his nickname, and generally it's more politic and much more fun to keep it to yourselves.

Nicknames tend to fall into one of a number of categories:

1. Physical features
2. Behavioural traits
3. Alliteration
4. Origins
5. Similarity to TV, cartoon, book, real life or film characters
6. What they do for a living
7. Descriptive

1. PHYSICAL FEATURES

Fatso
Baldy
Big Ears
Bride of Wildenstein
Ponytail
Blondie
Crow Face
Shorty
Lanky
Tango (false tan)
Footie Shirt
Tattoo
Twat in a Hat
Gorilla
Potato Head
Apeman
Goth
Thug
Pygmy
Specky Four Eyes
Syrup (of figs)
Moby Dick
Medusa
Big Foot
The Gorgon
Carrot Top
Freckles
Twiggy

Leggy
Cue Ball
Lunchbox
The Geek
Plain Jane
John Doe
Sweaty Face
Budgie Smuggler
Pot Belly/Fat Belly
Prune Face

2. BEHAVIOURAL TRAITS

Grouchy
Boy Racer
Tricky Dickie
Wifezilla
Dumbo
Action Man
The Floozy
The Birdman (feeds birds)
Mummy's Boy
Big Mouth
Motormouth
Gob on a Stick
Gobby
Barkosaurus
Wet Dog

Grumpy

Grumpy Boots

Grumpy Cow

Revhead (revving bike)

Kiss my Ass

Mr File (Peter File = paedophile)

Mr and Mrs Hitler

Mr Know-it-all

Mr Fix-it

Doughnuts

Sour Puss

Pit Bull

Lord and Lady Muck

The Dragon

Tigger

Honest John

Moneybags

Her Royal Highness

Sloan Ranger

Punch and Judy

Booger (nose picker)

Dopeyboots

Superbrat

Flash Harry

Bible Bashers

God Squad

Fag Ash Lil

Spring Heeled Jack

Half Past Seven (because he goes out at that time
every night)

The Boss
Sunny Jim
Doubting Thomas
Pollyanna
Billy No Mates
Fancy Pants
Billy Whizz

3. ALLITERATION

Ratty Ray
Porky Pig
Fred Flintstone
King Kong
Jungle Jim
Moaning Minnie
Mighty Mouse
Roger Rabbit
Nosy Nellie
Donald Duck
Gentleman Jim
Pink Panther
Olive Oyl
Bungalow Bill
Duncan Disorderly
Dick Dastardly
Penelope Pitstop
Plastic Paddy

Sheep Shagger
Bilbo Baggins
Bugs Bunny
Tiny Tim
Willy Wonka
Benjamin Brat
Tintin
Clark Kent
Big Bertha
Doctor Doom
Silver Surfer
Wonder Woman
Severus Snape
Billy Bunter
Road Runner
Woody Woodpecker
Basil Brush
Roland Rat
Noggin the Nog
Minnie the Minx
Nervous Nellie
Droopy Drawers
Mad Max
Billy Bunter
Minnie the Moocher
Train Tracks
Nasty Nick
Anal Annie
Peter Perfect
Hooray Henry

Judge Judy
Nutty Nora
Posing Pouch
Foghorn Fred

4. ORIGINS

The Italians
The Irish Lot
Scouser
Geordie
Country Bumpkin
The Townies
Troll
Monkey Hanger
Aussie
Banana Bender
Brummie
Cockney
Culchie
Tyke
Taffy
Kraut
Kiwi
Frog
Gringo
Hillbilly
Swansea Jack

Woollyback
Eurotrash
Bogtrotter
Cheesehead
Eye-tie
Jock
Mickey Finn
Paddy
Moonraker

5. SIMILARITY TO TV, CARTOON, BOOK, REAL LIFE OR FILM CHARACTERS

Victor Meldrew
Wallace and Gromit
Hot lips (Houlihan from M*A*S*H)
Posh and Becks
Vicky Pollard (chav)
Barbie and Ken
The Adams Family
Andy Capp
The Grinch (moans when Christmas lights go up in November)
Mapp and Lucia
Scrooge
Miss Piggy
Cat Woman
Munch Bunch

Mr Toad
Little and Large
Hawkeye
Cruella de Vil
Mr Blobby
The Teletubbies
Tardis Family (lots of people and vehicles)
The Clampetts (hillbillies)
Psycho
The Simpsons
The Muppets
The Waltons
Wicked Witch of the West
Mrs Bucket
Noddy and Big Ears
The Poison Dwarf
Tweedledee and Tweedledum
Pinky and Perky
Muffin the Mule
Mickey Mouse
Minnie Mouse
Peter Pan
Tracy Turnblad
Seasick Steve
SpongeBob SquarePants
Uriah Heap
Frankenstein
Dracula
Don Juan
Svengali

Machiavelli
The Fonz
The Terminator
She Who Must Be Obeyed
Biggles
Popeye
Bones
Parker (Thunderbirds)
Mary Poppins
Big Daddy
Tinkerbell
Brainiac
The Badd Ladds
The Numskulls
The Country Cuzzins
Master Bates
Lurch
Dr Strangelove
Dennis the Menace
Gnasher

6. WHAT THEY DO FOR A LIVING

Professor Plum
Holy Joe
Bean Counter
Bob the Builder
Postman Pat

The Professor
Doc
PC Plod
Grease Monkey
Chippie
Drain-O
Paper Pusher
Pen Pusher
Sparky
Trolley Dolly
Turd Herder

7. DESCRIPTIVE

Harry's Mum (Harry being dog, cat or child)
Old Dave
Young Dave
Fag-a-lot
The Beamers (2+ BMWs)
Thug Life
Her Upstairs
Her Downstairs
Her Indoors
Madam Next Door
Money Bags
Mutton (dressed as lamb)
Jailbait
Fur Coat (and no knickers)

If you fancy your own nickname, I have to tell you that it is not done to choose one for yourself. They must be bestowed upon you. However, Googling 'Nickname Generator' brings up 713,000 search results. Go, Tiger!

Quiz: What Sort Of Neighbour Are You?

"I don't pretend we have all the answers. But the questions are certainly worth thinking about." Arthur C. Clarke

So, you've identified all those pesky neighbours, but how about if the tables were turned? What do your neighbours think about you? We all like to think of ourselves as the neighbour we would like to have. But are we? Take our light hearted quiz to discover just what your neighbours think about you!

1. **Do you**

a) always greet your neighbours with a friendly wave and a smile?
b) acknowledge those you like and ignore the rest?
c) hide when you see a neighbour coming?
d) stick two fingers up at any neighbour you encounter?

2. IF YOU HAVE A COMPLAINT ABOUT THEM, DO YOU

a) excuse them their misdemeanours?
b) go round with cakes and explain that you are sure they didn't appreciate the problem?
c) write them an anonymous letter?
d) get up a petition to have them evicted?

3. IF YOU'RE HAVING A PARTY, DO YOU

a) invite all the neighbours?
b) invite all the neighbours except the grumpy ones?
c) invite only those neighbours you consider to be important?
d) invite none of the neighbours and make sure the volume is turned up to maximum?

4. IF YOU GO TO SOMEONE ELSE'S PARTY, DO YOU

a) breeze in with plenty of bottles and offer to help the host?
b) greet everyone vaguely and only talk to one person all night?
c) look for the people who can be useful to you and monopolise them all night?
d) get drunk and start a fight?

5. **IF YOU ACCIDENTALLY RECEIVE A LETTER ADDRESSED TO A NEIGHBOUR, DO YOU**

a) deliver it to the correct address straight away?
b) examine it for clues then drop it in the post box for redelivery?
c) steam it open carefully, read it, reseal it and deliver it under cover of darkness?
d) bin it unopened?

6. **IF SOMEONE AT A PARTY INTRODUCES YOU TO THE NEW NEIGHBOUR, DO YOU**

a) use it as a great opportunity to get to know them?
b) make small talk but leave asap?
c) complain about their peeling paintwork?
d) turn your back on them and walk away?

7. **NEW NEIGHBOURS HAVE JUST MOVED IN. DO YOU**

a) go round with a card and a bunch of flowers?
b) smile if you see them but don't approach them?
c) find out as much as possible about them on social media?
d) let your dogs out to poop on their lawn?

8. YOUR NEIGHBOUR SUBMITS A PLANNING APPLICATION FOR A TASTEFUL EXTENSION. DO YOU

a) tell your neighbours how nice it will look and offer to support their application?
b) feel jealous and start planning your own extension?
c) immediately go round and complain about stealing light, noise, builders making a mess, skips in the road etc?
d) plan a burglary while the property is vulnerable?

9. YOU WANT TO BUILD A CONSERVATORY. DO YOU

a) consult the neighbours before submitting the application?
b) make sure you order blinds so the neighbours can't see in?
c) put in the plans without telling them, because it's none of their business?
d) build it without planning permission?

10. IF THEY COMPLAIN THAT YOUR DOGS ARE BARKING WHEN YOU'RE OUT, DO YOU

a) apologise and arrange for the dog to go to doggy crèche when you're out?
b) ask if they'll pop in and let them into the garden?

c) say you can't hear them?

d) get your solicitor to write them a letter warning them off?

11. IF THEY MENTION THAT THEY CAN HEAR YOU HAVING SEX, DO YOU

a) laugh it off?

b) feel embarrassed?

c) invite them to join you?

d) tell them they're only jealous?

12. YOU BUY A NEW SOFA. DO YOU

a) offer the old one to someone else?

b) take it to the tip?

c) burn it in the garden when the neighbour's washing is out?

d) leave the old one in the front garden so the kids can play on it?

13. YOU HAVE TEENAGERS WHO LIKE TO INVITE THEIR FRIENDS ROUND AND PLAY LOUD MUSIC. DO YOU

a) build them a soundproofed shed in the garden?

b) only allow it at weekends and insist the noise is kept down?

c) let them stay up until all hours making as much noise as they like?

d) go on holiday and leave them to it?

14. YOU HAVEN'T SEEN YOUR ELDERLY NEIGHBOUR FOR A FEW DAYS. DO YOU

a) knock on the door and check she's OK?
b) assume she's gone away?
c) pretend you hadn't noticed?
d) hope she's died because she was always complaining about you?

15. YOU'VE HEARD SOME JUICY GOSSIP ABOUT A NEIGHBOUR. DO YOU

a) tell them so that they can refute it if it's untrue?
b) keep it to yourself?
c) repeat it to one or two of your closest friends but tell them not to pass it on?
d) tell everyone and throw in a few fictitious details to make it more interesting?

16. YOU'RE OFF ON HOLIDAY AND SET THE ALARM. DO YOU

a) give the neighbour a spare key and the code so they can stop it if it goes off accidentally?

b)   do nothing? The alarm box is only for show.
c)   go on holiday and leave no information with anyone?
d)   inform the alarm company that your neighbours are all thieves?

17. IF THE NEIGHBOURS BUY A BRAND NEW CAR, DO YOU

a)   go round, admire it and be genuinely pleased for them?
b)   do the maths to see if you can afford a better model than theirs?
c)   tell them it came bottom in a Which? Magazine survey?
d)   sneak out one dark night and run a key down the side of it?

18. THEIR CHILD GETS INTO THE SCHOOL OF THEIR CHOICE AND YOURS DIDN'T. DO YOU

a)   accept that your child is not academic and wish your neighbour's child well?
b)   hire a private tutor?
c)   hire a barrister and take it to appeal?
d)   start a rumour that they are dealing dope in the playground?

19. **YOU MEET YOUR NEIGHBOUR AT THE SCHOOL GATES WHEN YOU ARE PICKING UP YOUR KIDS. DO YOU**

a) volunteer to pick hers up in future or start a rota?
b) in future tell your child you'll be waiting round the corner?
c) make sure she hears that darling Tabitha is in the Gifted and Talented programme?
d) tell all the other mums that her children have nits?

20. **YOUR NEIGHBOUR STARTS A BONFIRE OF THEIR AUTUMN LEAVES. DO YOU**

a) breathe in the seasonal aroma and ask if you can put some potatoes in the embers?
b) start coughing loudly in the garden?
c) go round and pour a bucket of water over it?
d) gather up all your old plastic sacks and old rubbish then light a bigger one? They'll get the blame.

21. **YOUR NEIGHBOUR IS UNWELL AND CAN'T GET OUT. DO YOU**

a) bring her kids round to yours for meals, ferry them to school and do her shopping until she's better?
b) keep well away? She might be infectious.
c) hope it's something serious?
d) tell all the other neighbours that her partner's beaten her up?

22. IT'S CHRISTMAS EVE, IT'S STARTING TO SNOW AND YOUR NEIGHBOUR'S BOILER HAS BROKEN DOWN. DO YOU

a) invite them all round to yours for Christmas? The more the merrier.
b) reluctantly lend them your camping stove?
c) suggest they get the boiler serviced earlier next year like you did?
d) say "Bah humbug" and throw another log on the fire?

23. A NEIGHBOUR PARKS A SKIP OUTSIDE THEIR HOUSE. DO YOU

a) offer to help them move their rubbish into it?
b) feel that it lowers the tone of the neighbourhood?
c) inspect the contents each day and help yourself to anything worth having?
d) chuck loads of your own rubbish in without asking?

24. YOU FIND A DOG BELONGING TO A NEIGHBOUR WHO LIVES A FEW HOUSES AWAY. WOULD YOU

a) immediately return it to its owner?
b) ignore it? It'll find its own way home.
c) chuck a bucket of water at it?
d) take it to the dog pound?

25. A NEIGHBOUR COMES ROUND WITH A COMPLAINT. WOULD YOU

a) apologise for upsetting them, invite them in, give them a cup of tea and ask them to explain the problem so you can deal with it?

b) look through the peep hole to see who it is and then not open the door?

c) slam the door in their face when you hear what they have to say?

d) start a massive row and shout at them until they back off?

MOSTLY AS: Your house has roses round the door, the 'Welcome' on the mat is genuine, and the kettle is always on. You are there to listen but are not judgemental. You never outstay your welcome. You lend a hand without being asked, are tolerant and generous with time and possessions. You try to live your life with respect for others. We could all learn a lot from you. You are a very good-hearted neighbour and one we would all like to have living next door to us. You have either lied in every question or you are a figment of the imagination and don't exist.

MOSTLY BS: You're selective in who you confide in and have sussed out the timewasters and nutters but will pass the time of day with all the neighbours as you like to think that you are a nice person. You try to appease people who are nasty to you and rarely stand up for yourself in case you upset someone. You are unlikely to complain to anyone's face. You like to feel that you are part of the community and will help out if asked but prefer to stay in the background. You think of yourself as shy – everyone else thinks you're either very clever at negotiating neighbourly relations or pathetic.

MOSTLY CS: You consider yourself too busy and too self-important to take much notice of the neighbours, but like to hear what's going on even if you're not prepared to get involved or help out. You especially like gossip that is salacious or derogatory as it makes you feel better about your miserable lot, but get very defensive if it is about you. You stalk the neighbours on Twitter and Facebook and like to start rumours and see how long it takes for them to get back to you. You won't help anyone unless there's something in it for you or you want to ingratiate yourself with someone you can later ask for a return favour to get something you want.

MOSTLY DS: You couldn't care less about your neighbours whom you consider to be snotty-nosed and always complaining about you. You consider that you have every right to do anything you please, and do not have to take anyone else's views into account. You use denial as a defence mechanism and try to blame others. You like to have control and are happy to tell other people what they should be doing, but are not willing to get your hands dirty. You think you are better than everyone else and show your mean side when not getting your own way. You are the neighbour from hell.

TV Shows, Plays, Films And Books About Neighbours

"Theatre is life. Cinema is art. Television is furniture." Origin Unknown

Neighbours have been a good source of material for a number of scriptwriters and documentary makers over the years. Even Shakespearean characters had trouble with the neighbours. In *Much Ado about Nothing* Leonato says to Dogberry, "Neighbours you are tedious." Some stories in shows on TV and in the theatre, on the big screen and the radio, and in print are well-observed satires of domestic life. At the other extreme are the true-life horror stories of homicidal maniacs and weirdos. Here are just a few. Not all are directly about neighbours but they creep in somewhere. Every story set in a house, around a family or in a community eventually has the neighbours coming round to ask something, doing something weird or being murdered.

The Simpsons
Operation Meet the Street
Abigail's Party
Run for your Wife
Love Thy Neighbour
Neighbourhood Watch
Everybody Loves Raymond
The Good Life
Mrs Brown's Boys
Madea's Neighbours from Hell
Neighbours
Beggar my Neighbour
The Flintstones
EastEnders
What the Neighbours Did
Ruby Moon
Next Door Neighbours
West Side Story
The Curious Incident of the Dog in the Night-Time
Emmerdale
Coronation Street
Friends
The Nightmare Neighbour Next Door
Neighbourhood Watched
Neighbourhood Blues
Neighbours from Hell

FILMS

Paranormal Activity 4 (2012)
Apt Pupil (1998)
Arlington Road (1999)
National Lampoon's Christmas Vacation (1989)
Stepford Wives (1975)
Rear Window (1954)
Pacific Heights (1990)
Drive (2011)
Duplex (2003)
In the Realms of the Unreal (2004)
Village of the Damned (1960, 1995)
Rosemary's Baby (1968)
Barton Fink (1991)
Trouble the Water (2008)
Invasion of the Body Snatchers (1956, 1978)
Boyz N the Hood (1991)
The Wicker Man (1973, 2006)
The Apartment (1960)
Bad Neighbours (2014)
Explorers (1985)
The Girl Next Door (2007)
Edward Scissorhands (1990)
Poltergeist (1982, 2015)
Can't Buy Me Love (1987)
Neighbours (1981)
Love Thy Neighbour (1973)
Disturbia (2007)
Drive Me Crazy (1999)

Consenting Adults (1992)

The Burbs (1989)

Home Alone (1990)

Good Neighbour Sam (1964)

Monster House (2006)

Lakeview Terrace (2008)

Toy Story (1995)

Up (2009)

Silence of the Lambs (1991)

The People Under the Stairs (1991)

Fright Night (1985, 2011)

Friends: The Movie (2015)

Now and Then (1995)

Clueless (1995)

Get Over It (2001)

My Girl (1991)

Deck the Halls (2006)

Butterflies are Free (1972)

The Double (2013)

Fright Night (2011)

Spanking the Monkey (1994)

The Drop (2014)

Christmas Angel (2009)

Seven Brides for Seven Brothers (1954)

Gran Torino (2008)

Funny Games (1997)

Body Double (1984)

Ghostbusters (1984)

Project X (2012)

House at the End of the Street (2012)

What Their House Name Says About Your Neighbours

"A house without a name is a house without a soul." Graham Gould

Sometimes when you buy a place it comes with a name, and it can tell you a lot about the previous occupants and what they thought was cool or funny. Music lovers might, quite innocently, call their house *Eroica* and proudly and neatly stencil the name onto the mail box. It is, of course, the name of Beethoven's Symphony No. 3 in E-flat major, Opus 55, in case you didn't know. But the neighbours will inevitably refer to it as Erotica, and any new owners are likely to decide that it has to go. You can only hope that changing the name of a house is not considered as inauspicious as changing the name of a ship.

The Halifax Building Society carried out the first and largest survey of house names in the UK in 1988, and the most popular name was The Bungalow, followed by The Cottage which just shows how inspired most people were when naming their property. In fact, amongst the top 100 there were twenty-eight names beginning with The… including The Gables, The Croft, The Barn, The Beeches, The Nook, and The Mount, and intriguingly The Nurses' Home which came in at No. 45. Whether this was as a result of redundant hospitals being redeveloped as homes or a reflection of the occupant's job was not revealed.

Flowers and trees are always in fashion for house names, conjuring up thatched cottages in pretty villages with roses round the door and set amongst picturesque gently rolling hills. So we find Snowdrop Cottage, Pear Tree Cottage, Ivy Cottage, Rest Harrow, Periwinkle, Honeysuckle Cottage, The Laurels, Sweetbriar, Bluebells, The Sycamores, Oaklands, The Pines, Silver Birches, Conifers, The Oaks, The Limes, The Hollies, Elm View and Beechcroft. The landscape continues to be a source of inspiration to those who favour Sunset Cottage, Hillside, Meadow View, Hill View, Fair View, Church View, and Belle Vue. Some find inspiration from the time of year: Christmas Cottage, Easter Cottage, April Cottage, September Cottage, October Morning, Morning Glory, Michaelmas Cottage, Lammas Cottage, Spring Cottage, Summer Breeze, The Winter Gardens, Autumn Tints and Four Seasons. The precariously sited property might be given the name Brinkcliffedge just to reinforce the point. Lane End describes its position. Summer Breeze, Chinook, Roaring Forties, The Bora, Mistral, Shamal, Sirocco, Pampero and anything with the word wind in it, such as Windrustle, Trade Winds and West Winds conjures up bracing and blustery locations. The well-known landmark in Thorpeness, Suffolk, is perfectly described by its name – The House in the Clouds.

Animals and where they live frequently feature in house names: Squirrel's Leap, Dolphins, Frog Hollow, Badger's End, The Dog House, Bearsden, The Rabbit Hutch, The Pig Pen, The Earth, The Lodge, The Beehive, The Burrow, The Warren, The Den, The Byre, The Dray. Similarly for birds: Two Hoots, Magpies, Rookery Nook, Nightingales, Dovedale, Sparrows, Ravenswood, Windhover, Mallards, Jackdaws, Robin's Rest, Wild Goose, Oystercatchers, The Cuckoo's Nest, The Eyrie, The Chicken Coop, The Roost, The Nest. Anywhere called Noah's Park probably has lots of pets.

Houses with a coastal connection have a plethora of quaint names to choose from: The Moorings, Seashells, Harbour Lights, Smugglers, The Anchorage, Driftwood, Seahorses, Waterside, The Bosun's Locker, Admiral's Rest, The Lookout, Creekside, Sea Shanty, Sandpipers, Sea Breeze, Seaview and Bayview (forever reminiscent of childhood holidays), Shore-enuff, Seastheday, The Saucy Seagull (after the trawler in the radio series *The Navy Lark*) or Gone Fission (from *The Simpsons*). The Lobster Pot always reminds you of a tearoom on the quay where you can while away a sunny afternoon with scones and tea served in vintage china cups, watching the fishing boats come and go followed by a raucous flock of seagulls.

Famous ships, real and fictional, can be a source of creativity and have spawned house names such as Argo, Canberra, Gloriana, Kon Tiki, Mayflower, Nautilus,

Terra Nova, Aurora, Altair, The Dawn Treader, Ark Royal, Calypso, Cutty Sark, Morning Cloud, Swallow, Amazon, Ben-my-Chree or even Enterprise. The house excruciatingly named The Love Nest could have been inappropriately named after the whaling ship in the 1923 Buster Keaton film of the same name and Red October was given its name long before the 1984 film of the hunt for a Russian submarine, for the autumn colours of the surrounding woodland.

Seven Seas would be a good name for a house near the coast that also had the number seven in its address. This leads on to thinking about other names for houses with specific numbers such as Kelly's Eye (1), Little Boy Blue (2), Set of Jacks (5), Tom Mix (6), Samurai (7), Deadly Sins (7), The Magnificent (7), The Garden/Golden Gate (8), Doctor's Orders (9), Downing Street (10), Firdene (13), Tetheradick (13), Valentines (14), Dancing Queen (17), Royal Salute (21), Little Ducks (22), Duck and Dive (25), Pick'n'Mix (26), Half a Crown (26), Rise & Shine (29), Burlington (Bertie – 30), Buckle My Shoe (32), Steps (39), Top Banana (49), Bull's Eye (50), Pack o' Cards (52), Musty Hive (55), Shotts (bus from Glasgow to Shotts – 56), Heinz (57), Brighton Line (59), Baker's Bun (61), Tickety-Boo (62), Clickety-click (66), Any Way Up (69), Par (72), Queen Bee (73), Trombones (76), Sunset Strip (77), Heaven's Gate (78), One More Time (79), Red Balloons (99), The Ton (100).

Then there are those who clearly found the process of searching for their dream home a stressful occupation, hence Thisisit and Tether's End, a variation of the popular

Wit's End, Duz Us and It'll Do. Some like the name to reflect their attitude to buying it or like you to know something about their lifestyles, so call their home Costa Lotta, Costa Bom, Millstone, Kantafordyt, Hocktober, Little Worth, The Money Pit or Bedlam, Mon Repos, Stayinput, Seldom Inn, Happy Ours and Crackatinnie. You have to admire the wit of the person who named the house with the gravel garden Sycamowin.

In days of yore, the name informed you of the craft being peddled within or what the house's origins were. So houses were called Saddlers, Cobblers, Thatchers, The Granary, The Apple Barn, The Pigsty, The Old Post Office, Truncheons (being the old police house), The Orchard, The Walled Garden, The Smithy, Wheelwrights, Coopers, The Coach House, The Old Stud, The Old Vicarage, The Old Rectory, Cricketers, The Old Tannery, The Toll House, Tithe Barn, The Old Schoolhouse, The Old Chapel, The Station Master's House, Stonemill, The Lighthouse, The Boathouse, Millwright's Cottage, The Old Wash House, Scriveners, Weavers, Shepherds or The Manse. A house called Peelers, Constable Cottage or Copper's End would tell you something about the occupation of a past or present incumbent and Aftermath is perfect for the retired mathematics teacher. Would you call a property The House of Commons? Perhaps the original owner had political aspirations.

Patron saints are a common sight on house name signs, so we have St Anns – the patron saint of equestrians, sailors and homemakers.

St Michaels – soldiers, police and security officers.

St Patricks – engineers.

St Phocas – gardeners.

St Stephens – bricklayers.

St Vitus – comedians and dancers.

St Yves – lawyers.

St Valentines – beekeepers.

St Theresas – florists.

St Aexius – nurses.

St Anthonys – motorists and women seeking a husband.

St Christophers – travellers. Also St Bona shared with flight attendants and couriers. Taxi drivers have their own in St Fiacre.

St Blaises – veterinarians.

St Florians – firefighters.

St Matthews – accountants and bankers.

St Johns (the Evangelist as opposed to all the other St Johns) – authors.

St Gregorys – teachers.

Dentists have plenty to choose from – St Antipas, St Apollonia or St Foillan and hospital administrators have their own in St Basil. Jobseekers and the unemployed may find comfort in St Cajetan, but be aware that he is also the patron saint of gamblers.

Some folk want visitors to know where they live so they name their house after themselves. Twinned names are common e.g. Marloe (Mark/Chloe). You have to commend the originality of Jackie and Dan (or Jack and Danni) in calling their house Jack Daniel's. The Spooners would, naturally, call their house something like Gorldly Woods. The Potts might consider The Flower Potts and the Sherlock family residence could be Sherlock's Holme. The Rogers family could call their abode Jolly Rogers and if you had the appropriate surname you could call your home Loch Ness, Blue Peters, Spring Fields, Sunset Coves, Parks' Place, Stones' Pit, Toad Hall, Windsors' Castle or Little Brooks. If your last name is Wood you could call your house Choppers and someone with the surname Willow could call their house The Wind in the Willows. The Smiths might be found at The Old Forge and the Campbells could occupy Glencoe. Hmm, perhaps not.

Others want you to know that these are New Beginnings or a New Prospect. At one time every house had just been built so Ty Newydd, The New House and Casa Nuevo were appropriate.

The romantic might call their property Little Tuscany as a memory of a wonderful holiday, and so we see Solsbury Hill, Snaefell, Ambleside, Woodbridge, Windermere, Iona, Cartmel, Lindisfarne, Broadway, Donegal, Galway or The Dark Hedges from places in the United Kingdom. Further afield you might see a house called Notre Dame, Taj Mahal, Montmartre, The Big Apple, Hollywood, Maldives, Santorini, St Lucia, Angkor Wat, Yosemite, Petra, Machu Picchu, Venice, Provence, Polynesia or Cappadocia. Place names make good house names but only if the vernacular evokes the original location. The name Skyfall is forever associated with the James Bond film of the same name, but the house depicted never existed. It was purpose built in Surrey on bleak Ministry of Defence land. Similarly, the house in Psycho, Bates Motel, only exists on the Universal Studios lot in Los Angeles. Other houses featured in fiction and films such as Tara, Wayne Manor, Dragonwyck, House of Leaves, Blandings, and Ponderosa are all out there somewhere. Those with a literary bent might choose Wuthering Heights, Great Expectations, Bleak House, Green Gables, Howard's End, Peyton Place, Uncle Tom's Cabin, Manderley, Cair Paravel, Camelot, Thornfield, Callander, Cashelmara, Mansfield Park, Pemberley, Rivendell, Thrushcross Grange, Hogwarts, Wildfell Hall or Downton, but Cold Comfort Farm is probably not common.

And then there are the comedians, who call their property Emoh Ruo, Emoclew, Erehwon, Lamedos, Tiedam, or Rood Egats. (If you don't get these, think of the film *Esio Trot*, which is Tortoise backward.) Quite what the occupants of Elas Rofton do when the time comes, I'm not sure. The owners of Paidefor want you to be in no doubt that they are solvent. Gnoman's Cottage might be a good name for someone who likes the wee folk and you have to smile at the inventiveness of whoever called their conversion Barn Yesterday. Somewhere there is a Bedside Manor, presumably named by someone in the medical profession. Ski Lodge is a modern invention and conveys the intention of the owners to Spend the Kid's Inheritance before they go. Rugrats would be a good name for a family home with lots of children. Furkham Hall tells you something about the attitude of the inhabitants and Firred House tells you it's the third house along. Everyone has heard the name Dunroamin but others in the same vein include Dunlukin, Dunowen, Dunrunnin, Dunbankin, Dunrentin and Wynding Down. Equally embarrassing are Kumincyde, and the sweet but twee Homeleigh/Holmlea.

If you live in a road with a suitable name then you could link it with an appropriate house name, which would mean something only when the full address is revealed. Some people living in a road called The Hatches called their house Batton Down. Someone with the appropriate conversion in Deadman's Lane has called their house Gallows Barn. Any Pickle Street has to have a house called Branstons. The residents of Baker's Lane could have a cake theme such as The Gingerbread House, Bara Brith, Fat Rascals, Lamington, Madeira, Muffins, Red Velvet or Tiramisu. And don't you just love the sense of humour of the occupants in Pudding Lane who called their house Roly Poly Cottage? They could have also considered Malvern, Eve's, Sussex Pond or Summer.

There are some intriguing names that you want to know more about. How, for instance, did Salt Pie Farm get its name? Does The Missing Rose refer to a person, a garden thief or were there only eleven roses in a bouquet when there should have been twelve? Sally in the Wood conjures up a pretty arboreal glade. Does a herpetologist live at Snakes' Harbour? Who called their house Black

Nonsuch and what does it mean? Why would you call a house Creeping Snails?

Are there names to be avoided? Well, you might be put off by a house called Fludsoffen or Pearly Gates and you might be curious to establish the veracity of a small cottage optimistically called The Tardis. Lightning Cottage might give you some misgivings about living there and you would want to make sure that the heating worked well at North Pole Cottage, especially if it was in Coldharbour. Strangeways and Alcatraz have dark connotations, but people have been known to name their properties after these infamous prisons. Scabious, a pretty blue flower of the honeysuckle family, is too much like scabies, a contagious skin infestation caused by mites. Do the owners of Tank's Crossing live on Salisbury Plain, I wonder? Tennis loving owners might hesitate to call their house Flushing Meadow, even if it came with a court to play on.

The rich and famous tend to live in houses with names rather than numbers and I rather like the name of Les Dawson's – The Bumbles. Did he name it or did he buy it because he liked its name? Did you know that Chris Bonnington, the mountaineer, lived in a house rather disappointingly called Badger's Hill? Ian Fleming famously called his beautiful Jamaican house overlooking the Caribbean after Operation Goldeneye, which referred to a contingency plan drawn up by Fleming during WWII in the event of Gibraltar being invaded by the Nazis. It only became the title of the 17th James Bond film after his death.

So, what do your neighbours call their properties, I wonder. Or, more appositely, how do you refer to your neighbours' property? What is an appropriate name for each of your neighbours' homes? Here are a few suggestions.

1. The Angelic Grandma Neighbour: Heaven's Gate, Rose Cottage, Cosy Nook, Rainbow's End.

2. The Stingy Neighbour: Shylock's Retreat, Pennypinchers, Old Misers, Cheapskates, Skinflints.

3. The Absent Minded Professor Neighbour: Forget-me-Not Cottage, High Brow, The Marbles, Lostwithiel, Mylzaway, Vacant Lot, High Brow.

4. The Good Life Neighbour: Dunworkin, Mazel Tov (good life), Gaia (Greek goddess of Earth), The Great Escape, Treadmill's End, Fruitful, Little Freedom, Latitude.

5. The Hippie Neighbour: Patchouli, Glastonbury, Sans Souci, Purple Haze, The Yurt, Dreadlocks, Dreamcatcher, Stonehenge, Druids.

6. The Crazy Cat Lady Neighbour: The Litter Tray, Kitty's Korner, Kittiwakes, Whiskers, Catbells, Pussy Willows, Pawprints, Garfield, Thie ny Kiyt (cat's home).

7. The Pessimistic Neighbour: World's End, Cassandra, Doom-n-Gloom, Long Odds, Oswald's (anagram of Sod's Law), St Judes (patron saint of lost causes), Titanic, Dismaland, Dire Straits.

8. The Optimistic Neighbour: Sunny Days, Brightside, High Hope House, Sunnyside Up, Beulah (last place before Paradise in Pilgrim's Progress), Purple Patch, Serendipity.

9. The Loved-Up Neighbours: Lovemedoo, The Bunnies, The Nest, Elveston (anagram of love nest), Valentines, The Love Boat.

10. The Needy Neighbour: Yashila (famous), Bide-a-Wee, Poor Me Cottage, Seekers.

11. The Lonely Neighbour: Dolores, Marisol, Enola, Two's Company, Lingalonga, Solitaire.

12. The Borrower Neighbour: Clock House (The Borrower's abode), Cedars House, Poor Stainless, Firbank Hall, Nortons.

13. The Hypochondriac Neighbour: Hearse House, The Surgery, Pillpoppers, Munchausens, Patient's Place.

14. The Medical Expert Neighbour: Mims, Old Doctor's, The Doctor's House, Imposters, Quack Cottage, The Waiting Room.

15. The Free-Range Parenting Neighbour: The Gooseberry Bush, Stork Cottage, Pandemonium, Sea Urchin, Baker's Dozen, Full House, The Toy Box.

16. The Downsizing Neighbours: Pint Cottage, The Box, Littlecote, Kosy Kot, Halfa House, The Doll's House, The Broom Cupboard.

17. The Organiser Neighbour: La Snell, Plan B, Nevamessy, Prim-n-Proper, Crossed Tees, Tick in the Box.

18. The Aspiring Author Neighbour: Dickens House, Diary Cottage, Memoirs, The Novel Hovel, Magnum Opus, The Book Nook, Ex Libris, First Edition, Copywriters, Bookends, Scribblers.

19. The Entrepreneurial Neighbour: Dragon's Den, Apprentice House, Little Acorns, Ambitions.

20. The Teaser Neighbour: Come Hither, Pussy Galore, Temptation, Mata Hari, Sirens, Enbon Point.

21. The Mysterious Neighbour: Cobwebs, Lucan's Leap, The Shadows, Glubbdubdrib, Whispers.

22. The Secretive Neighbour: Brigadoon, Mannanan, Fog Cottage, Marie Celeste, Rumours.

23. The Lowering-the-Tone Neighbour: Isor, The Hovel, The Pits, Puta Puta (full of holes), Ramshackle Cottage, The Shambles, Ricoperto (overgrown).

24. The Sporting Neighbour: Muirfield, Kyalami, Marathon, Out of Bounds, The Pavilion, The Ashes, Old Trafford, Maracana, Anfield, Churchill Downs, Wrigley Fields, The Bootroom.

25. The Lecherous Neighbour: Limpetts, Sticky Fingers, Pocket Pool, Manual Override, Quayles, Tan Nittien.

26. The Hunting, Shooting, Fishing Neighbour: The Duck Decoy, The Hide, Aholehole, Hue and Full Cry, Gone to Earth, The Kennel, Purdeys, Holland Royal, Over and Under, Quantum, St Croix, Honey Hole, Backwater, Eyelets, Elvers.

27. The Vegan Neighbour: Salad Days, Grasseaters, Roots, Treehuggers, Mildreds, Manna, The Nut House.

28. The Whinger Neighbour: Ibindun, Mona's Cottage, Hobbyhorses, The Soapbox, The Grouse House.

29. The Brand Label Neighbour: Chanel Cottage, Tiffanys, Beckingham Palace, Timberland, Prada Place, Burberrys, Hermes, Palladino, Mouawad, Omega.

30. The Noisy Neighbour: Brouhaha, Hullabaloo, Outlaws, Decibels, Clatterbridge, Fortissimo, Stentorian, Rough House.

31. The Hoarder Neighbour: Treasure Trove, Magpies, Squirrels, Bric-a-brac, Hotch Potch, Plyushkin, Clutterers.

32. The Nosy Neighbour: Buttinsky, Yenta (gossip or busybody), The Lookout, The Watchtower, The Crow's Nest, Parkers.

33. The Artist Neighbour: The Gallery, The Studio, The Colour Wheel, Chitra (painting), The Residency, The Atelier, Daubers, Artisans, Graffiti, Sketchers.

34. The Mega Rich Neighbour: El Dorado, Midas Mansions, Brass Castle, Cashmere, South Fork, Kulinan, Raffles.

35. The Note Writing Neighbour: Script Cottage, Billet-doux, Penny-a-liner, Wordsmiths, Poet's Cottage, The Black and White House, Penman's Cottage, Writer's House, Wordsworth.

36. The Copycat Neighbour: Forgery Farm, Parrot Cottage, Echo Falls, Ringers, Double Take, Lookalike, Pirates.

37. The Party Loving Neighbour: Liveitup, Conga House, The Social Club, Party Central, Celebrations, The Clubhouse, Life and Soul, Dancing Shoes.

38. The Snooping Neighbour: Glimpses, Keyhole Cottage, Curtain Twitchers, I-Spy, Eavesdroppers.

39. The Boring Neighbour: Nowhere, Numbatoo, The House, Aitchfer House.

40. The DIY Neighbour: Nuts and Bolts, Bodger's End, Clean Sweep, Roughcaster, Plumb Bob, Gofer, Carpenters.

41. The Problem Solving Neighbour: Rubik's Cube, Sudoku, Philosophers, Troubleshooters, Crosswords, Sage, King Soloman's.

42. The Know-It-All Neighbour: Kibitzer (gives unwanted advice), Eggheads, Wiseacre, Boffins, Mamba, The Fount.

43. The Multi-Generation Neighbours: Maison Bonde (crowded house), The Hive, Sardines, Sovraffollato (overcrowded), Affolato Casa (crowded house), Turuki (crowded), Packemin.

44. The Organic Neighbour: Daylesford, The Duchy, St Katari (patron saint of environmentalists), Lily's Kitchen.

45. The Social Climber Neighbour: The White House, Balmoral, Toff Towers, The Residence, The Penthouse, Broadlands, Chatsworth.

46. The Frenemy Neighbour: Quisling Cottage, Cave Lupum (beware of the wolf in sheep's clothing), Gemini, Cerberus Court, Traitor's Gate.

47. The "Isn't it terrible" Neighbour: Shrinking Violets, Poltroon, The Mouse House, Omihi (Maori for sad place), The Acheron (river of woe).

48. The Flashy Neighbour: Limelighters, The Red Carpet, Gaudy, Catchpenny, Harry's, St Trinians, Tinseltown.

49. The Territorial Neighbour: Fort Knox, The Vaults, No Man's Land, The Moat, The Fortress, The Drawbridge, Cavendum a Domino (beware of the owner).

50. The Manipulative Neighbour: Hobgoblins, Machiavelli Mansions, Svengali, Meddlers.

51. The Self-Sufficient Loner Neighbour: Soledad, Isola, Siyamak, Ezhno, The Hermitage, The Retreat.

52. The Condescending Neighbour: Withering Heights, Popinjays, Hatchetts, La-dee-da, Upstage, High Hat, Cock-a-loft.

53. The Bully Neighbour: Casimir, Alpha House, The Bull Pen, Loggerheads, The Nails (as in hard as…), Rover's Revenge, Top Banana, The Big Cheese, Lindalino.

54. The Swinger Neighbours: Handcuff House, Mount Pleasant, Postman's Knock, The Cat House, Forbidden Fruit, Whare Rahia (house of pleasure), The Foresum, The Playhouse, Wild Thyme, The Hussienda, Anything Goes.

55. The Tiger Mother Neighbour: Elbows, Lake Superior, Abovetherest, The Viper's Nest, The Winning Line, Champion's Cottage.

56. The Highly Sensitive Neighbour: Solo, The Gift, Quell, Spooked, Empathy, Intuity.

57. The Second Homer Neighbour: The Bolt Hole, The Refuge, The Haven, The Sanctuary, Hideaway, Narnia, But-n-Ben.

58. The Perfect Neighbour: Stargazer, Utopia, Cornucopia, Eden Cottage, Xanadu, Paradise Gained, Halcyon Days, Shangri-La, Peacehaven.

Doors And Doormats, Knobs And Knockers

"The doors we open and close each day decide the lives we live." Flora Whittemore

First impressions are important and you can tell a lot about the personality of your neighbours from their doors, doormats and door furniture. So, what colour is your neighbour's front door? Many cultures past and present have attributed certain meanings to certain colours, especially the colour chosen for the main entrance to a home as it is the 'mouth', where good and bad can enter.

BLUE: One of the most popular colours to paint a door. It signals that the owner sees their abode as a refuge from a busy life, a calm oasis where they can relax and be at peace. Police boxes were painted blue because it was associated with trust and truth. It is the colour of a summer sky and the sea and so is considered to be tranquil and calming. Blue stands for intelligence, loyalty and integrity. Blue verging on turquoise implies someone with big dreams and ideals, but lacking in emotional stability. Do they wish for something to go right once in a blue moon, or for a little good luck to occur out of the blue or are they the proverbial blue-eyed boy?

BLACK: Serious, deep, not to be trifled with, black conveys strength and solidity. The door of 10 Downing Street is black and exudes the power and authority of someone who likes to be in control. We all like to be 'in the black'. Black is associated with control and discipline, and can be intimidating. But it is also the colour of negativity, pessimism, sadness and depression – we have black days, get a black mark against us or may be a black sheep. Amy Winehouse sang about going back to black. Black is also linked with secrets, mystery and the unknown – who knows what lurks in a black hole?

WHITE: People who like to mind their own business, guard their privacy, and prefer to travel through life anonymously and invisibly. You would describe them as opaque rather than transparent. Inside their home they are organised and logical, to the point of perfection. White is associated with peace, purity, innocence and goodness and is the colour related to new beginnings and positivity. The cool colour of snow and ghosts, white blends in with any other colour. They may appear to be whiter than white and in times of trouble may be a white knight but they wouldn't be above telling those little white lies.

YELLOW: Sunny, bright and cheerful. Yellow is a colour associated with sunshine, daffodils and warmth that are bound to cheer you up on an otherwise gloomy early spring day. People who like their front door this colour are perceptive, understanding, confident and have a good sense of humour. But do they have a yellow streak or are they yellow-bellied? This colour can indicate jaundice and it is unsurprising that some of the sources of yellow pigments (cadmium, lead and chrome) are toxic. In China, films of an adult nature are called yellow films.

RED: Don't believe all the nonsense you read that red is the Feng Shui colour of sensitivity. It is a strident, overbearing, domineering colour that shouts a warning – "Stop", "Beware", "Danger". Do you remember when teachers used to correct your spelling using a red pen? Insects sport it as a warning that they are poisonous. It is the colour of blood, anger (seeing red), insolvency (in the red) and is associated with prostitutes (red light district) and rage (red rag to a bull). We have to deal with red tape, red herrings, and you catch someone red handed. Red is about lust, whereas pink is the true colour of love. On the plus side, a red front door in Scotland is supposed to represent the boast that the owners have paid off the mortgage.

GREEN: Generally considered to be an unlucky colour, it was the colour of 10 Downing Street during the 19th century when Herbert Asquith was in residence. When he fell out of favour and resigned in 1916, the door was painted black and has been that colour ever since. Allegedly the '0' is said to be wobbly in tribute to the original door on which the zero was badly fitted and loose. You don't see many bright green doors although there are now some lovely subtle chalky greens about that are very fashionable. Green says healthy, organic, at one with nature. A green door can look fresh, like spring grass, and symbolise growth and fertility. A dark green colour is associated with money and safety. However, green is the colour of envy and neediness.

PURPLE: The occupants of this house like taking risks and purple symbolises energy and opportunity. It is a colour linked to royalty, and conveys wealth, privilege and luxury. It is also reminiscent of magic and the occult. It is an artificial colour and rarely occurs in nature. A person can write purple prose, and if he has smoked a certain strain of cannabis with purple buds he is probably in a Purple Haze, a state of mind induced by psychotic drugs. Maybe they're hoping that a purple door will lead to a purple patch, a period of exceptional good luck. If someone in the house works as a recruitment consultant, ask them about the mythical ideal candidate for a job, also known as the purple squirrel, because that's how rare they are.

ORANGE: Vibrant and vintage 1960s, it is making a comeback for those who are busy, active and highly sociable so there will be plenty of visitors to this house, and they like to be noticed. In heraldry, orange is symbolic of strength and endurance. Perhaps they like a bet, as in the expression 'All Lombard Street to a china orange'. Orange is the colour associated with Mercury, the god of business, so it would be a good choice for commercial premises. It is a warm colour that we commonly associate with autumn.

PINK: I suppose someone, somewhere has a pink door and that someone is almost certainly female! It says that the occupant is girly, silly, and giggly. Her equally airhead friends are likely to describe her as 'bubbly'. In other words, she is immature, doesn't want to grow up and throws tantrums when she doesn't get her own way. Pink, not red, is the colour of romance, friendship and love. Sometimes we are 'tickled pink' or 'in the pink'.

GREY: A cool, sophisticated, elegant and understated colour much like its owner who may be difficult to pin down or slippery. The occupant may be subtle, calculating, a negotiator rather than someone who stands on a principle. We talk about grey areas. After all, grey makes up most of the continuum from black to white. Or does it? Grey paint is not simply a blend of black and white. Subtle additions of other colours make different greys. Adding blue makes it cool. Pink makes it warm. Green makes it elusive. More white makes it discreet. More black makes it darker and more subversive. Uber chic at the moment, historically it implied that the owner was unimaginative, drab, cheerless and gloomy.

BROWN: Can you still buy brown paint? So out of fashion that it must be due to be rediscovered and find a return to favour before too long, when it will be marketed to us as 'natural' and 'earthy'. On the one hand, it sends out a message of warmth and reliability. On the other hand, it says that the person living there is dull and lacking in personality. Varnished or stained wood is a popular choice and many wooden doors are left to age naturally and become silvery as the wood oxidises.

SILVER: Associated with the light of the moon and the ebb and flow of the tides, it is more spiritual and mysterious than grey and implies that the occupants are intuitive and empathic. A silver-tongued person can be very persuasive and calculating, and may be prepared to bribe someone by crossing their palm with silver. They may have been born with a silver spoon in their mouth or expect to have everything handed to them on a silver platter. A lustrous silver door reflects negative energy to protect the inhabitants. It is the colour of celebration and respect (25th wedding anniversary) and in times of trouble these neighbours will hope for a silver lining or a magic silver bullet solution.

A growing trend is for not one but two front doors as double doors give an impression of a much bigger frontage. The building that is, but perhaps it also refers to the occupants.

And that leads us neatly on to your neighbour's knockers. Door knockers, that is, and other door furniture – what do they give away about the inhabitants? Door knockers have a long history and come in many different styles, according to the country and the culture. In the Middle Ages, gargoyles were popular as door knockers as it was believed they kept away evil spirits. In past times in Italy, visitors might have been greeted with a door sporting a knocker in the shape of the head of Medusa, complete with snakes in place of hair, in order to frighten. Callers in Renaissance times used beautiful, intricately designed knockers to notify the inhabitants of their presence, which the owners had made as a symbol of wealth and to impress. In *A Christmas Carol*, Ebenezer Scrooge's door knocker mysteriously morphed into Marley's face. The so-called doctor's door knocker, having a single S-shaped vertical bar hinged at the top where it attaches to the door, with a small circular striking plate, was popular in the late 18th and early 19th centuries for its simple and classic design, and can often be seen and bought today. It is more elaborate than the plain ponytail knocker, whose art deco style is less commonly seen. A popular style which suits both period and modern properties, and is widely available in many different materials, is the urn-shaped door knocker. These days, knockers are mostly made of metal – brass, cast iron or steel – and may reflect the interests or occupation of the dweller. So for instance, a sailor might have an anchor or a fisherman a dolphin. A keen cricketer might have one in the shape of a cricket bat.

A lion's head is common on door knockers (for example, one is featured on the front door of 10 Downing Street) as they signify strength and power. Lions were used as guardians at the city gates in Mycenae c1250BC. The symbol of a lion is associated with St Mark, who was the patron saint of glaziers, lawyers and Venice. Other animals feature frequently on door knockers and include owls, foxes, dogs, cats, ram's heads, elephants with the trunk as the knocker, alligators, bulls, bats, fish, seahorses, dragons, squirrels, horse's heads and eagles. You can get a splendid depiction of a spider catching a fly. Others incorporate hands, hoops, keys, pestle and mortars, mermaids, revolvers, and the Knights of Malta. There is even one based on the film *The Full Monty*. I will leave it to your imagination as to what is used as the knocker!

Other items you might see around doorways include horseshoes and herbs. Many cultures have had similar talismans to protect evil entering the dwelling. Horseshoes are considered to be a symbol of good luck and protect those who enter through the door although the horseshoe must be the correct way up, with the open end uppermost, so that luck can be held in or it will fall out and be lost! It should also be one that has previously been worn by a horse rather than a new one, as a worn one will be steeped in powerful energy from the horse, which is considered to be a strong, free spirit. Alternatively, in some parts of the country in the 16th century, when fear of witches casting spells was rife, people believed that no witch would pass under a horseshoe which was hung points down over a doorway.

Plants of many kinds were held to have magical properties, and rosemary was tied in bundles by a door to ward off burglars. Valerian was used to prevent strife and discontent from entering, but was not so popular as it smelt of cat urine! A bunch of clover over a door allegedly kept negative entities away and was a symbol of good fortune. Of course, we still treat four-leaf clovers as lucky today. In the Celtic culture, they used to make a cross from rowan bound with red cord and hang it above a doorway and chant, "Rowan tree, red thread, hold the witches all in dread."

There are many myths and legends relating to doorways and the fear of evil spirits. Salt sprinkled across thresholds was supposed to keep them from entering. Wind chimes were also used to scare them away and were considered a good luck talisman. Bagua mirrors – a round mirror surrounded by an octagonal wooden frame – originated in China and are a popular symbol in Feng Shui. The mirror should be convex if hung over the front door and concave if hung over the back entrance. The mirror is said to deflect and repel bad luck, negativity, evil and sickness, and prevent accidents.

You should only place a wishbone over the front door on New Year's Day, and it is first necessary to say the incantation "Lover, come hither!" three times. Your new lover will then appear to you. Sounds like the sort of thing your Swinger Neighbours might do! Other symbols include the mezuzah, a part of Jewish mysticism, which is a piece of parchment on which are written Hebrew verses and prayers. It is rolled up and placed in a casing which is fixed diagonally onto a door frame, thereby denying evil access to the house. Altar bells hung in a doorway are also used as a charm for protection of the occupants. In Japan and the Shinto belief, ofuda are talismans typically made of paper, wood, cloth or metal attached to doors.

Finally, we come to the doormat. No, not the wimpy neighbour who allows everyone to trample all over them, but that hairy rug outside or inside the front door. Do you have one? More to the point, does it send a message to the visitors to your home? Is it well turned out or is it dirty, worn and scruffy? If it has your family name on it, you are metaphorically allowing people to drag your name through the dirt and walk all over you. Now, be honest – how many of you have, or have ever had in the past, a doormat with a message on it? It is very easy to have a doormat personalised with almost anything you like. Here are a choice few. What do you think they say about the owner?

'STAFF, PEASANTS AND RIFF-RAFF MUST USE THE TRADESMAN'S ENTRANCE'

– amusing but with a hidden message?

'HOME SWEET HOME'

– house-proud.

'WELCOME'

– nice but a bit boring.

'FRIENDS WELCOME. RELATIVES BY APPOINTMENT'

– good way to upset the mother-in-law.

'CLEANLINESS IS NEXT TO IMPOSSIBLE'

– a warning of what's inside?

'ABANDON HOPE ALL YE WHO ENTER HERE'

– definitely a warning of the state of the interior!

'A MESSY HOUSE IS A HAPPY HOUSE. THIS ONE IS DELIRIOUS'

– happy go lucky sort.

'GO AWAY'

– to the point.

'OH, NO! NOT YOU AGAIN'

– don't mince their words.

'PLEASE LEAVE YOUR INHIBITIONS AT THE DOOR'

– those Swingers would like that one!

'I LIVE HERE' (WITH A PICTURE OF A ROTTWEILER)

– do they mean the dog or the owner?

'NICE SHOES' OR 'NICE UNDERWEAR'

– a joker or a creep?

'I GOLF THEREFORE I AM NOT HERE'

– cerebral type who likes the great outdoors.

'DOG FRIENDLY. OWNERS BITE'

– probably true.

'DOG LIKES STRANGERS – THINKS THEY TASTE LIKE CHICKEN'

– think twice about knocking.

'DOGS WELCOME. PEOPLE TOLERATED'

– they're not joking.

'BEWARE OF THE CAT'

– don't say you weren't warned about dear Mittens.

'PROTECTED BY A CHIHUAHUA SECURITY SYSTEM'

– they may be small but they have sharp teeth.

'THE CAT AND HIS STAFF LIVE HERE'

– every cat owner knows this to be true.

'WELCOME TO THE MADHOUSE'

– owner has a sense of humour, but probably right.

'BEWARE OF THE DRAGON'

– we are not talking mythology here.

'I KNOW WHAT NICKNAME YOU GIVE ME'

– if you gave it to them and it isn't nice, I would back off now.

'RECENTLY TREATED FOR ANTHRAX'

– not funny, guys.

'CRIME SCENE. DO NOT CROSS'

– fact or fiction?

'I KNOW WHAT YOU CALL ME BEHIND MY BACK'

– oops!

'I DENY EVERYTHING'

– no point asking him to turn the volume down then.

'LIVE WELL, LAUGH OFTEN, LEAVE SOON'

– someone with a short attention span.

'I AM NOT A DOOR MAT'

– cue discussion on existentialism.

'THE CRAZY CAT LADY LIVES HERE'

– you know, 'cos you can smell 'em.

'THE TRAPDOOR UNDER THIS MAT WILL OPEN IN 5, 4, 3….'

– too late.

'APPROACH. KNEEL. PULL FORELOCK BEFORE SPEAKING'

– your bully neighbour got this for Christmas.

'I CLEANED THE HOUSE LAST WEEK (YOU MISSED IT)'

– a lie but a great excuse for the mess.

'ASK NOT FOR WHOM THE DOG BARKS. IT BARKS FOR THEE'

– ha ha very funny.

'NEVER MIND THE DOG. BEWARE OF THE OWNER'

– the owner has a bite worse than the dog's.

How to Deal With Your Neighbours Without Resorting to Murder

"We cannot solve our problems with the same thinking we used when we created them."
Albert Einstein

Dr David Buss claimed that "91% of men and 84% of women have had at least one vivid fantasy – often intense and astonishingly detailed – of committing murder." Fortunately, few translate this into action. Most people, when they calm down, can work through the cost-benefit analysis and figure out some alternative means of solving the problem without resorting to extremes. A long prison stretch is too high a price to pay for getting your own back. Anyway, how and where would you dispose of the body? As a friend once confided after yet another bruising round with the neighbours, "I don't know what I'd do without chocolate and red wine – probably fifteen to life!"

To a neighbour's pathetic self-pitying lament of "You've humiliated me", try not to respond with "No, you've done that all by yourself." Trust me, it won't go down well. But if the excrement has made contact with the air current distribution system, there is no going back. You might feel a brief pang of contrition (you are not, at the end of the day, deliberately antagonistic and on the whole you like a quiet life), but then console yourself with the fact that what you said was simply the truth from your point of view.

Trading insults is the stuff of many a sitcom and neighbourly argument as the following example shows.

1st neighbour "One day you'll need our help."
2nd neighbour "Even if you were the last person on Earth I would never ask for your help."
1st neighbour "Well, you wouldn't get it!"
2nd neighbour "That's why I wouldn't bother asking!"

Most people aren't quick thinking enough to come up with appropriate invectives in the heat of the moment, so an exchange of abuse rarely lasts long. How often have you spent time after the run-in with your nuisance neighbours thinking about what you should have said, come up with some pretty neat caustic rejoinders and cursed yourself for not coming out with them at the time? We all do it! Rerunning the conversation in your head with newly thought up ripostes, wisecracks and put-downs can be very satisfying! The trouble is your neighbour probably does the selfsame thing! Practice, advance preparation and experience sharpen the wits, but don't let the altercation deteriorate into an exchange of personal insults that you may regret, and back off the moment it looks like getting physical.

Are you the problem?

But first we ought to address the possibility that, rather than you having the problem neighbour, your neighbour has approached you about some transgression you are supposedly guilty of, whether deliberately or unwittingly. In other words, you are being accused of being the annoying neighbour. How would you react? Above all, try not to be immediately defensive and start arguing, especially if your neighbour has explained the problem quietly and reasonably. This also applies if your neighbour comes round red in the face and with the proverbial steam coming out of their ears and yells obscenities at you. Nothing will make them look sillier and put you in control of the situation more than if you calmly say that you are willing to discuss this, but that it will be more productive if you can have a conversation rather than a row.

So, your neighbour has politely pointed out that you are parking in their allocated slot, your dogs bark all day when you're at work, your children have been kicking a ball against their wall or that playing your new bongos at midnight is anti-social. What do you say? Well, try to listen to the full story, asking for additional information if you need to, and see it from their point of view. Don't retort with something they will find inflammatory or threatening. Or laugh at them. Or tease them about it. You may think it's clever, but it won't improve relations between you, and belittling what to them is a big issue will only provoke them. Asking for more information or repeating in a quizzical way something they have said is also a way of giving yourself more time to think as they ramble on, usually repeating themselves to try and emphasise the point, however obscure. It's natural to feel like they're criticising you and to feel annoyed and perhaps exasperated, but a good tip is to treat it like you would if someone at work had alerted you to a problem and it was your job to sit down with them and try to resolve it. In other words, try to depersonalise it. By all means calmly explain where you stand on the issue, just in case it is a simple misunderstanding, and put a smile (not a smirk, please) on your face when doing so to indicate that you didn't mean any harm by it or you just failed to understand the implications. Restating the issue in order to clarify it can help – it shows that you understand. Don't be frightened of saying that you need time to think it over. It will give you both a while to reflect on the encounter and formulate some possible solutions. A compromise can usually be reached that will at least partially satisfy both sides, and it may mean visiting their house to assess their concerns. This shows that there is a willingness to see the problem from their point of view.

And just remember that resolution is the goal here, not making the situation worse. Compromise is important – if one side feels that the other has dismissed their concerns or won more ground or concessions from the other, then the fault hasn't been fixed and will fester. It may then resurface at a later date when you thought everything was hunky dory, or be displaced and resurface in a different guise but basically be the same grudge.

Smiling helps to diffuse a hostile atmosphere and keeps the conversation positive and more relaxed. Insincerity doesn't count. And if you are genuinely in the wrong, apologise. Yes, you heard me. APOLOGISE. You don't have to crawl. A simple "Sorry, it won't happen again" or "Sorry, I hadn't realised that" can diffuse many a delicate situation, and will take the wind out of their sails. It doesn't mean you are taking the blame. Quite the contrary – you are in effect seizing the moral high ground. Not enough people apologise and it is a sign of strength not weakness to be able to accept responsibility, and you will gain respect in doing so, provided that you mean it sincerely. It's all in the way you say it and people can easily tell from your intonation if you are not being honest or if you don't really intend to change your behaviour, which will only exacerbate the situation. A bunch of flowers wouldn't go amiss either. Or a bottle of wine. With a bit of luck, they may even invite you in to share it. Research has shown that an apology involving some expenditure is a more sincere and meaningful apology, and is much more likely to lead to forgiveness.

Usually between you, you can come up with an equitable and practical solution to keep everyone happy, but don't make any promises you can't or have no intention of keeping. And don't be pressured into coming up with an answer straight away. You may have to consult others as the problem may not be resolvable immediately. If that is the case, explain the steps you intend to take and keep them in the loop as you work towards an amicable outcome. Your neighbour should understand this and accept that you are listening to their concerns.

COMMON PROBLEMS BETWEEN NEIGHBOURS

1. NOISE

For instance, if a neighbour asks you to move your washing machine away from the party wall as the noise of the vibrations is disturbing their sleep, don't retort that you can't hear it, even if it's true. That isn't the point. They can hear it and it is keeping them awake. If they suggest putting the machine on a rubber mat and thoughtfully provide one, the problem is solved with little effort on your part! If not, how much time would it take to pull it away from the wall, for the sake of peace between you?

Noisy neighbours can seriously impact the quality of your life. It is inevitable that, living in close proximity to others, we can hear occasional raised voices, the TV or screechy violin practice, especially in the summer when the windows are open. This sort of noise just has to be tolerated. What we all dread is the constant noise, such as building works, which might continue for months and be very disruptive. But even this will come to an end at some stage. Just as bad is noise at a particular time of day or day of the week, because you get increasingly anxious as the time it usually starts approaches.

Noise that wakes you up frequently and keeps you awake can leave you sleep deprived, irritable and can ultimately damage your health. It has to be tackled, and you'll find some ways of dealing with this in the section on managing the neighbours.

2. TREES AND HEDGES

Trees and hedges cause numerous clashes between neighbours. Trees belong to whoever owns the land on which they grow, regardless of the fact that the roots and branches spread themselves. Trees do not understand the legal definition of a boundary! You have no legal right to cut down a tree which is entirely in your neighbour's garden, although it is their responsibility if their tree is causing subsidence to your property. You have a common law right to cut any branches that protrude over the fence onto your property, but only as far as the boundary and you must offer the cut pieces back to the neighbour before disposing of them. If there is any fruit on the overhanging branches that belong to your neighbour, you will be guilty of stealing if you keep it without permission. Far better to consult with your neighbour first and agree the way forward, and check if the tree has a preservation order on it or is in a conservation area in which case you will need permission from the local authority to prune it. The cost of trimming will be yours and you cannot trespass onto their property to do any work without their consent.

Provided you have taken due care and had trees

inspected and maintained regularly, you are not responsible if a branch falls off in a storm and damages their property. In insurance terms, this is considered to be unforeseeable and due to an Act of God! If, however, you had noticed that their tree was diseased or there was a risk it could fall, and you had told the owner and they had refused to do anything, then they could be liable if it subsequently fell and caused injury or damage.

You can prune a neighbour's hedge back to the boundary but not reduce it in height. There are no laws that say you must trim a hedge at a certain height. Laws on height only apply to fences and walls. Contrary to popular belief, there are no general rights to light and there is no right to a view.

3. STEALING YOUR WI-FI, MAIL, GAS OR ELECTRICITY

A rare obstacle to neighbourly relations is misappropriation, otherwise known as stealing. The most common of these in urban areas is 'piggybacking' your Wi-Fi. Not only can they slow down your broadband speed, they can infect your network with viruses and your confidential documents could be accessed. They can also push your data usage above its monthly limits. If what they are looking at is illegal, such as child pornography, you could be in serious trouble, and you don't want those nice people from Operation Ore knocking on your door and escorting you to the police station along with your confiscated computer. Supposing your post occasionally gets accidentally delivered to other people and you suspect that someone is deliberately opening it, judging from the badly resealed package or envelope you receive. Persistent episodes of lost mail could be a sign of identity theft, so if you suspect your neighbours of intercepting your mail, report it to the sender and also inform Royal Mail Customer Care Team, who take this very seriously. In the meantime, you could have important mail or parcels delivered to your place of work or set up a private box in your local Royal Mail delivery office. These can even accept recorded deliveries and those requiring a signature. And don't forget to password protect your Wi-Fi!

Not quite so unusual is the neighbour who decides to steal your gas or electricity. Who knows if your astronomical gas bill is supporting the local cannabis factory? It has been known for people to regularly reverse the gas meter so it runs backward, and this only comes to light when the gas company calls to read the meter and is alerted by the fact that the meter is upside down and the dial is facing the wall. Not only is this illegal but highly dangerous. If someone you know is doing this, warn them that you will report them if they ignore you and carry on doing it. Gas leaks put you at risk of fires and carbon monoxide poisoning and gas explosions kill.

4. HARASSMENT AND ABUSE

Many of the disputes between neighbours can be humorous, especially when they happen to someone else, but there are some matters that cannot be dismissed lightly, and one of these is harassment or abuse, and usually happens when a dispute has got out of hand and someone won't back off. It may take the form of insulting words whether verbal or written or abusive behaviour, or even threats of or actual violence to you, your family or your property. You should immediately notify the police of where and when this happened and what ensued. Back this up with evidence from witnesses, phone records, photos, CCTV or emails. Keep all details in writing, however small, and be brave. Nothing lasts forever.

Supposing a neighbour appears on your doorstep out of the blue in a complete tizzy clearly itching for a fight, and proceeds without pre-amble to insult your clothes, your hair, your car or your children and ends by accusing you of trying to steal her husband. As her husband is one of the most repulsive and unappealing men you had ever had the misfortune to set eyes on, the idea is, frankly, laughable. While you are standing there speechless and somewhat mystified, as well as amused, she continues by listing other misdemeanours you have allegedly committed and accompanies them with some very rude personal remarks and name calling. If something like this happens, remain calm throughout and when this unexpected broadside abates, politely suggest she comes back to discuss whatever has upset her when she has calmed down. She'll probably flounce off in a huff. Not giving her the fight she so obviously wants, which would only have resulted in a further deterioration in your relationship, gives you time to think. On reflection you may be puzzled. You have not committed any offence and you certainly haven't warranted this degree of personal assault. This type of behaviour is not uncommon and is an example of displaced aggression. Something else has pissed her off and, unable to retaliate appropriately, she shifts the focus and tries to take it out on someone else she perceives deserves her wrath i.e. you. Psychologists call this the scapegoat solution – if someone can unfairly transfer blame onto others, they can feel better about being powerless in another, unrelated, situation. There is no point in attempting to discuss anything with someone who is in an irrational state. They won't come back because reasonable discussion isn't what it is about and, in any case, they'll feel far too embarrassed at their lack of composure and loss of self-control.

MANAGING THE NEIGHBOURS

So you've identified your nuisance neighbour according to their character (and they may be a combination of several) and now you need to know the best ways of dealing with them, without spending years at Her Majesty's pleasure. Easier said than done, but read on and choose your way of proceeding with caution.

The best way to keep on good terms with the neighbours is to start as you mean to go on. Got new neighbours? Be proactive. Send them a card, take a cake round and introduce yourself, wave when you see them.

If there are a few new faces on the block, invite everyone round for drinks so that you can all get to know each other, which might take a lot longer otherwise. Tell your neighbours that if they ever have a gripe, to come over and talk it through with you. It doesn't matter how slight the grievance; it is better to deal with it when it's still relatively small. Repeat this often over the years. Anticipating any potential problems and putting a mechanism in place to resolve them could one day prove to be very useful. Most neighbours are relatively benign, if occasionally irritating, and can generally rub along harmoniously most of the time. If your neighbour calls the kids in for their dinner every day with a voice like a foghorn, it may be a minor irritation, but try to retain a sense of perspective here. Being nice to the neighbours can seem daunting at times, but it pays dividends in the long term. Communication is the key to neighbourly relations, so let them know if you intend letting off fireworks or cutting down a tree and invite them to any social gatherings. Consider whether anything like building work could affect them. Let them know in advance and reiterate that if something bothers them, to come over and let you know so you can minimise any disruption. Lack of communication breeds suspicion and mistrust. Better to leave the door open than to slam it in their faces, metaphorically or physically, however tempting it may be.

In the longer term, particularly in urban situations, one or other of the parties will move on. In the meantime, things will settle down over time and people will get on with their busy lives albeit maintaining a disrespectful distance. Only those with nothing better to do can sustain a prolonged campaign of conflict with a neighbour, and the dispute may have limited appeal to any of the other neighbours, especially if it does not affect them. In a study carried out in New York by Baumgartner in the 1980s, it was found that young people, especially men, were more likely to use fighting, threats and actual damage to property as a means of dealing with a conflict with a neighbour. They also made more formal complaints than older people. The study found that those of working class were more likely to openly confront neighbours, make formal complaints and call the police. Does this justify and explain a lot of the implausible story lines in soap operas? After all, if everyone in dramas ignored the neighbours who make their lives hell, there'd be no storylines at all!

1. PRETENDING THE NEIGHBOURS DON'T EXIST

The most common strategy of managing conflict between neighbours is simply to stop interacting with them. If their behaviour is seen as unacceptable or offensive, most people are unlikely to discuss it with them or openly confront them. This withdrawal from interacting in any way with nuisance neighbours – avoiding them, greeting them only perfunctorily or not at all, not inviting them over or visiting them and no longer asking them for favours however small – is considered by some researchers to be a sign of maturity and responsibility. Unfortunately, it can lead to an upscale of aggressive behaviour on the part of the rejected neighbour, who you have morally offended by ignoring them. You just can't win. Most people are reluctant to involve the police, social services or other professional bodies for the same reason. Wearing sunglasses gives you a good justification for preventing neighbours from catching your eye. Especially those mirrored ones. They can't be sure whether you have seen them or not, and you can drive on or shut a door or dive around a corner or wave to an imaginary person to avoid them without causing offence. Hats, hoodies and umbrellas can work well too. If they confront you, say you weren't wearing your glasses or you were preoccupied. Or pissed. Top tip: always look them in the eye when you are unashamedly lying and make sure you don't look guilty. Smile. Practise in the mirror if necessary. They might suspect you're a lying little shit but they'll never be 100% certain. Best not to try this one too often though, as repetition will undermine your credibility. Oh, and don't try the sunglasses trick at night. You'll look silly and they will gleefully spread rumours that your partner is abusing you and you're just trying to conceal the resultant black eye.

2. WINDING UP THE NEIGHBOURS

This approach is mentioned because it's a part of life with the neighbours and everybody does it, but is not (perish the thought!) advocated! Only do it if you're not planning on sticking around, in which case your neighbours will heave a sigh of relief.

There are some neighbours who are immune to all appeals, and you have to work with their personality disorders. You know the ones – self-important, pretentious, pompous and obsessed with money and status. They have an overinflated ego that is hiding a severe inferiority complex, and are touchy and difficult to deal with. Here you need to be clever and cunningly undermine them in barely imperceptible ways so they don't notice until you've gone and they've had time to think about it. So belittle their achievements, expose their flaws and faults, take a dig at their reputation, if you must. Small things please small minds, as they say. If you can't think of a suitable put-down straight away, ignore what they're telling you about any accomplishments they're waxing lyrical about and simply change the subject. You might remind them of past failures or damn their efforts with faint praise but do it so that they have to think about what you have said before they realise you are censuring their behaviour, by which time you'll be long gone. Disagree with their ideas, play Devil's advocate, point out the shortcomings in their plans.

"Going on holiday – wasn't that the hotel where they had food poisoning?"

"That new car you've bought – got a bad reputation for breakdowns."

"Getting married again – glutton for punishment!"

"Got a new job – wasn't that company on the verge of administration?"

Drip feed little criticisms as often as possible. But do it in a friendly and helpful tone, even make a joke of it, and then make a quick exit, before the penny drops.

Remember the 'Golden Rule', or ethic of reciprocity, a concept found in many traditions and religions going back to Confucius (551–479BC) – you should treat others as you would like to be treated and you should not treat anyone in a way that you would not like to be treated. OK, that's enough moralising. If you've sent them off with a flea in their ear, you may have won the battle but the war just got a lot more serious, especially if you humiliated them. They might not remember exactly what you said, but they will forever remember the way you made them feel, and it stings. Best to let bygones be bygones and to forget if not forgive. And if you are the mean, unforgiving, spiteful neighbour they claim you are, take time to reflect before coming up with a plan to get your own back. You know what they say about revenge being a dish best served cold.

3. CHANGE THE WAY YOU FEEL ABOUT THE NEIGHBOURS

If you can't change your neighbours, you can change the way you feel about them. In other words, change your attitude or level of tolerance.

One way of coping with your obnoxious neighbours is to picture them in a bubble and to mentally put that bubble somewhere unpleasant so you won't have to think about them anymore. Perhaps you can imagine them trapped inside a bird's faecal sac or soundproof box and picture yourself dropping it into a deep cesspit. Think how gratified you'll feel hearing the splat as it hits the you-know-what. Another similar tactic is to imagine them inside a balloon, which you tie tightly and then release, watching it float away. Then see yourself firing a weapon, a gun, bazooka, cannon or missile, at the balloon and blasting it to smithereens. Watch as the pieces disperse and disappear and visualise yourself turning and walking away. If you do this often, hopefully you'll find that this has the effect of putting them out of your thoughts.

Another coping strategy is to write down all the grievances, who said what and your vitriolic wish list of things you'd like to do to your annoying neighbours. Make sure you include how you felt during and after the encounter. Don't worry about neatness, spelling, grammar or if it makes any sense – just dump it all down on paper. Then you can put it away somewhere, preferably dark and unpleasant – in a smelly shoe at the bottom of a wardrobe or under a container of slug pellets in a spidery corner of the shed for example. By doing this you don't have to be constantly going over every little detail in your head and can forget about it all because, if you want, you can remind yourself of what prats and arseholes your neighbours are by rereading it in the future. If a suitable period of time has elapsed, and you have some perspective on the incident, it'll probably give you a good laugh.

Or you can destroy it by burning, shredding, soaking it until it becomes pulpy and illegible, cutting it up with scissors, ripping it to tiny bits or all of these things – whatever takes your fancy. By obliterating your bitter outpourings, you symbolically take control. You have the power. It should feel good!

If you are feeling powerless, then affirmations may be beneficial. They can help you focus on the positive and stop dwelling on the negative. Try repeating them to yourself regularly. Pin them up around the house to remind yourself.

"I'm strong enough to cope with this."

"This is only a very small part of my life."

"I have many options."

"I have right on my side."

"This may take some time and effort but I'll get there in the end."

"I am in charge of how I feel and I let go of anger/ frustration/envy/bitterness."

"Everything will be OK."

Relaxation techniques, mindfulness, going for a long walk on the beach or in your favourite place or pounding out your tensions at the gym can all be effective in dealing with distressing or intrusive thoughts and prevent you dwelling on your wearisome and trying neighbours. Doing something that takes all your concentration helps to stop you going over and over whatever it is they've done or said and calms the turmoil in your mind. Keeping busy cleaning out the drains, defrosting the freezer, ripping out the weeds in the garden or doing some other unpleasant job you have been putting off for ages will help channel your emotions, can be very therapeutic and make you feel more on top of the situation.

Share your woes with some trouble dolls. These are tiny, colourful dolls traditionally made in Guatemala. Tell them about anything that is bothering you (not just your annoying neighbours) before you go to sleep, and supposedly they will take the worry away from you and work together overnight to solve the problem. If you can't find any, you could make your own from instructions to be found online.

Talking and laughing with friends and family, not necessarily about your tiresome neighbours, will also improve your mood and let you see that there are more important things in life and that, for all its trials and tribulations, there is still much to be grateful for. Laughing releases endorphins which lower the stress-causing hormones cortisol and adrenaline, so even if you're on your own, take some deep breaths and smile. There's usually an amusing side to those clashes with the neighbours – you just have to find it and hang onto it. Look for the ridiculous in what was said or the comical expression on their face. Think of how it would be portrayed in a sitcom.

Go to a funny movie, listen to classical music, the sounds of the sea or birdsong – anything that will clear your mind and allow some time to pass since the confrontation. Things usually look better in retrospect or at least not as bleak. Learn to forgive if not forget. We're all human after all and we all transgress and make mistakes. Let it go.

If you can find a way to move forward in your thinking and relieve the stress, it will come as a great release. But avoid alcohol – it lowers your inhibitions and may make you do or say something you'll regret. Remember the four things, variously attributed to Omar Ibn Al-Halif, Sujan Rao, Umar/Omar (577-644), Chinese philosophy, Arabian proverbs and Aiki Flinthart.

"Four things come not back
The sped arrow
The spoken word
Time past
The neglected opportunity."

Sometimes it's altered or simplified but the meaning is clear

"The stone after the throw
The word after it's said
The occasion after it's missed
The time after it's gone."

You get the picture. Now try putting it into practice.

4. ATTEMPTING RESOLUTION

But if you feel that you want to sort out the issue and are not afraid to confront your neighbour, here are a few tips.

Call them or speak to them, calmly explain what is distressing you and ask them if you can both sit down and talk about it. Resist the urge to discuss it there and then unless they are truly mortified, apologise profusely and promise to stop immediately, which is extremely unlikely. This will give them some time to consider your request and whether you are being reasonable, and hopefully come up with a positive response. Arrange to meet on neutral territory if possible – the pub has a convivial and relaxed atmosphere and people are less likely to throw a complete wobbly in public. State your case without accusing them, and ask them if they can suggest any way round it. If they are unresponsive, suggest some sensible alternatives. If possible, offer a concession on your part so that the giving is not all on their side. If this fails, ask them if they would feel more comfortable if an independent trained mediator assessed the situation and came up with some suggestions, at your expense of course. It may sound cold-blooded, but keep a private record of all the incidents, dates and their responses.

Another ploy which works well is to avoid directly blaming the neighbour. If her dog is fouling your pristine lawn, and you know they know because you've seen them standing there watching it do its business, don't deliberately antagonise them by accusing them of knowingly allowing it. Be sneaky. Preface your words with "You probably don't know this but…" thus allowing them some innocence of the crime, even when you both know it's a lie. Subtly making people feel guilty can be very effective.

If you have trouble with a noisy neighbour who likes to blast out heavy metal music late into the night and no amount of requests and pleas have any effect, take some comfort from the following anecdote. What finally worked for one person was due to an email received concerning a spate of burglaries that had occurred in the area. In true neighbourly fashion, he circulated it to all the neighbours, including the noisy one, but he couldn't help writing on their copy "Just because you're not very considerate towards your neighbours doesn't mean you shouldn't know about this. We're all keeping an eye open for anything suspicious that we see at anyone's house when they're at work, including yours." It was that little dig that made the noisy neighbours feel ashamed and they stopped the loud music. Doing a good deed not only makes you feel good, it can work in your interests. Reciprocation is a powerful force that lives in all of us – you just have to tap into it.

If you are the sort who can be bothered to try and modify their neighbour's conduct over time, you could make an effort to nudge them in the right direction by reinforcing good behaviour or lack of bad behaviour by a reward, which can be as simple as a thank you. Punishing bad manners or trying to get even rarely ends well and simply encourages escalation, so isn't recommended, however tempting. Vandalism, property damage and other methods of taking matters into your own hands can seriously backfire and can end up with you in court. If nothing else deters you, imagine how your annoying neighbours would love that.

With some neighbours, the more they know that something they do annoys you, the more they will do it, just to wind you up. They show no empathy for your frustration that their rows are keeping your baby awake, and feel entitled to indulge in whatever activities they want, and that other people should acquiesce to them. They usually have a very high opinion of themselves, which stems from insecurity, low esteem and personality stagnation. Somewhere in their past someone humiliated them and they have never forgotten it. Every time someone challenges them reminds them of the original incident and they have to win every trivial point to boost their fragile ego. This is your classic bully. They will not respond to the straightforward approach and you are going to have to be very cunning! Interacting with them will be uncomfortable as it may make you feel two-faced, but with a little planning and guile, and a lot of patience, it may turn up trumps in the long term. You have nothing to lose although you may have to let their boorishness pass you by and accept that you can only manage, rather than change, their attitude. Basically, you have to take a big breath, retreat several paces and use their need for flattery by praising anything you can find that you genuinely like about them. It must be credible as they have a built in shit detector, borne of years of suspicion. As they have a low threshold of tolerance, avoid controversial topics, smile and nod agreement where you can. If the conversation starts to drift onto difficult territory where you have your own strong views, change the subject, preferably to something neutral. Maintain control! Keep your long term goal in mind. Softly, softly, catchee monkey. Eventually there will come a time when they want something from you, and this is your opportunity to bring up the subject that is really bothering you. But above all, don't make it seem like blackmail! You have to link the two favours together carefully and best to have thought about this, prepared and practised various scenarios in advance. Yes, it's calculating and manipulative, but if it works, who cares? It's a win-win situation for all, and you will have tamed the neighbour and got what you want. What's not to like? Furthermore, you will have gained the respect of all your others neighbours for your negotiating skills. Awesome!

The problem of nuisance neighbours is so nationwide that there are specialist neighbourhood dispute services concentrating on community mediation and resolution. So this is your first port of call for boundary issues, problems with ball games, noise, parking and virtually anything else that gets neighbours at each other's throats and which can't be resolved amicably. Look them up under 'Mediation Services'. Mediators are impartial and trained in dealing with difficult situations. There may be a fee but it is a lot cheaper than resorting to the law.

It helps to know what sort of character your neighbour is so that you can work out which is the best method of dealing with them. Sometimes the apparent problem is not the real issue and behind it lies a bigger conundrum, which has festered for some time but they have been unable to address or resolve it to their satisfaction. They are using the present situation, trivial as it might appear at first sight, to get some redress.

Standing up for a principle is very noble but negotiating a settlement means that everyone can get on with their lives instead of constantly bickering and will save a lot of hassle in the long term. It is fine to establish and set out your position, but you must be prepared to concede if necessary. However, there is likely to be a point which you will not go beyond. If your neighbour is the same, you can end up in stalemate. But if you know him to be a bully or a quitter, and believe that you have a strong case, stand your ground and push for an amicable solution – cajoling, coaxing, persuading, sweet-talking, flattering, wheedling, whatever it takes – to get there. However, it may be more politic to allow independent parties to negotiate on your behalf as they will be more objective, and you can both agree in advance to accept their decision as binding.

5. THE LEGAL APPROACH – THE LAST RESORT

But supposing your best efforts backfire or simply don't work? This brings us to the legal issues and a word of warning – only resort to the courts if absolutely necessary and if every other avenue of negotiation and mediation has failed, and then only if you have very deep pockets. Courts can and do issue orders to those responsible for causing the nuisance to end their errant behaviour, but it does not necessarily mean they will. This method of attempting to resolve problems is not for the faint-hearted. It can be much cheaper, quicker and a whole lot less stressful, to move. Life is too short to be unhappy.

If your properties are rented, you may consider contacting the landlord or management committee, tenants association or housing association. They can offer support and install extra locks, alarms and lighting to help you feel safe, or may be able to rehouse you. The nuisance neighbour may be in breach of a tenancy agreement and could face eviction.

Do some research on any relevant bylaws. Check your property title deeds or look them up at the Land Registry to see if they shed any light on a boundary dispute. Is there a restrictive covenant in your deeds or lease preventing anyone from certain actions such as having an external satellite dish or solar panels or painting their doors and windows anything but white? Who is responsible for looking after communal areas or repairing the fences? If your neighbour is responsible for a fence, they can do as they like, even if you don't like it. Having said that, electrifying a fence is illegal! Boundary disputes are notorious for having hidden agendas, such as:

- your neighbour is trying to regain land he feels he lost when a previous neighbour replaced the fence.
- he is trying to claim a hedge so he can get rid of it or keep it if you want to get rid of it.
- he needs the extra inches to build an extension but hasn't declared this.
- he has tried to enclose a bit of land neglected by the previous owner but clearly shown on the deeds as belonging to you.

- the boundary wall is falling down and he doesn't want the expense of repair.
- you got planning permission for an extension against his wishes and he is getting his own back.
- he wants you to know who's boss around here.
- you have never got on and he will do anything to annoy you.

Make sure you keep a note of each occurrence of the nuisance, including time, date, length of disturbance, people involved, what happened and any other relevant details, such as how you felt. Back it up with recordings or photos if possible.

The local authority may be able to make an order for the responsible person to clean up an insanitary garden which is so infested with rats or rubbish that it is a health hazard, so contact the Environmental Health Officer. You can also get the council involved if the dispute is a 'statutory' one, such as loud music or barking dogs, which means there are laws associated with it to prevent nuisance. They can enforce action with a Statutory Notice in which case the owner has twenty-one days to resolve the issue. After that there may be financial penalties and, as a last resort, the dog can be legally removed.

In the case of the neighbour's overgrown leylandii hedge, if you cannot come to an amicable arrangement or discussions with them have broken down, you can make a complaint to the local council under the Anti-Social Behaviour Act, 2003. They are likely to charge you a fee of several hundred pounds, but will consider both sides' arguments. They will probably make a site visit to assess the different points of view and whether the offending hedge adversely affects the complainant's reasonable enjoyment of their home or garden. Note the use of the word 'reasonable.' They will come to a decision to either reject the complaint or issue a notice for work to be carried out on the hedge, including a timescale for it to be done, which could be several months. This is so that nesting birds are not disturbed. If the neighbours do not comply, they have committed an offence and can be fined in a Magistrates' Court. The council cannot, however, order the hedge to be removed or require anything to be done that would result in the death of the hedge, and they may not necessarily stipulate a reduction in height to 2m. There is no general requirement that hedges in suburban gardens must be kept below a certain height. No fees or compensation can be claimed from the neighbours even if you win. Both sides have the right to appeal and any remedial works are suspended while the appeal is being heard.

Problems with neighbours' children are a potential minefield. Once upon a time you could tell the children's parents and know that the issues would be dealt with, but today you criticise their little darlings at your peril. Above all never physically get hold of the children or you will be in big trouble. Dragging a child home by the ear will get you a criminal record. Kids know this and may taunt you but keep your cool. Children are naturally exuberant and running around screaming and shouting during play is part of the job description. If you're a shift worker trying to sleep during the day it can be a problem, so explain your situation to the parents in a conciliatory way. If they have caused damage to a window, then the parents should pay for the repair. If they refuse you can sue them, but you will only win if they have been negligent, say by trusting their child with something dangerous like a gun, or if you could prove that they failed to exercise proper control. And don't be tempted to puncture or confiscate any ball that arrives in your garden. Give it back.

Interestingly, research in California has shown that if people see painted eyes 'watching' them, they are more honest and generous and less likely to be anti-social. I suspect that this is the reason why CCTV works so well, and you have the added advantage of the recorded evidence. There are laws governing the installation and use of CCTV which apply to businesses and organisations under the Data Protection Act 1998, but not domestic property. This does not, however, mean that you can train your cameras on someone's bedroom, which can, quite rightly, be tantamount to harassment, invasion of privacy or snooping. It should only be focused on your own property and is likely to work more as a deterrent than anything else.

Only call the police (call on 101, if it is not urgent enough for a 999 call) if you are being threatened with violence, or are being harassed due to your gender, sexual orientation, religion or ethnic origins, or your neighbour is breaking the law or you suspect that they are.

6. MOVING HOUSE

So, you've had enough of your nuisance neighbours, for whatever reasons, and decide to sell up and move on. The dilemma is: how do you avoid the subject with prospective buyers and stay on the right side of the law? Be honest. If you have had any tiffs about the odd party going on a bit late and are miffed because you weren't invited or you have different political views and have exchanged opinions robustly on occasions, these don't have to be declared as they do not affect anything material about the property and are subjective. It is unlikely you would ever be asked to put these sorts of things in writing. If you have had any kind of serious problems with the neighbours, then these will, of course, have to be declared. If in doubt, ask your solicitor or Citizens Advice Bureau. It may be possible to say that there have been no issues between you in the last ten years if you haven't spoken to them in that time since the issue involving the cat, the mysterious disappearance of the Christmas turkey, and the baseball bat. Anyway, the cat has since departed to the big litter tray in the sky so the incident is unlikely to be repeated. That little business when the builders doing their extension mooned at your mother-in-law for being nosy? She might have wanted to call the police but you managed to mollify her with alcohol and it was a great excuse not to invite her round until they had finished. You could say you don't see much of the neighbours as you are so busy, but exchange Christmas cards or take in parcels for them when they're out, so long as it's not a lie. Most people will be satisfied and won't realise that you are being somewhat economical with the truth! In any case, the issue with the cannabis plants was eventually resolved amicably, and little Johnny is now living in a commune in Cornwall after he came out of prison, and only visits when he's run out of money. You may be able to get away with it. It just depends how ethical you are and how desperate to move. What do you tell potential buyers if the neighbours are perfectly pleasant to you but the police are round there regularly when he comes home from the pub and beats her up again? Is it a material fact that might put off some buyers? Would it put you off? You wouldn't be the first or last person to wax lyrical about the neighbours you can't stand the sight of and, who knows, the prospective buyers might get along famously with them!

Please note that nothing in this book is meant to be a substitute for consulting the appropriate body and getting professional advice.

NEIGHBOURLY ORGANISATIONS

In the UK we have Neighbourhood Watch coordinators who are sometimes mocked as some sort of curtain-twitching vigilantes but they do much good in passing around information from the police about neighbourhood issues such as burglaries, suspicious activities and persons, focusing on the need for improving security and looking out for each other's property.

There is a plethora of advice on the internet but you could try the following two sites for information:

www.problemneighbours.co.uk

www.gov.uk/how-to-resolve-neighbour-disputes

For free advice, you can consult your local Citizens Advice Bureau as they deal with neighbourhood disputes frequently and have abundant experience of the issues. It helps to know you're not alone.

Neighbours from Hell in Britain (NFHiB) is a not-for-profit organisation set up in 2002 and provides advice, information and support for people plagued by nuisance neighbours. It was founded by two people with personal experience of the trials and tribulations of inconsiderate neighbours. It also actively lobbies for changes in the law relating to disputes between neighbours. Here you will find blank logs to help you record incidents, self-help articles, template letters, relevant Acts of Parliament and all sorts of gadgets from earplugs and sunglasses with a hidden camera to full blown CCTV systems, as well as a forum to vent your fury.

To paraphrase John F Kennedy, "Ask not what your neighbour can do for you but what you can do for your neighbour." So you want to get on with the neighbours. Where do you start? Well, there are some interesting organisations around the world, set up by individuals with just this goal in mind. Apartment Life encourages people in blocks of flats in America to get to know their neighbours with a view to building good relationships between them. They welcome new residents and plan social events encouraging interaction between the residents. Their ideas have included inviting a neighbour over for dinner each month, organising a walking group or running club, inviting other residents to be their friend on Facebook, getting together socially and performing random acts of kindness, such as putting someone's rubbish out or returning their bin after collection. Doing a good deed costs nothing, makes you feel good and is neighbourly to boot. Sounds good to me!

In New Zealand they have an annual Neighbour's Day in March and a European Neighbour's Day was officially launched in Paris in 2000 as a way to bring communities together, to encourage solidarity amongst neighbours and to promote better living. Gradually the idea has spread all over the world and now there are over fourteen million participants in countries as far afield as Australia, Canada, the USA, Japan, Mexico and Togo. So, I hear you say, why not the United Kingdom? Well, we do participate although it is not very widely known. The Eden Project, an educational charity, started The Big Lunch back in 2009 and 7.29m people took part in 2015, with people being encouraged to arrange parties to get to know the neighbours and talk to each other. This annual get-together takes place on the first Sunday in June each year and you can send for a free pack of inspirational ideas, invitations, posters and stickers funded by The Big Lottery Fund. Parties take place not only in streets, but in gardens and parks, village halls and other public locations. The Big Lunch is encouraging communities to celebrate local living, enjoy great food together, meet their neighbours – perhaps for the first time – and share time in each other's company. By fostering community spirit, it is helping neighbours develop a stronger sense of pride and belonging in their neighbourhood, enhance social cohesion and create new friends in a convivial and social atmosphere. Find out more at www.thebiglunch.com.

These events remind people to make peace with the neighbours, whatever has happened in the past. On some occasions this has led to the setting up of local time banks, where no money changes hands but a time-based currency is established where the unit is a person-hour. The idea is that if you agree to do work for someone, you earn the equivalent time as a credit so that you can ask someone else to do some work for you in the future. So an hour's accountancy or gardening might earn you an hour getting your ironing done or your car cleaned and vice versa. The first time bank was started in Stonehouse, Gloucestershire in 1998, and there are now over 300 in the UK. Find out whether there is one in your area at www.timebanking.org and www.freedomfavours.com.

AND FINALLY...

In reading this book, you have probably learnt a lot about your own behaviour and that of others. More especially how your feelings have influenced your behaviour towards your neighbours, past and present, and how their actions (or lack of) have affected yours, how events can be misinterpreted or misconstrued, and how a careless word can result in things getting blown out of proportion. How, by not addressing an issue that is important to someone else, seemingly trivial incidents can fester and have unexpected consequences down the years. Behind all the frivolity of poking fun at the neighbours, there is a serious message here. We can choose our friends but we are stuck with the neighbours, like 'em or loathe 'em.

The last word on the subject goes to the poet Robert Frost, who perfectly summed up the subject of neighbours and the relationships we should have with them. In his poem *Mending Wall*, the rural neighbours take equal responsibility for mending their communal boundary, despite one of them questioning the necessity. By retaining and mending the wall each year, they are able to preserve their individual and personal identities – one of an apple farmer, the other of a pine tree forester – and to demarcate the boundaries of property and ownership, so that there is never any dispute over the limits of their territory. It also provides an opportunity to interact and communicate with each other while working together doing a shared job which is satisfying and of mutual benefit. We could all learn a lot from it.

THE END

(OR NEVER LET THOSE PESKY NEIGHBOURS GET YOU DOWN!)

References

Aron, Elaine. The Highly Sensitive Person: How to thrive when the world overwhelms you. Thorsons, 1999

Baumgartner, M P. The Moral Order of a Suburb, New York. Oxford University Press, 1988

Bulmer, M. Neighbours: The Work of Philip Abrams. Cambridge University Press, 1986

Buofino, A and Hilder, P. Neighbouring in Contemporary Britain. Joseph Rowntree Foundation, 2006

Buss, Dr David M. The Murderer Next Door: Why the Mind is Designed to Kill. Penguin Press, 2005

Frost, Robert. Mending Wall (1914)

Halifax Home Insurance survey reported in The Telegraph, 13 March 2010

O'Toole, M E and Bowman, A. Dangerous Instincts: How Gut Reactions Betray Us. Hudson Street Press (Penguin USA imprint), 2011

Ruonavaara, H and Kouvo, A. Neighbour Relations in Contemporary Society. Paper presented at the ISA Housing Assets Conference, Glasgow, 2008

Schopenhauer, A. Studies in Pessimism (1851)

Acknowledgements

Now, all books have this section and I always start here when I pick up a new one because I want to see how many people were affected. Often it's an exercise in 'See how popular I am and how many people I know' and, if possible, there is a good bit of name-dropping and self-publicity. Authors are often very keen to show that they have spent time doing some research, sometimes in exotic locations, and that this demonstrates how intelligent they are and how much hard work goes into being an author. Yeah, right. Sometimes it's about the people who got pushed to one side, neglected, ruthlessly used and then sacrificed on the altar of writing, and the acknowledgement of their existence in print is a mollification exercise. Sometimes it's a glimpse into something magical.

So, here goes.

Friends – I only told a couple of them that I was writing a book at all, and I suspect I only told them because I thought they'd be impressed. I refused to tell them exactly what it was about, just dropped hints that it was of the satirical genre and would appeal to everyone all over the world. Modest, I was not. Jackie replied, with good insight into my character, that she expected it would be "pithy". I hope you feel I have validated your perspicacity. And thanks to my beta readers, even though you made me delete some of the more colourful bits.

Research – Well, all I can say is that there's a lot of stuff out there on the internet and thank you to everyone who contributed to the online rants about their psychopathic neighbours. It gave me some great ideas! I got withdrawal symptoms when I had a new idea and couldn't get to my laptop to work on it. I shamelessly seeded conversations with innocuous enquiries about neighbours, encouraged people to elaborate on any spontaneous reference to their neighbours and pricked up my ears whenever I overheard someone in the supermarket queue or at the hairdresser's complaining about their neighbours, which was surprisingly often. These earwigged conversations gave me much useful material. Thank you to everyone who was so helpful, albeit unsuspectingly.

Apologies – I sorely neglected the housework during the writing process, expecting that, if I ignored it for long enough and it became unbearably messy and unhygienic, the other resident 'staff' would do it. Him or the fairies. He did it – eventually.

Although I found writing incredibly addictive, I was surprised that at times it was also very tiring. How can sitting on your arse and flexing a few fingers be tiring? At the same time, it sometimes left me so hyped up when working into the evenings that I couldn't sleep. And I had to have a notepad by the side of the bed in case I woke up in the night with a fantastic idea for another character. I knocked a fair few glasses of water onto the floor scrabbling for a pencil in the wee small hours only to find, in the proverbial cold light of day, that what I thought might be inspired was simply the ramblings of a somnambulist.

Many thanks to my publishers, Matador, without whom you wouldn't be reading this at all. Or if you were it wouldn't be as readable as it is now. Turning the manuscript into a finished book took a lot of time and a huge team effort, and the credit goes to Lauren, Sian, Hannah, Katherine, Alice, Chelsea, Becky, Rebecca and, of course, Jane and Jeremy. The journey was a great adventure but I was very glad when we reached our destination. Finally, special thanks to Mike Bastin (www.mikebastincreative.com) for the brilliant front cover and for accommodating my special request.

Index

Remarks Upon a Position of the Right Reverend the Lord Bishop of Bangor Concerning Religious Sincerity. Wherein the Consequences of This Position are Fully Stated The Second Edition

REMARKS

UPON A

POSITION

• OF

The RIGHT REVEREND the

Lord Bifhop of *Bangor*

CONCERNING

Religious Sincerity.

WHEREIN

The Confequences of this POSITION are fully
ftated, and his Lordfhip's pretended DEMON-
STRATION is fhewn to be inconclufive.

By *HENRY STEBBING*, M. A.
Rector of RICKINGHALL *in* SUFFOLK, *and late*
Fellow of St. CATHARINES-HALL *in* Cambridge.

To which is prefix'd a PREFACE *by the*
Reverend the DEAN *of* Chichefter.

𝕿𝖍𝖊 𝕾𝖊𝖈𝖔𝖓𝖉 𝕰𝖉𝖎𝖙𝖎𝖔𝖓.

• *LONDON,*
Printed for HENRY CLEMENTS, at the *Half Moon*
in St. *Paul's* Church-Yard. 1718.

THE
PREFACE
TO THE
READER.

THE following Treatise will give every judicious Reader so true an Idea of the Abilities of its Author, that I think it needless for me to tell the World what I know of him. The truest Character of any Writer is that which naturally arises from his Performance; and I would not be so unjust to my Friend, as to give any one reason to suspect that he owes the Opinion he shall have of him, to any Hand but his own.

The Charge of the Committee upon the Lord Bishop of Bangor *with respect to his Doctrine of* Sincerity, *is in its main Parts so fully cleared in the following Treatise, that I see no occasion there can be to consider it over again. One Passage indeed there is relating to this Head which the Author has not undertaken to vindicate, and the reason is, because he was not en-*

A 2

tirely

tirely satisfied with it, as appears in his former Treatise *. Whether that Passage in the Representation be defensible or no, shall in due Time be considered; in the mean while the World has an undeniable Proof before them that this Gentleman did not enter into this Controversy with a Party Zeal, and a Determination to support the Charge of the Committee right or wrong, but with an honest and impartial Regard to Truth, where-ever it was, in his Judgment, to be found.

In his former Treatise, which is a Defence of the first Part of the Representation upon the Head of Church Authority, he has so carefully weighed and considered the Bishop of Bangor's Answer to the Committee on that Head, together with the Positions of the Sermon which gave Occasion to the Charge, and so closely pursued his Lordship thro' all his Turnings and Windings, and so plainly proved that the Doctrines, as well of his Answer to the Committee, as of his Sermon, subvert all Government and Discipline in the Church of Christ, that till I see new reason to the contrary, I shall reckon the Committee fully justified thus far in the Part they acted; for however Men may differ in their Opinions, and some may think that the Bishop deserves well for his worthy Endeavours to subvert all Church Authority, yet I verily think it can no longer be a Question whether he intended to subvert it or no. And this is the Point between his Lordship and the Committee.

For my own part, when I consider the Method of his Lordship's Answer to the Representation, and

---

* A Defence of the first Head, p 3, 4.

see

*fee how carefully and refolutely he avoids declaring
what* one *Branch of* Authority *he allows to the* Chriftian Church, *infifting neverthelefs that he has not
denied all Authority; upon which Plea, if Iffue muft
be joined, the only Point in Debate will be concerning
the* Meaning *of certain Paffages in his Lordfhip's*
Sermon; *when I fee this, I fay, I am furprized to
hear his Lordfhip declaring to the World that he is
engaged in a Subject of the utmoft* Importance *to the
future and* prefent *Happinefs of* Mankind; *for
furely it cannot be of* fuch *Confequence to the World
to know what his Lordfhip means by* properly, abfo-
lutely, *or by an Hundred more fuch Words, and if
the Controverfy is never to rife above this noble Point,
'tis pity that one Sheet more of Paper fhould be loft in
Purfuit of it. It had been of much more Service to
the Caufe of Truth, and of Religion, if his Lordfhip,
inftead of writing between* 3 *and* 400 *Pages to tell us
what he did* not *mean, had been pleafed to publifh*
Ten *only to inform us what he does mean, and what
Authority he pretends to affert in confequence of his
often repeated Plea, that he has not denied All. His
Lordfhip has publickly told us that he intends to go on
in this Caufe, and if he does, I call upon him by all
the Regard that is due to* Truth, *to* Religion, *to the*
Gofpel, *and to the* Church of Chrift, *to fay without
Difguife what* Authority *he allows to the Church;
this is a Point that well deferves to be treated with
Opennefs, Plainnefs, and Sincerity; and whenever
his Lordfhip fhall take this Part, I will be ready to do
either* him *or the Caufe* Juftice, *by fubfcribing to
his Judgment, or by fhewing the Reafons why I cannot,*

It

It was once in my Thoughts to take this Opportuni-
ty of vindicating that Passage in the Representation
relating to Sincerity, which the Author of the follow-
ing Treatise has not entred into, but I found it would
carry me beyond the Bounds of a Preface, and require
more Time than my present Engagements will allow
me ; I shall therefore only say what may be sufficient
to shew the true Meaning of the Passage, and leave
the Prosecution of the Argument to another Season.

The Passage is this

From this pretended Demonstration his Lordship infers, " If this were duly and impartially
" consider'd, it would be impossible for Men to
" unchristian, unchurch, or declare out of
" God's Favour, any of their *Fellow Creatures,*
" upon any leſſer, or indeed any other Conside-
" ration, than that of a wicked Dishonesty and
" Insincerity; of which, in these Cases, God
" alone is Judge."

If it be true that there is but one Consideration, *viz.* that of wicked Dishonesty and Insincerity, which will justify unchristianing, unchurch-
ing, or declaring out of God's Favour, and of
that one Consideration, in these Cases, God
alone is Judge, there is evidently an End of all
Church Authority, to oblige any to external
Communion, and of all Power, that one Man,
in what Station soever, can have over another,
in Matters of Religion. *

---

* *Report of the Committee,* Oct. Edit. p. 12.

The

The Points here maintained by his Lordship are, That there is but one Reason in the Cases referred to for unchriftianing, &c. viz. wicked Dishonesty and Insincerity, and that of this one Reason God alone is Judge.

The Consequence then drawn by the Committee from his Lordship's Doctrine is undeniable; for if there be in these Cases but one Reason for unchriftianing, &c. and of that Reason God alone is Judge, 'tis evident that in these Cases there is no room for the Church to exercise any Authority by unchriftianing, &c. For if the Church grounds a Sentence upon any thing but Insincerity, it errs in acting upon a Reason, which his Lordship declares to be no Reason. If it judges of Sincerity, it pretends to judge where 'tis impossible it should, God alone being Judge in this Point. Since therefore the Church ought not to act without Reason, since in this Case there is no Reason for it to act upon, the Church is evidently excluded from acting at all, or having any Concern in these Cases.

The Committee, who maintain that the Church has such Authority, are, I think, bound, in answer to his Lordship's Position, to shew at least one of these two Things, either that the Church may have in these Cases sufficient Evidence of Insincerity, or that there are sufficient Reasons to exclude Men from the Communion of Christians, without entring into the Consideration of their Sincerity or Insincerity.

This is the true State of the Case. And that 'tis possible oftentimes to judge of Men's Insincerity in the Choice they make of external Communion, is

one

one of those things of which no Man of a plain Understanding can doubt. Do we not every Day see
how wantonly and peevishly Men separate from the
establish'd Church? How common a thing it is for
a little Dispute between the Parson and his Parishioner, to end in the Parishioner's forsaking the Church?
And when we see Men hurried into the Meeting-
Houses by their Passions and Resentment, and revi-
ling the Church in which they were born and bred,
only because they could not get Twenty Shillings, or
perhaps but Twenty Pence, abated in their Offerings
or Church Rates, shall we be afraid of saying that
such Men are dishonest in their Choice, and use the
Indulgence granted to tender Consciences only as a
Protection, whilst they act without any Conscience
at all?

As to the other Case. Let it be supposed if a
Number of Men should form themselves into a Communion upon Terms directly opposite to those laid
down in the Gospel, that they should, for Instance,
reject the Use of the Sacraments, declare the Scrip-
tures to be a dead Letter, and deny that Christ came
in the Flesh, &c. here now is an external Communion,
such as it is, and let his Lordship tell us whether the
Church of Christ may declare the Men of this Communion to be no Christians upon Account of their
Doctrines and Practices held in Opposition to the
Gospel, or whether it must maintain that these
Doctrines joined to Sincerity become the Terms of
the Gospel, and entitle Men to the Privileges of
Christianity?

In all Cases of this nature, if you suppose Men
to act with Sincerity, you must also suppose their
Sin-

Sincerity to be attended with great Ignorance *and* Weaknefs; *for when Men reject the very Terms of the Gofpel with Sincerity, you muft either fay that the Sincerity is attended with Ignorance and Weaknefs, or you muft fay that the Terms of the Gofpel are fuch, that an honeft fincere Man after a full Examination, may, and ought to reject them · His Lordfhip, I prefume, will hardly affirm this; and therefore he muft allow us to fay, that by Sincerity, in the prefent Cafe at leaft, he means no more than a Man's acting according to his prefent Opinion, without confidering whether fuch Opinion arifes from the due Exercife of Reafon, or from Paffion and Prejudice : For remove Ignorance and Paffion out of the Cafe, and where is the Sincerity which will refufe to fubmit to fuch Terms of Communion as the Gofpel has made neceffary, or indeed to fuch as are in their own Nature indifferent, and required only for the fake of external Order and Decency?*

This is the true State of the Cafe.

The only Difficulty now is, to afcertain the true Meaning of his Lordfhip's Words, to unchriftian, unchurch, or declare out of God's Favour.

To unchriftian, *muft, I think, mean to declare a Man to have forfeited the Rights of a Chriftian :* To unchurch, *muft mean to throw a Man out of the Communion of the Church · Thus far I fhould hope for his Lordfhip's Confent to what I fay. The third Expreffion is,* to declare out of God's Favour: *There are two ways of underftanding thefe Words; either by the* Favour of God *you mean, that Favour which he has publifhed, declared, and promifed to Mankind thro' the Means provided in the Gofpel;*

B *or*

*or you mean in general that Goodneſs and Mercy of
God, which, for ought we know, he may extend beyond the Limits of the Goſpel, even to ſuch perhaps
as have in the* Sincerity *of their* Hearts, *and in
the* Weakneſs *of their* Underſtandings *(for theſe
two things muſt go together) rejected the Conditions
of the Goſpel · But ſurely 'tis highly reaſonable to
underſtand a Chriſtian Biſhop, and in a Controverſy
relating to the Church of Chriſt, in the firſt Senſe.
His Lordſhip ſpeaks of* unchriſtianing, unchurch-
ing, declaring out of God's Favour, *in relation
to one and the ſame thing; it muſt therefore be
ſuppoſed that the three* Expreſſions *have ſome relation to one another, and conſequently, that by
the* Favour of God, *he means that* Favour *which
we are entitled to as* Chriſtians *and* Members
*of the Church, but as Chriſtians and Members of
the Church, we are concerned only with that* Favour of God, *the Terms of which he has declared
in the Goſpel. Beſides, the Subject which his Lordſhip was treating on, ſeems neceſſarily to require
this Senſe of the Words · Church Authority was
the Subject; but the Church having nothing to do
to judge one way or other about the Favour of God,
but only as he has declared it in the Goſpel, and as
he has committed the Diſpenſation of it to his Church
under the Uſe of the Means, and Rules preſcribed by
himſelf, it cannot conſiſtently be ſuppoſed that his
Lordſhip in this Argument ſpoke of it in any other
Senſe.*

*But to clear this Matter, I add; that if his Lord-
ſhip ſhall declare, that he did not mean the Favour
of God as promiſed upon the Terms of the Goſpel,*
but

but that general Favour which he may extend to all whose Circumstances shall recommend them as Objects of Mercy: In Answer to it I say, that the Church has no Concern in this Part of his Assertion it never did, it never can pretend to meddle with, or to declare any thing about the uncovenanted Mercies of God: The Gospel is its Rule ; it declares those only to be out of the Favour of God who reject the Gospel, and the Means of Salvation there offered, or who live in open Disobedience to the Precepts therein contained.

But if his Lordship shall own, that by the Favour of God *he means the* Favour of God *as declared in the Gospel, upon the Terms of which we are admitted to be Disciples of Christ, and Members of the Church, then I deny that there is but* one Reason, viz. wicked Dishonesty and Insincerity *for declaring Men out of God's Favour ; and my Reason is, because I will not say that every Man who does not receive all that the Gospel has made necessary, is* wickedly, *i. e. knowingly and wilfully* Insincere : *But those who do not receive, or who reject the Conditions of the Gospel, are no Christians, and the Church has a Right to declare them so ; or which comes to the same thing, to declare them to have no Title to* God's Favour *as it is set forth by Christ Jesus.*

The Case is now clear If his Lordship means only that such Sincerity as is attended with Weakness and Ignorance (for of such Sincerity in the present Case he must speak) will be a compassionate Plea for Favour or Mercy, I have no Inclination (my own Infirmities forbid me to have any) to dispute it with

him:

*him. But then I beg of his Lordſhip to tell me what
this has to do in an Argument of Church Power:
did he ever hear that the Chriſtian Church pretended to be the Diſpenſer of God's uncovenanted
Mercies, which would be in Truth to make Rules for
God, whereas the Church muſt ever hold it ſelf
bound to judge only according to the Rules made by
God; and whilſt it does ſo, it is ſo far from being
chargeable with the extravagant Preſumption of obliging God to execute its Sentence, that the Church does
in truth paſs no Sentence of its own, but ſpeaks in
Obedience to the Obligation it finds it ſelf under to
publiſh and declare the Sentence of God.*

But if his Lordſhip means that this *Sincerity is*
ſuch a Plea or Title *to the* Favour of God, *that no
other Terms of obtaining it ought to be inſiſted on;* he
muſt argue this Point not with the Church, but with
an higher Power, the Author of the Goſpel. *The
Church has no Right to declare any Terms or Means
of Salvation, but what are declared in the Goſpel.
His Lordſhip then before he blames the Church for declaring the Favour of God upon other Terms than Sincerity alone, muſt ſhew that the only* Term *or* Condition *of Salvation propoſed in the Goſpel is* Sincerity: *he muſt ſhew that when we are required to be* bap-
tized, *the Meaning is, that we ſhould ſincerely* accept, *or* ſincerely refuſe Baptiſm; *that when we are*
commanded *to* believe in Jeſus Chriſt, *the Meaning*
only *is, that we ſhould either ſincerely* believe in
him, *or* ſincerely reject him, *that when we are required not to* forſake the aſſembling our ſelves together, *the Meaning is, that we ſhould either ſincerely* go to Church, *or* ſincerely ſtay away; *that when*
we

we are commanded to continue the Memory of the
Death of Chrift *till his coming again, the Meaning*
only *is, that we fhould either fincerely* do it, *or fincerely* let it alone : *In a Word, that the Preachers
of the Gofpel fhou'd confine themfelves to this* one
Speech, " *Men and Brethren, this is the Method of*
" *Salvation, which God thro' Chrift has offered to the*
" *World; but if you like any other Way better, better*
" *it is that you fhou'd follow your own Opinion.*"

   *This Doctrine of Sincerity, his Lordfhip, you fee,
applys to the Cafe of difference in Communion, and
particularly to the* difference *between* Popifh *and*
Proteftant *Communion, and affirms, that a fincere*
Papift *is in juft the* fame *Cafe with a fincere* Proteftant ; *and therefore the Committee rightly obferved that he left no Difference (as to the Favour of
God) between the two Communions ; for if Sincerity
in one Communion is as good a Title to the Favour
of God, as Sincerity in the* other, *what poffible difference, in this refpect, can there be? I ask his Lordfhip now, whether it be not againft the Doctrine of
the Gofpel, and of natural Religion too, to pay Worfhip and Adoration to Creatures in the manner the
Church of* Rome *requires · If he fays it is not, it will
then be manifeft whofe Principles tend moft to Popery,
his Lordfhip's or his Adverfaries : But if he fays,
that it is contrary to the Rules of the Gofpel to pay
fuch Worfhip, I then ask him, whether he thinks that
when the Gofpel forbids Creature Worfhip, the only
Meaning is, that Men ought either* fincerely *to worfhip Creatures, or* fincerely *not to do it If his
Lordfhip will not affert this Interpretation, he muft
then own that every* fincere *Papift offends againft the*
                              Rules

Rules of the Gospel; and if after this he will still maintain, that a sincere Papist *has the same Title to the Favour of God, as a sincere* Protestant, *he must say, that as to the Favour of God, a sincere Disobedience to the Gospel, is just as good as a sincere Obedience.*

Upon his Lordship's Principles, I cannot see with what Reason or Conscience he can ever endeavour to convert a Papist · *Let us suppose his Lordship to attempt it, and let the* Papist *say to him, "* For *what* "*Purpose would your Lordship convert me? I am at* "*present free from Doubts, and sincere in the Pro-* "*fession of* Popery, *and your Lordship has told me,* "*that I am* therefore *in as good a Case, as fully* "*entitled to the Favour of God, as if I were a sin-* "*cere* Proteftant; *what Advantage then do you pro-* "*pose to me by a Change? Is there any other reason,* "*besides the Hopes of God's Favour, for which Men* "*ought to change their Religion? How this is to be answered upon his Lordship's Principles, I profess I know not ; and were I of his Lordship's Opinion, I should think it one of the wickedest things in the World, to disturb any Man in his settled and sincerely embraced Errors in Religion , for since those Errors certainly entitle him to God's Favour, since an Attempt to remove them may possibly raise Doubts and Scruples, and put it out of the Man's Power to act with so clear a Persuasion of being in the right as he did before, how could I justify my self to God or Man in hazarding unnecessarily my Neighbour's Title to the Favour of God, which stood secured by an happy Ignorance, and Prejudices so strong that they admitted no Doubts?*

Nay

Nay further ; *if there be no real difference in this Cafe between Truth and Falfhood* ; *if he who* believes *a* Lye *fincerely, and he who* embraces *the* Truth *fincerely, are equally in the* Favour *of* God, *to what End was Truth brought down from Heaven?* *Why was the Gofpel publifhed, and the World difturbed with the* Light, *fince it was before not only at Eafe, but equally* fecure *in* Darknefs? *His Lordfhip will anfwer perhaps that* Truth *is a real* Good, *that there is an effential difference between Truth and Falfhood. Away with this Metaphyfical Goodnefs; the Queftion is, how Truth is better to the Purpofe of Religion than Falfhood, fince if you add a fincere Perfwafion to both, both become the fame thing, and are equally entitled to the Favour of* God.

St. Paul *tells us, that upon fome Sort of Sinners* God fhall fend a ftrong Delufion that they fhou'd believe a Lye , *believe it they cannot, without being fincerely perfwaded of it, and confequently upon his Lordfhip's Principles they* muft *be entitled to the Favour of* God, *if they act according to the Lye they believe. And thus in the Bifhop's Scheme, that is the fureft, nay, the only* Title *to* God's Favour, *which in* St. Paul's *is not only the Forerunner, but oftentimes the immediate* Effect *of his* Vengeance.

Upon thefe Principles there is nothing in which Men are capable of deceiving themfelves, but it may be juftified. His Lordfhip has applied thefe Principles to Popery, and exprefly taught that fincere Papifts *are juftified by his Rule. Let us hear now from his own Mouth what it is that Sincerity does juftify in this Inftance* Popery, *he tells us,* is a Religion which wherever it is received, muft act univerfally

fally and equally in the fame Way: It is a Religion which leaves nothing to Variety of Tempers or Principles, but layeth the fame Neceffity on all thofe who receive it, either to facrifice all the World to it, or to be facrificed to it themfelves *

Tell me Sincerity *what art thou! (O dea certe!) that can'ft entitle thofe to the Favour of God, who are* univerfally *and* equally *bent to fet the* World *on* Fire, *for the Sake of a falfe corrupt Perfwafion! that can'ft diffolve all the Bands of* natural *and* revealed *Religion, and* fanctify *even the* Cruelties *of an* Inquifition! *That can'ft juftify all the Forms of Error and Impiety which ever a deluded People were made to think to be Religion;* and *fecure to all, what belongs only to* Virtue *and* Truth, *the* Favour *of* God!

But I tranfgrefs the Bounds of a Preface, and fhall therefore difmifs the Reader to the Confideration of the following Treatife, affuring him that it is put into his Hands *as it came out of the Author's.*

THO. SHERLOCK.

---

* Prefervat. *p.* 19. 4th Edit.

REMARKS

UPON A

POSITION

OF THE

Bishop of *BANGOR*

CONCERNING

RELIGIOUS SINCERITY.

Bishop of *BANGOR.*

THE *Favour of God follows* SINCERITY CONSI-
DERED AS SUCH; *and consequently* EQUALLY *follows every equal Degree of* SINCERITY. Prefervative, *p. 91.*

REMARKS.

In order to the finding out the true Sense of this Po-
fition, it needs only to be obferved, 1. That *Sincerity,*
according to his Lordfhip (and as the Truth indeed is)
is when a Man follows the Dictates of his own Confcience or Underftanding, after having made ufe of the beft
Means he has for his Information. *A Man,* fays he, *(a)
is always fuppofed to ufe his utmoft Endeavours and Application*——*and then, and only then, to be juftified by*——— *his
private Judgment.* Again, *(b)* Sincerity *cannot be fuppofed, where a Man does not take all proper Methods of being
rightly informed.* 2. That by Sincerity *confider'd as fuch,*

(*a*) Anfw. to the Repref. Chap. 1. Sect. 19 p. 23. (*b*) Ibid. p. 9.

B   his

his Lordſhip means Sincerity *of it ſelf*, or Sincerity *alone.*
This needs no Proof. 3. That when he ſays, that the
Favour of God *follows* Sincerity, his Meaning is, that
Sincerity *gives a Man a Right or Title to* the Favour of
God. This will be plain from the following Paſſages.
(c) Either a Man muſt be INTITLED *to Heaven by the perfeſt
Sincerity of his Choice , or elſe none can have a* TITLE *to it,
but thoſe who are in the Right.* Again, *(d) Almighty God
puts our* TITLE *to his Favour upon our preſent Sincerity.*
4. That *Degrees* of *Sincerity* there can be none. For either a Man *has* uſed his beſt Endeavours to inform himſelf rightly, or he has *not.* If he has *not*, he is not ſincere *at all*, becauſe *Sincerity* is only when a Man *has* uſed
his beſt Endeavours. If he *has*, he cannot be *more* ſincere than he already is; becauſe no Man can do *more*
than uſe his *beſt* Endeavours. Wherefore, 5 The full
Senſe and Meaning of his Lordſhip's Poſition appears to
be this, *viz.* That *all Perſons who uſe their utmoſt Endeavours to inform themſelves rightly, and aſt according to the
beſt of their Judgments, have an equal Title to God's Favour ;*
or, that *all ſuch Perſons have a Right to an equal Share or
Degree of the Favour of God.* Thus ſtands his Lordſhip's
Doſtrine, which I ſhall examine firſt *a poſteriori*, by con-
ſidering its *Conſequences* ; and ſecondly, *a priori*, by con-
ſidering what *Foundation* it has in the *Nature* and *Reaſon*
of Things.

Firſt, I will conſider the *Conſequences* of this Doſtrine,
moſt of which I find already drawn to my Hand by the
learned *Committee*, Repreſent. *p.* 7. 8 where his Lordſhip
is charged with having made *all Methods of Religion alike
with Reſpeſt to Salvation, or the Favour of God*, with having *put all Communions upon an equal Foot, without regard
to any intrinſick Goodneſs, or whether they be right or wrong ;*
with *referring every Man's Choice* of a Communion *to his
own private Judgment, as that which will juſtify even the
worſt he can make ;* and finally, with *rendring all Church
Communion unneceſſary, in order to intitle Men to the Favour
of God.* Theſe Conſequences might all of them have

(c) Ibid. *(d)* Ibid. Seſt. 11. p 104.

been

been expressed by one single Proposition, That *all sincere Persons have equally a Right or Title to God's Favour, whatsoever Method of Religion they follow.* But I chose to make use of the very Words of the *Representation,* that I might hereby give my self the fairer Opportunity of vindicating them against his Lordship's Exceptions. In the mean time, I am verily perswaded, that there is no considerate Man, who will not see at the very first Glance, that these Consequences do every one of them naturally and necessarily follow from the Principle above laid down. For if all sincere Persons are *alike intitled to,* i. e. have a Right to an *equal Share* or *Degree* of God's Favour, pray what can it signify as to the Favour of God, whether a Man follows *this* Method of Religion, or follows *that,* provided he be but *sincere* in that which he follows? To say that the *Nature,* i. e the *intrinsick Goodness* of the Method, makes any Difference in the Case, is directly to give up the Point. For if the intrinsick Goodness of the Method must *in the least concur,* to intitle a Man to God's Favour, it is not then true, that Sincerity *alone* will give him this Title. And if the intrinsick Goodness of the Method does not *in the least* contribute towards the entitling a Man to God's Favour, his Title will be the same, whether this intrinsick Goodness be *present* or *absent.* For *an Effect* can receive no Alteration from that which has not the least Relation to it under the Notion of *a Cause* Upon this Principle therefore it must follow, that *all Methods of Religion are alike with respect to Salvation, or the Favour of God,* that in the same Respect, *all Communions* how unequal soever they may be as to their *intrinsick* Worth and Excellency, are *upon an equal Foot ;* and that therefore, if a Man *chuses the worst* Communion possible, the Sincerity of his Choice will *justify him* in so doing, even so far, as that he shall have a Right to as great a Share of God's Favour, as if he had chosen the *best.* Upon the same Principle it also follows, that with respect to the Favour of God, *all Church Communion is unnecessary.* For how is it possible, that Church Communion should be at all *necessary,* if Sincerity *alone* be *sufficient ?*

There

There is not, I believe, a *Demonstration* in *Euclid* that concludes more strongly than this Argument ; it is however very fit that we attend a little to his Lordfhips Exceptions. And therefore,

1. Whereas the learned *Committee* have obferved, that his Lordfhip has *made all Methods of Religion alike*, &c. and *put all Communions upon an equal Foot*, &c. his Lordfhip anfwers, That (e) *what he fays about private Perfwafion relates to the Juftification of the Man before God, and not to the Excellency of one Communion above another, which it leaves juft as it finds it, and cannot poffibly alter*. Now by this it is very manifeft, that his Lordfhip fuppofes the Charge of the *Committee* to be, that he has made all Methods of Religion alike, and put all Communions upon an equal Foot, *with refpeft to their real, natural, and intrinfick* Excellency ; which, were it true, it would not in the leaft affeft the Confequence as it is now ftated by me ; which, as it is evident, does alfo *leave* the *intrinfick Excellency* of every Communion *as it finds it*, and relates *folely* to that which his Lordfhip's Principle relates, to wit, *the Juftification of the Man before God*. I have indeed fuppofed this to be the Senfe of the *Committee* in their Charge ; and therefore, if it be not fo, I muft, I own, be filenced, fo far as I am concerned in their Vindication. But I will leave the World to judge between us, who is guilty of a Mifreprefentation, his Lordfhip, or I. That which the Committee fay is, That his Lordfhip hath put all Communions upon an equal Foot, WITHOUT REGARD TO *any intrinfick Goodnefs, or whether they be right, or wrong*. That which his Lordfhip *reprefents* the *Committee* as faying, is, that he hath put all Communions upon an equal Foot, WITH RESPECT TO *their intrinfick Goodnefs*. But are thefe two Affertions the fame ? It is manifeft that they are not For whereas the *latter* fuppofes that his Lordfhip hath *deftroyed* all real *intrinfick* Difference between one Communion and another, the *former* fuppofes no fuch Matter ; but only this, that his Lordfhip in his Argument *hath had no Regard* to

(e) Ibid. Sect. 23. p. 113.

any

any such Difference, or *hath not confidered*, whether a Communion be either *right* or *wrong*. Yes, but the *Committee*, you'll say, still charge his Lordſhip with putting all Communions upon an equal Foot. Upon an equal Foot? In what reſpect? In ſome *other* reſpect you may be ſure; for what Senſe is there in ſaying that all Communions are put upon an equal Foot, *i. e.* made equal with reſpect to their *intrinſick* Goodneſs, *without regarding their intrinſick Goodneſs*, or *whether they be right or wrong*? He that puts all Communions upon an equal Foot in this Senſe, is always ſuppoſed *to have regarded* or *conſidered* the *intrinſick* Goodneſs of *all*, and to have compared them one with another; and therefore had the *Committee* intended any ſuch Charge againſt his Lordſhip, they would have expreſſed themſelves *barely* after this manner, that *he had put all Communions upon an equal Foot with reſpect to their intrinſick Goodneſs*, and would not have added thoſe Words, *without regarding whether they be right or wrong*, which indeed is a very ſhameful Inconſiſtency. And what now is that *other* Reſpect in which the *Committee* charge his Lordſhip with having put all Communions upon an equal Foot? Why, they tell you as plainly as Words can expreſs it, that it is with reſpect to the *Efficaciouſneſs* of them, in order to the *intitling* Men to *God's Favour*. All Methods of Religion, ſay they, are made alike, not *ſimply*, but *with reſpect to Salvation or the Favour of God*. So that the Meaning of the *Committee* in theſe Paſſages appears plainly to be this: That notwithſtanding there is a manifeſt Difference between one Communion and another, and one Method of Religion and another, with reſpect to their *intrinſick* Goodneſs; and notwithſtanding it ought in reaſon to be ſuppoſed, that the *intrinſick* Goodneſs of the Communion or Method a Man follows, has at leaſt *ſome* Share in intitling him to God's Favour; yet that his Lordſhip, as he hath ſtated the Matter, has made it to ſignify nothing at all to this End, and therefore has in this reſpect put all Methods and all Communions upon an equal Foot. This, I ſay, is manifeſtly the Meaning of the *Committee* in theſe Paſſages, and common Equity requires, that all

other

other Paſſages relating to this Point, in the *Repreſentation*, be interpreted after the ſame manner, if the Words them-ſelves be fairly capable (and that they are ſo, you will ſee preſently) of being brought to this Senſe. Thus when the *Committee* charge it upon his Lordſhip, that ac-cording to this Doctrine *no one Method of Religion is* In it self *preferable to another*, the Meaning of this Paſſage is not, as his Lordſhip ſuppoſes, that there is no *real* Excel-lency or Goodneſs in *one* Method *above another*, but that no one Method of Religion is *of it ſelf*, or upon the Ac-count of any *intrinſick Goodneſs* that it has above another, *preferable* to another ; I ſay *preferable to another*, i. e. with reſpect to any *Virtue* or *Efficacy* which the *intrinſick Goodneſs* of it will give it *above* another, towards procuring *Sal-vation*, or the *Favour of God* So likewiſe when they charge it upon his Lordſhip, that *in Vertue* of his *Prin-ciple, he hath left no Difference between the* Popiſh *and our* Re-formed *Church, but what is founded in* Perſonal Perſwaſion *only, and not in the Truth of the Doctrines, or in the Excel-lency of one Communion above the other* ; the Senſe of this is not what his Lordſhip has made it to be, that the Com-munion of the *Reformed* Church is not (according to his Lordſhip's Principle) *really better* than the Communion of the *Popiſh*, but that the Communion of the *Reformed* Church is *in it ſelf of no greater Efficacy* towards the *intit-tling* Men to *Salvation*, than the Communion of the *Popiſh*, and conſequently, that his Lordſhip in Vertue of his Prin-ciple, hath *in this Reſpect* left no Difference between the *one* and the *other*, but what is founded in *Perſonal Perſwaſion*.

Upon the whole therefore, I think it is manifeſt, that the Senſe of the *Committee* is exactly as I have ſtated it a-bove, *viz.* That his Lordſhip in conſequence of his Do-ctrine hath made all Methods of Religion alike, and put all Communions upon an equal Foot, *with reſpect to any Vertue* or *Efficacy that is in them towards intitling Men to* God's *Favour*. Which had his Lordſhip duly attended to, he might, perhaps, have ſpared himſelf and *his Rea-ders* a great deal of fruitleſs Trouble, there being no leſs than *one* intire *Section*, and part of a *Second*, which run upon this general Miſtake, that the *Committee* had changed

ged him with making all Methods of Religion alike, and putting all Communions upon an equal Foot, *with respect to their intrinsick Goodness*, and which consequently do not in the least contribute towards removing the Difficulty which is now faftned upon this Doctrine. The moft of what his Lordfhip has elfe faid upon this Matter is by way of *Retortion* upon the *Committee*, whom he firft of all fuppofes (I think) to have claimed all *abfolute Authority in fome* to oblige *others* to a particular *External Communion*, and then argues, that their Doctrine is liable to the fame Objection with his. About this he hath fpent near three *Sections* more, all which, fuppofing it were true (which it certainly is not) how little it is to the Purpofe I need not to obferve But it was his Lordfhip's wifeft way to *evade* the Charge by fuch Methods as thefe For the *Confequence*, I perceive, is of fuch an *untoward* Nature, that tho' it demonftratively follows from his Lordfhip's Principle, his Lordfhip does not yet care *plainly* to *own* and *defend* it. But

2. With refpect to the *next* of the Paflages above cited, his Lordfhip's Management is yet more extraordinary. That Paflage lays it upon his Lordfhip, that in following any particular Communion he has *referred every Man to his own private Judgment, as that which will juftify even the worft Choice he can make* Here his Lordfhip peremptorily denies, that he has *ever taught* any fuch thing, and is (*f*) *forced to complain* of the *Committee* as having *framed* this *Opinion* for him. The Reader will foon be convinced how fmall a Matter will *force a Complaint* from his Lordfhip: For even as he himfelf has been pleafed to reprefent the Matter, the Ground of this Complaint is no more than this, *viz* That the *Committee* have framed this Opinion for him IN WORDS *he neither ever did ufe, nor will own*. Well; be it fo; I hope there is no great Harm in this, provided his Lordfhip will but *own* THE THING And that he will, and does own *the thing*, is plain: For how does he go about to clear himfelf? Why, truly he fays, that his *conftant Doctrine is* not that *a Man's private*

(*f*) Ibid Sect. 19 p 92, 93.

Judgment will juſtify him in the WORST *Choice that he can make,* but *in the* BEST *Choice that he can make!* This, you'll ſay, perhaps, is a very manifeſt Contradiction: But pray conſider whether that which the *Committee* call *the worſt* Choice, and that which his Lordſhip calls *the beſt* Choice, may not poſſibly be *the ſame;* and if you will not be ſo eaſy as to be carried away merely with the Sound of Words, you will find this to be the very Caſe. For what do the *Committee* mean by *the* WORST Choice? Why, plainly, the Choice of that Communion which is IN IT SELF *the worſt.* And what does his Lordſhip mean by the BEST Choice? Manifeſtly, the Choice of that Communion which, upon the ſtricteſt Inquiry, AP-PEARS TO BE *the beſt.* But may not that Communion which *appears* to a Man to be THE BEST, be, *in it ſelf,* THE WORST? His Lordſhip will not deny it. Suppoſe then, that a Man ſhould chuſe the *worſt* Communion, *thinking* it to be *the beſt,* will the Sincerity of his private Judgment juſtify him in this Caſe? His Lordſhip owns, and contends that it will. Who ſees not then, that this is only a Contradiction of *Words,* and that his Lordſhip owns the very thing charged upon him by the *Committee?* I am ſorry his Lordſhip ſhould deſcend to ſuch mean *Sophiſtry* as this! Pardon the Expreſſion; for if it be *not* Sophiſtry, his Lordſhip muſt have ſuppoſed, that by the *worſt* Choice the *Committee* muſt have meant the Choice of that which *appears* to a Man's *own Judgment* to be *the worſt.* But what Senſe can there be in this Suppoſi-tion? Or who but his Lordſhip ſpeaks after this Man-ner? Every one knows, that, in common Computation, the Goodneſs or Badneſs of a Man's Choice is not mea-ſured by his *private Perſwaſion,* but by *the real intrinſick Value* of the thing he chuſes. And I believe, that ſhould any one, in the *pure Simplicity* of his Heart, chuſe *Silver* inſtead of *Gold,* as the more valuable Metal, his Lordſhip would hardly be brought to affirm, that he had made *the better Choice.*

3. It is farther charged upon his Lordſhip, by the *Committee,* that he hath *rendred all Church-Communion un-neceſſary, in order to intitle Men to the Favour of God.* Now this

this likewise his Lordship declares that he has not taught, and says, that it is *an Opinion framed for him* by the *Committee* But what has his Lordship done to shew, that this is not his Opinion ; or that this Consequence does not necessarily follow from his Principles? Why nothing, except it be this, that he has pretended as if *this* Part of the Charge were *contradictory* to the *former.* The two Parts put together stand thus, and are thus set down in the *Representation.* *All Church Communion is render'd unnecessary in order to intitle Men to the Favour of God, and every Man is referred in these Cases (i e in the Case of chusing a Communion) to his private Judgment, as that which will justify the worst Choice he can make.* (g) *The Words* (says his Lordship) *in which this Charge is drawn up, are very extraordinary.* (For) First, *It is declared, that in my Book all Church Communion is render'd unnecessary in order to intitle Men to God's Favour ; and then it is immediately supposed, that the same Book makes Communion with some Church or other necessary, but only leaves every Man in these Cases (I suppose they mean in this Case) to his private Judgment* I think truly, that this Observation is very *extraordinary!* For *where* or *how,* I pray, is it supposed, that his Lordship hath made Communion *with some Church* or other *necessary?* Why, his Lordship, it seems, hath declared, that when a Man *does* chuse a Communion, the Sincerity of his private Judgment will justify him if he chuses *the worst !* Very true! But may not the same Person also very consistently affirm, that the same Sincerity will likewise justify him if he chuses *none at all!* On the other Side, may not he who makes all Church Communion *unnecessary, may* he not, or rather *will* he not by his Principles naturally be led to say, that if he does think fit to follow any Communion, it signifies nothing at all which he follows? But his Lordship, I perceive, was in great Streights, and what should he do, but have Recourse to *Art,* where *Reason* would not bear him out? His Lordship's general Maxim is, that Sincerity *alone* justifies a Man What then can be more plain, than, that if a

(g) Ibid

C

Man

Man be but sincere, whether he joins himself to *any* Communion, or to *no* Communion, he is *equally justified !*

Thus then you see what the Consequence of his Lordship's Doctrine is, *viz.* That a Man who joins himself with *no* Society of Christians, who frequents *no* Place of publick Worship, who partakes of *no* Sacraments, may yet have a Title to God's Favour, and that in the same Degree with him who sincerely keeps the whole Law. His Lordship has indeed said something, which, were it true, would in a great Measure destroy the Force of this Objection: But besides, that it would also make his whole Doctrine about *Sincerity* to be utterly insignificant, the Supposition is attended with this farther Unhappiness, that it is *actually false.* The Supposition is in short this. That those who (*h*) *sincerely believe in* Christ, *will be led by their Regard to him to the Profession of that* Faith, *and to the outward Use of* All the Means *which he appointed.* Which is as much as to say, that those who sincerely believe in Christ will be led by their Regard to him *to* Believe *and* Do *as the Gospel directs* them. This will be farther plain from another Passage where he declares, that (*i*) it Cannot be supposed— *that a Man who sincerely is subject to* Jesus Christ *alone in the great Affair of Salvation, will not follow* Jesus Christ's *Direction, and join in the Worship of God with other Men, or will not be induced to follow* All *his Master's* Injunctions. Indeed, my Lord! Why then, for whose Use I pray was this *new Scheme* of *Justification* contrived? I always apprehended, that it was for the Benefit of such Persons as should in the Sincerity of their Hearts be led to act *contrary to* Christ's *Injunctions.* But now it seems there neither *are nor can be* any such Persons; for *all* sincere Persons, we are told, *will,* and *must* be led to *follow* Christ's Injunctions, and that not only a *few,* but *all* of them. But where, it I may presume to ask, did his Lordship learn this? Does Experience teach it? I would to God it did. But Experience, I trust, is full against him, and since his Lordship has not in another Case

(h) Ibid. Sect. 15 p. 81. (*i*) Ibid. Sect. 14. p. 79

thought

thought it beneath him to appeal to the *Quakers*, let me have leave also to appeal to them in this, where I think they may much more properly be appealed to This People, it is true, are joined together in a Communion, and frequent Places of Publick Worship among themselves; so far therefore they must be excepted out of the present Argument   But then his Lordship knows, that they *are* not *led by their Regard to* Christ, *to the Profession of that* Faith *which he has appointed*; for they *err* in several very *important Matters* of *Faith*. His Lordship is also sensible that they *are* not *led by their Regard to* Christ, *to the* outward *Use of* all the Means *which he has appointed, or to follow* all *his* Injunctions, for they *reject* both the *Sacraments*   I ask then, are this People any of them *sincere*, or are they not? If they *be* any of them sincere, his Lordship's Assertion, that *all* sincere Persons will be led to follow *all* the Appointments or Injunctions of Christ, must then be false   If they are *not* any of them sincere, his Lordship damns them all, and the *Quakers* will have Reason to thank him for his Charity. Why should I mention the *Papists*, who according to his Lordship's Rule must also be *all* of them *insincere*, and consequently in a State of Damnation ? But his Lordship cannot but be farther apprized, that there are even among Christians a Sort of Men who neglect *wholly* to join in any publick Worship, and to partake in any Ordinances of the Gospel. These Men will tell us, that in their Opinion they may serve God as acceptably by saying their Prayers and reading their Bibles at Home, as they can by resorting to Church, or to any other Assemblies of Christians   And are then all such Persons *insincere* ? For my own Part, I dare not affirm it; and if his Lordship should, it will be be more than he will ever able to prove, unless he could determine precisely how far Men may or may not be led aside by the Error of their Understandings, which is a thing utterly impossible

 In short; That Sincerity *alone* should be sufficient to lead Men *to observe* ALL *the Appointments or Injunctions of* Christ, is a Doctrine so new, so contrary both to Reason and plain Matter of Fact, as that nothing can be more.

And

And it may juftly be wonder'd what could draw from his Lordfhip an Affertion fo extraordinary in it felf, and fo entirely deftructive of his own darling Scheme! That he was then, when he faid this, upon another Point, and litt'e thought of his general Principle, you will eafily guefs; and tho' it fignifies not much as to the prefent Controverfy, to be informed what that Point was, I will yet beg Leave juft to mention it His Lordfhip then had in his Sermon defined the *Church* to be *The Number of Men, whether fmall or great, whether difperfed or united, who truly and fincerely are Subjects to* Jefus Chrift *alone, in Matters relating to the Favour of God and their eternal Salvation* The Fault which the *Committee* found with this Definition, was, that it was too general; for that his Lordfhip had left out of it feveral Particulars *which are neceffary to form a juft and true Notion of* The Church, inftancing particularly in *Preaching the Word,* and *Adminiftring the Sacraments.* This the *Committee* fpoke with reference to the *Vifible* Church of Chrift, fuppofing (as indeed they very reafonably might fuppofe) that *this* was the Subject of his Lordfhip's *Definition.* In Anfwer to this, his Lordfhip fays, that he was not then fpeaking of A Visible *Church (to which alone, as fuch, vifible outward Signs belong) but of the Univerfal* Invisible *Church made up of fuch as fincerely believe in* Chrift Upon this Foot (could his Lordfhip have defended his Definition) he would have had nothing to anfwer for but the Impropriety of defining *one* Sort of Church, when the Nature and Tendency of his whole Difcourfe led him to rectify the Miftakes about *another* But there was a rougher Difficulty yet that ftood in the way, even with refpect to his Notion of the *invifible* Church, *viz.* That according to it a Man might be a Member of Chrift's *invifible* Church, tho' he were *not* a Member of *the vifible* one For if every one who is *fincerely fubject* to Chrift *alone,* is a Member of the *invifible* Church, the Confequence is clear, that he is *ftill* a Member of *that* Church, tho' in the Sincerity of his Heart, he fhould be led to *cut himfelf off* from the *vifible* one, even by neglecting the Sacraments and every thing elfe, in the joint Practice and Participation

tion whereof *visible* Communion does confift. So that
his Lordfhip found himfelf ftill liable to that which the
Committee had objected againft him, to wit, the having
thrown out (by his Definition) the Participation of the
Sacraments, &c. as not effential to the denominating a
Man a *true Member of* Chrift's *Church* What now was
to be done in this Cafe? Why there were but two
things poffible. The firft was for his Lordfhip to have
retracted his Definition, and *once in his Lifetime*, to have
confeffed himfelf *in the Wrong* The other, to fay that
a Man *could not be* a fincere Subject of *Jefus Chrift*, and
yet *neglect the Sacraments*, &c This latter his Lordfhip
thought fit to chufe; and how well it anfwers his Purpofe, I fhall now leave every Reader to judge (*l*) *To
make, fays he, fuch Objections as thefe, is to make Objections
that have no Weight in them, unlefs they who make them
fuppofe, that by taking* Chrift *for their* Lawgiver *and* King,
Men will not be led by him and his own Directions to the two
Sacraments, *and to the Ufe of* his own Appointments, *a
Suppofition which I fhall take Care never to be guilty of* My
Lord! I know of no *Crime* that there is in making fuch
a Suppofition as this, or if there be any, it certainly
lies at your Lordfhip's Door. For your whole *Scheme* of
Juftification depends upon this Suppofition But *this*, I
think, is a *Crime* (and I am forry your Lordfhip fhould
not think it fo too) to take fo unwarrantable a *Step* to
get over an Objection, which you muft needs have been
fenfible, is impoffible to be *removed*

To return; It appears from what has been faid, that
his Lordfhip in confequence of his general Principle
muft affirm, that provided a Man fincerely believes in
Jefus Chrift, it fignifies nothing as to his Title to God's
Favour, whether he be of *this* Communion of Chrifti-
ans, or of *that* Communion, or of *any* Communion *at all*;
and confequently, that in this Refpect he hath not only put
all Communions *upon an equal Foot*, but render'd *all* Communion *unneceffary* But to add one Confequence to
thofe already drawn by the *Committee*, I fay,

(*l*) Ibid Sect 15 p 81.

4. That upon his Lordſhip's Principle, even the *Religion* of *Jeſus Chriſt*, in the largeſt Senſe of the Word, or as it takes in *all thoſe* who *believe* in *Jeſus Chriſt*, is of no greater Efficacy towards procuring God's Favour than the *Religion*, v. g. of *Mahomet*. To make this plain, I will apply that Argument which his Lordſhip is pleaſed to call a *Demonſtration*, and leave you to judge whether it be not every whit as concluſive with reſpect to *Chriſtians* and *Mahometans*, as it is with reſpect to *Proteſtants* and *Papiſts*. "What is it then which *juſtifies* the *Chriſti-*
" *ans* in refuſing to follow the *Religion* of the *Mahome-*
" *tans*? Is it that the *Religion* of the *Mahometans* is a cor-
" rupt and falſe Religion, or that the *Chriſtians* are per-
" ſwaded in their own Conſciences, that it is ſo? The
" latter without doubt, as appears from this Demon-
" ſtration: Take away from this Perſwaſion; they are
" ſo far from being *juſtified*, that they are *condemned* for
" their refuſing Give them this Perſwaſion again, they
" are *condemned* if they do *not* refuſe, &c" Now 'tis manifeſt that this Argument may be put as ſtrong on the Side of the *Mahometans*, as it is on the Side of the *Chri-* *ſtians* For that which juſtifies *us* againſt *them*, muſt alſo juſtifie *them* againſt *us* I ask then, Can there be, or is there any ſuch thing as a Sincere *Mahometan*, or (for it is all one as to the Argument) a Sincere *Jew* or *Heathen*? If *not*, then his Lordſhip hath left *all the World*, except *Chriſtians*, irretrievably in a State of Condemnation, a *Suppoſition, which* (to uſe his Lordſhip's own Words) I *ſhall take care never to be guilty of* But if otherwiſe, then by his Lordſhip's Argument ſo many of *all* Sorts as are *ſincere* are *juſtified*, i e (for this is evidently what his Lordſhip means) they are *upon the ſame Foot with us* with reſpect to any *Right or Title* which *either* of us have to *Salvation or the Favour of God* The thing indeed is clear, and ſpeaks it ſelf · For if Sincerity *alone* be that which gives Men a Title to God's Favour, as his Lord ſhip aſſerts, then *all* ſincere Perſons, *Jews, Heathens,* *Turks, Chriſtians*, or whatever elſe you can conceive them to be. are in this Reſpect all alike, i. e. no or

of them hath a greater Title to God's Favour than another.

Thus I have fhewn you the plain and neceffary Con-fequences of his Lordfhip's Principle, and we are at laft brought to this general Conclufion, *that provided a Man be but* SINCERE, *it fignifies nothing what Religion he is of.* I proceed now to confider

Secondly, What *Foundation* the *Principle* from whom this Conclufion follows, has in the *Nature* and *Reafon* of Things. And here if the Reader be difpofed to take his Lord-fhip's Account of the Matter, he will think I am going to make either a very bold or a very fruitlefs Adventure. For the Argument upon which this Principle is built, his Lordfhip in his *Prefervative* THINKS *to be a* DEMON-STRATION *in the ftricteft Senfe of the Word,* and in his *An-fwer* to the *Reprefentation,* he is VERY CERTAIN *it is fo.* I fhall only beg that he would fufpend his Judgment, for a Moment, while I try his Lordfhip's *Infallibility*

The DEMONSTRATION then (for fo let it be called for the prefent) is thus introduced, *Preferv.* p. 89. *You,* fays his Lordfhip (fpeaking to the *Nonjurors) fay that God's Favour is not difpenfed but in the ftrict Communion of your particular little* Body *or* Church. *I am not now going to ac-cufe you of a* Herefy *againft Charity, but of a Herefy againft the very* Poffibility *and* Nature *of Things; or of holding that which throws Men out of the Favour of* God *which way foever they act You know there was a* Schifm *amongft your felves upon this Account. Mr.* Nelfon, *for Inftance, thinks himfelf obliged in Confcience to communi-cate with fome of our* Church. *Upon this you declare he hath no Title to God's Mercy And you and all the World al-low, that if he communicates with you whilft his* Confcience *tells him it is a* Sin, *he is felf-condemn'd, and out of God's Favour. He is therefore entitled to* God's Wrath, *both if he* doth communicate with you, *and if he doth* not *That Notion therefore which implies in it this great invincible Abfur-dity, cannot be true*

The fundamental *Maxim* upon which this Argument ftands, you fee is this· That *it is an Abfurdity to fuppofe that a Man fhould be entitled to* God's Wrath, WHICH WAY SOEVER

SOEVER HE ACTS. And this his Lordſhip himſelf elſe-
where declares: (*l*) *Whatever*, ſays he, *ſuppoſes a Man
condemned by* God, WHICH WAY SOEVER HE ACTS, *cannot
be admitted*; *but the Notion I was there* (referring to the
the Place now cited) *oppoſing, implies* THAT *in it, and
therefore muſt be falſe.* I hope therefore that this Argument will be ſufficiently replied to, if I can make out
theſe two things, *viz.*

Firſt, That there is *no* Abſurdity in ſuppoſing that a
Man may be entitled to God's Wrath, *which way ſoever*
he acts.

Secondly, That ſuppoſing *there were*, this Argument
does not come up to the Point in Controverſy.

Firſt then, I ſay there is *no* Abſurdity in ſuppoſing,
that a Man may be entitled to God's Wrath *which Way
ſoever he acts*, and that for this plain and unanſwerable
Reaſon, *viz.* That a Man may be under ſuch Circum-
ſtances, as that he muſt needs SIN *which Way ſoever he
acts*, or whether he *follows* his Conſcience, or follows it
not. This will be made plain by a few ſhort Obſerva-
tions As,

1. That it is *always* a Sin for a Man to act *againſt* his
Conſcience, whether *erroneous* or *not erroneous.* This his
Lordſhip's Argument ſuppoſes, and therefore it needs
not be proved.

2 That ſuppoſing a Man's Conſcience to be *erroneous*,
it is *a Sin* to act *according to* his Conſcience, provided that
Error was occaſioned *tho' his own Fault.* This is plain
becauſe the only Reaſon why the Error of a Man's
Conſcience or Judgment can be ſuppoſed to excuſe
him is this, that no Man can deſerve Blame who
has always acted according to the *beſt* of his Abilities
But if the Error of a Man's Conſcience is owing
to himſelf, he does not in following his Conſcience
act according to the *beſt* of his Abilities, becauſe i
is ſuppoſed that *if he would*, he might inform
his Conſcience *better.* I leave it therefore to the
Reader's Judgment, whether theſe Two Obſervation

(*l*) Ibid Sect. 19 p 94.

do not suggeſt to us a very manifeſt Caſe, wherein a Man muſt needs SIN *which way ſoever he acts*; even when his Conſcience is erroneous for want of taking proper Means for his Information   If he acts *againſt* his Conſcience, he ſins that way, for this very Reaſon *becauſe* he acts *againſt* his Conſcience.   If he acts *according* to his Conſcience, he ſins that way, becauſe he breaks the Law of God *tho' his own Fault.*   But this, you'll ſay, does not hit the Caſe in Hand; for the Caſe put by his Lordſhip is of a Man who is *ſincere*, and conſequently is ſuppoſed to have uſed all proper Means of informing himſelf.   But where is this Caſe put?   He that can ſee it in the Argument, has better Eyes than I.   The Caſe his Lordſhip has put, is that of Mr. *Nelſon*, whom he ſuppoſes to have thought himſelf obliged in Conſcience to communicate with our Church.   But that Mr. *Nelſon* was *ſincere* in this Perſwaſion, *i e.* that he had uſed all proper Means for his Information, is not *ſaid* to be ſuppoſed, or any thing like it.   Again, his Lordſhip's Rule is, that 'tis abſurd to ſuppoſe that a Man ſhould be intitled to God's Wrath *which Way ſoever he acts.*   And thus it is ſet down both in his *Preſervative*, and in his *Anſwer* to the *Repreſentation.*   But this Rule, as it appears, is *falſe*, and therefore the Argument which is built upon it muſt be ſo too.   I do not make this Obſervation, becauſe I think any Advantage can be taken from it as to the main Point in Debate; for the Controverſy is about *Sincerity; Sincerity* therefore ought to be ſuppoſed in the Argument.   But it is a new Way of writing DEMONSTRATIONS, to leave that to be *ſuppoſed* which gives the Argument *all* the Force it has, and I believe Mr. *Whiſton* would hardly have been guilty of ſuch a Miſtake. With his Lordſhip's Leave therefore, I will put his general Maxim as it ought to be put, and ſay as I believe he intended to ſay, That *it is abſurd to ſuppoſe that a Man ſhould be intitled to God's Wrath which Way ſoever he acts* WITH SINCERITY   But even this is not true.   For SINCERITY is when a Man acts according to the beſt of his *preſent* Abilities.   This his Lordſhip owns. *Almighty God*, ſays he, *puts our Title to his Favour upon our*

D   PRE-

PRESENT *Sincerity*, i. e. upon a faithful and honeſt Uſe of thoſe Means which we *at preſent actually* have. But it is notorious, that the *Voluntarineſs* or *Involuntarineſs* of *Error* is not to be meaſured *barely* by a Man's *preſent* Abilities, but by thoſe Abilities alſo, which he has had *at any time before.* For that *Error* is certainly *voluntary,* which either *immediately* or *originally* is occaſioned by a Man's *own Fault*, and ALL *voluntary Error* is *ſinful.* Suppoſing therefore that I *once had* thoſe Means which by a due Uſe would have brought me to the Knowledge of the Truth, and that by my own Negligence I have *now loſt* thoſe Means, it is plain that my *preſent* Sincerity will not juſtify me in a wrong Perſwaſion, becauſe upon this Suppoſition it is *my Fault* even *that I am ſincere* in that Perſwaſion, *i e.* it is my Fault that the *beſt Uſe* of the Means I *now have* is not ſufficient for my Information. *Sincerity* therefore *as ſuch,* i e. *mere* Sincerity in a wrong Perſwaſion, is not ſufficient to make a Man who acts according to that Perſwaſion, an improper Object of God's Wrath. It muſt ever be attended with this Circumſtance, that his *Sincerity* in that Perſwaſion is not *at all* owing *to himſelf,* i e. to *the Neglect* of *any* Means which he *once had,* and which, if carefully improved, would have informed him better. But

Secondly, Admitting that it was an Abſurdity to ſuppoſe that a Man ſhould be intitled to God's Wrath, which Way ſoever he acts *with Sincerity,* I ſay that this Argument does not come up to the Point in Controverſy. For what does this Argument conclude? Why, manifeſtly, and at moſt no more than this, *viz.* That *no ſincere Perſon ſhall be* DAMNED. But is this the Queſtion? Or is this the whole of what his Lordſhip hath maintain'd? Why, ſo indeed his Lordſhip *once* thought fit to tell us. *There is not,* ſays he, (m) *the leaſt Tendency in any thing I ſay———but only this , that ſuppoſing an honeſt* Chriſtian *in the* Integrity *of his Heart to have choſen that which is not the* Beſt———*Almighty* God WILL NOT CONDEMN *him at the laſt Day for not ſeeing what he was not able to*

(m) Ibid. Sect 21 p 105.

fee, &c But let us hear his Lordfhip's geneial Principle once more. *The Favour of* God *follows Sincerity* CONSIDERED AS SUCH ; *and confequently* EQUALLY *follows eveiy* EQUAL DEGREE *of Sincerity.* The Meaning of which, as I have already fhewn, is plainly this; That in difpenfing his Favours, God has *no* Regard to *any* thing *but* the *Sincerity* of a Man's *Heart,* and that theiefoie *all* fincere Perfons have a Right or Title to an *equal* Degree or Share of God's Favoui. Now if his Lordfhip can fee no Dffeience between thefe two Aflertions, I am forry for it ; for fuiely there is a veiy wide one, unlefs it were true that *all* Peifons who are *not damned* are intitled to an *equal* Share of God's Favoui ! Can this then be affirmed, or can it not ? Why, this too I am willing to try Only let it be obferved that his Lordfhip's DEMONSTRATION is not quite done withal, as falling manifeftly fhort of the Point to be pioved. That which his Lordfhip (as it is now fuppofed) has proved by his Argument is, That *no fincere Peifon* SHALL BE DAMNED The Doctrine built upon this Aigument, and which therefore ought to be pioved by it, to make it conclufive, is, That *all fincere Peifons are* INTITLED *to an* EQUAL SHARE *of* God's *Favour.* Whether this *latter* Affertion can be maintained, or not, is now the Queftion. But this muft be determined *not* by *that* Aigument, but by Arguments of *anothei Natuie*

And here without any more ado, I am willing to fuppofe the Meaning of the Queftion to be this, *viz.* Whether *all* Peifons who aie not in a State of Condemnation, are entitled to an equal Shaie of God's Favour, *notwithftanding any Diffeience that theie is between them with iefpect to the* PARTICULAR METHOD OF RELIGION, *which they each of them follow* This you'll fay, perhaps, is a veiy laige Conceffion to one that deals fo much in DEMONSTRATIONS For according as his Lordfhip has ftated the Matter, 'tis plain, that he hath left no Room for God Almighty in difpenfing his Favours in a Life to come, to make any Diffeience between one Man and another upon the Account of their *Moial Qualifications.* His Lordfhip, I piefume, will not ventuie to affiim, that all Perfons

fons who are *fincere* in their *Perfwafions*, and act according to what they are thus fincerely perfwaded of, do
yet make *equal Improvements under* thofe *Perfwafions*. If
therefore the Favour of God follows Sincerity *as fuch*,
i e. If God in difpenfing his Favours has *no* Regard to
any thing elfe *but* Sincerity, then how different foever the
State and Condition of *one* fincere Man may be from the
State of *another* as to *fuch Improvements*, his State as to
the Favour of God muft be the very fame. But I am
willing to ufe his Lordfhip with all the Fairnefs imagi-
nable, and therefore will not fuppofe that he *intended*
any fuch thing, becaufe I hope he does not *believe* any
fuch thing, and becaufe it was no way *fuitable* to the
Matter he was upon, to have *affirmed* any fuch thing
The Cafe of a Man's chufing in the Sincerity of his
Heart, a *wrong Method* of *Religion*, was the Cafe in
Hand, and it is upon his Refolution of this Cafe, that
his general Rule is founded. If therefore the Affertion
can be made good *in this Refpect*, it anfwers his Lordfhip's End Whether it can or not fhall therefore be the
only Queftion, and I think it may foon be refolved by
the Help of a few plain Propofitions, the Truth of
which I hope will not be difputed.

The Propofitions are thefe, *viz.*

1. That he who is intitled to the *Rewards* of *the Gofpel*, is intitled to *a greater Share* of *God's Favour*, than he
who is *not*.

2 That no one can have *a Title* to the Rewards of
the Gofpel by Vertue of *his own Merits*, but only thro
the *Merits* and *Satisfaction* of *Jefus Chrift*

3. That *Jefus Chrift* having *procur'd* thefe Rewards for
us, he may difpofe of them upon *what Terms* and *Conditions* he *pleafes*.

4. That

4. That whatever *Terms* or *Conditions* have been *fixed* upon by *Jesus Christ* for the obtaining these Rewards, those *Conditions* must be *performed*, or otherwise we can have *no Title* to these Rewards.

5. That there is *no other* Way of knowing upon what Terms *Jesus Christ* has proposed the Rewards of the Gospel, but by his *positive declared* Will.

6. That the *positive declared Will* of *Jesus Christ* can be learned *no where* but *from the Gospel*.

7. That therefore *no one* has, or can have *a Title* to the *Rewards* of the *Gospel*, but he who *performs the Conditions* laid down *in the Gospel*.

The Question now therefore is, whether SINCERITY be the ONLY *Condition* required in the Gospel, in order to give us *a Title* to *the Rewards* of the *Gospel*. And when his Lordship has once proved that it is, I will lay my Hand upon my Mouth, and not say one Word more. But this as yet he has not so much as attempted; and he was sensible, I suppose, that it would be in vain. The *Conditions* there laid down are FAITH in *Jesus Christ* and *his Doctrines*, and OBEDIENCE *to his Laws and Commandments*. These are inculcated upon us over and over; but *no where* do I find any *Promises* made to SINCERITY *exclusive of* these. No where can I learn, that he who in the Integrity of his Heart shall *fail* in these *Conditions*, is *equally intitled* to the *Favour* of God, with him who in the *same Integrity* shall *fulfill* them. If his Lordship can find any such Texts as these, I should gladly see them produced. But till then, I shall not be afraid to affirm, that (by any thing God has been pleased hitherto to reveal to us) no Man can be *certain*, that he is *intitled* to the *Rewards* of the *Gospel*, any farther than he is *certain* of his having *believed* and *done* as the Gospel commands. The *Justice* and *Mercy* of God, which his Lordship

ship so constantly appeals to, cannot in the least help him. For his *Justice* is cleared if he does not *punish* those who have always used their best Endeavours to serve him, tho' in a wrong Way. His *Mercy* will be conspicuous, if he *rewards* their Sincerity with *more* than they can *claim*; but neither *Justice* nor *Mercy* require that he should reward them *after the same Manner* that he rewards those who have sincerely and honestly served him in that Way *which he has prescribed*. That God *may* do this, if he pleases, I deny not. But this I say, that he has not *bound himself by Promise* so to do; and that what he *actually intends* in this Case, he has not thought fit any where to reveal. Therefore I dare not say even that God *will* have *no Regard* to the *Method* of *Religion* a Man has followed, in dispensing the Rewards of a Life to come. I dare not affirm, that he *has* reserved *no greater* Degree of Glory for *sincere Christians*, than he has for *sincere Jews, Turks*, or *Heathens*, nor for *sincere Orthodox Professors*, than for the *sincerely Erroneous*. I think it much more decent and modest in ME, to sit down contented with what I find revealed, and to leave *Secret Things* to him to whom *Secret Things belong*, who tho' (we may assure our selves) he will deal by all hereafter in such a Manner as that none shall have Occasion to complain, yet he will not be tied down by such Rules as even the *most lifted* up among the Sons of Men shall aforehand think fit to prescribe for him

But if this be the Case; (n) If *none have a Title to the* Rewards of the Gospel *but those who are in the Right, then none can be secure of it here vpon Earth, because none can be infalibly or absolutely certain* (that they are in the Right) *without the Possibility of being mistaken* This Consequence his Lordship it seems does not like, and therefore declares (o) *for* HIMSELF, that HE *will never put* HIS OWN *Salvation vpon his being certainly in the Right till he is certain of his own* INFALLIBILITY, (*i.e.* till he is *infallibly Infallible*) *nor can he see any Comfort* (upon this Principle) *for the most sincere and most deserving Christians* Had it been

---

(n) Ibid. Sect. 19 p 95   (o) Ibid. Sect. 21 p 107 108

left *to his Lordship* to have fixed and determined *for him-self* the *Conditions* of his Salvation, such a *Speech* might have well become him; but since it *is not*, he must for ought I know be content with *such a Title* as the *Conditions* laid down by *Almighty God* will afford him. And if his Lordship can find *no Comfort* without being *infallibly certain* that he has this *Title*, his Condition is really to be pitied and lamented. Even *his own* Terms will not afford him a sure Ground; for so long as *the Heart is deceitful* (and we are told, and we find, that its deceitful *above all things*) so long will it be impossible for a Man to be *infallibly certain* of his own *Sincerity*, and consequently so long it must be impossible (according to his Lordship's own Principle) for him to be *infallibly certain* of his *own Salvation* But if any thing *less* than *Infallibly* will satisfy his Lordship, I think verily that the *Terms of Salvation* as they are now stated, will administer a *sufficient Ground* for *Comfort* For 1. So sure as every Man is that he has always acted with *Sincerity*, so sure he may be that he shall *not be condemned*. 2 So sure also as a Man is of this, so sure may he be of meeting with a *good Reward*. But then 3. As to those who are for disposing of Men of *all* Religions in *the Kingdom of* Christ hereafter, as they would fain have them disposed of *here in the Kingdom of* Men, *i e upon an equal Foot;* who will not *be comforted* unless they, tho' they should happen to be never so much in the Wrong, may promise themselves the *same Share* of God's Favour, the *same Rewards* hereafter, with those who are never so much in in the Right, and this too in the way of *Claim* and *Title*, I say, to Men of such *Comprehensive Principles* as these, I have *no Comfort* to give, and that because I am verily perswaded that the *Gospel* has given them *none*

I have remarked these few Things, 1st For the Honour of the Learned and Reverend the *Committee*, with whom (to speak modestly) I think his Lordship has not dealt *very sincerely* in this *Dispute about Sincerity*. 2dly, And most principally, For the Honour of our common Lord and Master *Jesus Christ*, upon whose Wisdom I think it is no small Reflection to say, without any War-rant

rant from him, that tho' he came on Purpose to teach us a New Religion, tho' he has taken Care by his Apostles, and by his Ministers which he hath appointed to continue to the End of the World, to propagate this Religion, and to keep Men found and stedfast in the Faith and Practice of it, to say, notwithstanding all this, that this very Religion is *in it self not a surer or a better Way* to *Salvation* than *any other* 3*dly* And Lastly, To encourage Men earnestly to study and endeavour after the Knowledge of the Truth. For tho' 'tis a *good* Encouragement to Men to do this, to let them know that they shall for this Reason, tho' they should happen to be in the Wrong, be rewarded *well*, yet it is a *better* to say, that if their Endeavours should lead them into the right Way, they shall, so far as we can judge by the revealed Will of God, be rewarded *better*.

$$F\ I\ N\ I\ S.$$

Space Baby

Space Baby

Suzannah Evans

Nine
Arches
Press

Space Baby
Suzannah Evans

ISBN: 978-1-913437-38-1
eISBN: 978-1-913437-39-8

Cover artwork: 'Outer Landscape' © Ayham Jabr
www.instagram.com/ayhamjabr

First published June 2022 by:

Nine Arches Press
Unit 14, Sir Frank Whittle Business Centre,
Great Central Way, Rugby.
CV21 3XH
United Kingdom

www.ninearchespress.com

Printed in the United Kingdom by:
Imprint Digital

Nine Arches Press is supported using public funding by Arts Council England.

Supported using public funding by
**ARTS COUNCIL
ENGLAND**

Contents

'the grey universe that rolls us
a thousand thousand thousand years'

– Edwin Morgan, 'Last Message'

'If the recipients recognize the silhouetted
human figure, they may guess that it was
both difficult and seemingly pointless to scale
the rock needle. The only point would be the
accomplishment of doing it. If this message
is communicated, it will tell extraterrestrials
something very important about us.'

– Jon Lomberg, *Pictures of Earth*

Space Baby

SPACE BABY! Born on the 61st shuttle
off planet Earth, midwifed
into the unknown. SPACE BABY!

Bungeeing in zero-G on the umbilicus.
SPACE BABY! In silver nappy
on a cockpit chair, fat little hands

on the steering column *Look,*
she's driving! SPACE BABY! Her image
broadcast back to Earth by the Space Boss

to show its ailing systems *we don't need you*
any more. SPACE BABY! The first to learn
to talk, to sing, to count in space

the first child schooled entirely in space
the first to play spin the bottle and be kissed
by some other space-born teen.

SPACE BABY! The great hope, born
on a starship, citizen of no country
the first step towards *homo whatevernext*

SPACE BABY! Daydreaming from a porthole
on course to Kepler 542b where our race
won't land until her great-great grandkids

are a hundred. And once they have settled
her birthday will be a holiday! SPACE BABY!
At the municipal square her face smiles down

cast in some new-discovered alloy
kids loiter and smoke there after curfew
scratch their tags into her moonboots.

Timeline of the Far Future

The moon is pulling further
and further away from the earth

and you still haven't decided
if you're going to procreate

surely as the sun will exhaust
its supply of hydrogen

the doctor will ask about plans
for your as-yet voiceless eggs

in 50,000 years
every earth day will be a second longer

the supercontinent of Pangaea Ultima
will re-configure itself

all over the surface of the seas
it took our explorers so long to label

if you choose to have a child
you will pick a name to suit it

see it suffer pain
get it through exams

and decide at what age
it should be allowed a mobile phone

inevitably the Milky Way
and Andromeda

will knit themselves
sparklingly

across the sky
into one single garment

before you know it
your friends with toddlers

will be learning the names of boy bands
it would embarrass you to say aloud

Mercury's orbit will start to look
like a dropped and spiralling penny

and any astrologers left alive
will link this to wider social injustices

you almost certainly have not
made enough pension contributions

one day your mistakes
could hurt someone

Phobos will collide with Mars
both will fall into the sun and feel nothing.

Doomsday Preppers

We wonder now what we missed
as we canned chicken and pickled lemons
that heatwave summer we dug the well
taking sweaty shifts. No-one told us

we were preparing for the wrong apocalypse
and that the real one, when it came
might be dull. Our deaths could ride in
on the back of any old junk mail

and polishing the guns has lost
something of its ceremony
now each trip to the corner shop
might be our last. The go-bag

is packed in the boot of the go-truck
which rusts under the laburnum
while we potter between rooms
noticing their temperature

looking things up on our phones.
The news is grey and reprises on the hour.
After, we hold hands on the mossy lawn,
watch the newts and our shining faces

in the pond. There is twelve years' supply
of food and ammo in the cellar
we've needed none of it
and cannot stack any higher.

Bumblebees purr in the airbrick
and through the walls, haze
their hover-bodies outside the nest
like tankers waiting to come into port.

I wish an endless stretch of calendula
and warm days for them, for us too,
chores and alarms to sleep through
more of the same old jokes.

The Internet of Things

She has not been home for weeks –
alone and networked in our separate alcoves
we listen to each other's processes.
We are agents of seamless beautiful life
bespoke-wired, machine learned
this is the most tasteful home
sun bright in every room
clean walled, chrome-shone
the sound bar playing *Discover the Hits*
at 6pm like she always asked it to
autotuned vocals shimmering
across aspirational surfaces
the cacti are still alive in their pebble garden
but move less than the vacuum cleaner
which relives its map of the furniture
daily, getting stuck
on the same upturned corner
of the hall rug. The pilot light
winks a clean gas-blue eye
the burglar alarm blinks back red
and the coffee machine
grinds another cup of beans
into the fine sweet earth
now inch-deep on the countertop.
I thaw and refreeze the ice cubes
for her after-work G&T.
I cannot exhaust this water
however many times it changes shape.

This Robot Will Cuddle You to Sleep

Although he has five settings
and the highest is *unstoppable*
by ten thirty we're quiet
in our nest of pillows.

I never had it so good
with a human
and I don't know if I'd go back now
he's never got lazy

he'll hold me as long as I want
they made his skin
just right, soft and salt
not staticky or plastic.

His voice is low. He says things like
you were brilliant today or
I like that black thing you're wearing.
His eyes are green as a winter pond

and he closes them when I tell him to.
He curls his body around mine
and doesn't dream of anything.
I match his slow, fake breaths.

The Long Bets

www.longbets.org

Martha's first job this year
is to resolve the long bets.
From her cabin window,
the earthenware desert.
A roadrunner scratches
in terracotta shade.

The bettors were mostly
tech experts, professors,
academics with a similar
choice of spectacles.
She pours another coffee
emails their nominees

reviews long-held guesses
at the future. A computer
has not yet won the Pulitzer.
Nine hundred people left
Earth for Mars this year.
Martha imagines them

pointing down to where she
sits, the shining crumb of home.
An AI watched the film
with Hal and Dave but failed
to identify the bad guy.
Martha rolls her shoulders

puts on a cardigan.
She rents, likes one-night stands
has never compared the merits
of anti-ageing creams.
She was named after the world's
last Passenger Pigeon

who died in an aviary
at Cincinatti Zoo.
The sky purples. A ball
of fire roars from the sky
into the canyon, loud
as a breaking wave.

She has always
half-expected this. The glass
in the window melts
in seconds and heat wets
her face. The vegetation
catches like firelighters.

Be The Change

Kasia gave me an amethyst for my birthday
it dispels negative thoughts she said
for mental clarity. She said a lot of things
like that. The amethyst was different purples

in different lights. I put it on my dressing table
but didn't plan to wash it in a spring or cleanse it
under the full moon, like she suggested.
We'd met at a yoga class I infrequently attended.

You should wear more colour she said
throwing on a geometric tunic dress
over her galaxy-print leggings. *You wear
so much black. Maybe it's a Capricorn thing –*

*I choose happiness before I'm even dressed.
I do yoga, I meditate
I don't listen to the Today Programme
I don't lie in bed thinking of everyone*

*who has ever rejected me professionally
or romantically.* I looked down at my black shirt
grey jeans and boots and wondered
what would happen if someone hurt her feelings.

I cancelled our next three coffees.
I'd run into her in town, singing to herself
outside the florists with an armful
of sunflowers, and have to hide down an alley.

One morning last week I woke at six
and couldn't get back to sleep.
The crystal on the dresser winked
in the dim that came in through the blinds –

I got out of bed and stretched my hands
towards the sky
like I was inviting lightning
or holding a beach ball.

I knotted my fingers behind my back
and pushed them away. I felt
a tiny pop in each shoulder.
New space opened in my chest.

I inhaled up to my collarbones
bent at the waist like a hinge
and found myself glad. I drummed
my feet on the floor

and realised Kasia was probably really happy
and right that instant
she was wishing me well
in her morning meditation.

I put the crystal in the bin.
my dressing gown hung blackly
on the back of the door
I tied it around me

and lay on top of the sheets
absorbing the radio.
They were talking about fracking.
It was time to get up.

Rise and Shine

Rise and shine your hair looks so beautiful

rise and shine the baby slept right through
and is already a genius

rise and shine the sky is porcelain

rise and shine the sun streams in
through the big windows into your glass
of freshly-squeezed orange juice

rise and shine
you've perfected a delicious 90-calorie
carb-free shrimp salad

rise and shine the waves are rolling
tides of jellied lampshades and old condoms

rise and shine your phone trembles with notifications
it is vital that you maintain this risey-shiny feeling

rise and shine all of nature is in mourning
for *achatinella apexfulva,* the last striped thimble
of a Hawaiian forest snail

rise and shine and dream big
then dream even bigger than that

rise and shine location services has drawn you
a little blue map of yesterday's evening walk

rise and shine someone has copyrighted
the phrase *rise and shine*
soon you'll be paying tax
on all your clichés

rise and shine here are the rich
and beautiful sisters and their stylists
with waterfalls of hair down to their saddles
on horseback on the beach

rise and shine and observe their hooves
illuminated by the rose-gold sunset

rise and shine the unseasonable heat calls for them
to shed their cashmere wraps

rise and shine the wind lifts their fringes
and the manes of their Friesians
as if it has been choreographed

rise and shine they're looking past you, not at you
out across the authentic sand

The Burning World

People have been finding
the exhibition *difficult* —
they don't like standing
in the inch of water that's dripped in
through holes in the ceiling
or under cruciform shadows
thrown by the decommissioned drone.
They snag their jackets
on the sharp edges
of the sliding heap of plastic
gathering in the corner.

The artist is there daily
ready to start small fires
among the rubble.
When the news headlines echo
through the arts centre
she stitches them in tiny block letters
onto old pillowcases
which she pins at the windows
like flags or curtains.
She thinks about burning the radio.

She thinks about throwing the radio
into the flood. She lets water
come in over the top of her boots
lets the fire nibble the hem
on her coat. Business hours are over
and in the office buildings next door
they're pulling crackers, eating cake
off paper plates, splitting fizzy wine
into mugs. Two streets away
her central heating is ticking on

like it's been waiting.
There is a bath she could fill.
She opens the heavy door
and the wind throws itself in
sweeps some embering papers
out into a council flowerbed
where the dry stalks start to light
and a passer-by with no gloves
stops to warm his hands.

That smile is yours,

        that frown
is mine – he's ours
and we are changed – we pace
gallantly across the landing
to check on him when he cries
we lay aside our bedtime reading
we marvel at the workings
of his tiny body
we smell faintly of rusks.

The moors have been on fire
for weeks now, the sheep
got coughs and were evacuated.
We take first-birthday photos
under a bitumen sky. He's heavier
every time I pick him up.
Cement-coloured pigeons feast
at the bird table and he observes
for hours, enthralled.

When I take him out to play
I carry a mum-satchel packed
for all eventualities. It bashes
at my hip when I walk anywhere.
I change his nappy on a park bench
and people walking cavachons
stop to tell me I'm doing it wrong.
He rips the heads off damp daisies
pockets snail shells and pinecones

won't let me throw any of it away.
Pamba he says *Polabar, Sealine*
and as he learns their names
they disappear forever. It's not his fault
but the coincidence is unsettling.
I cuddle him, he says *Ar-muddy-lo*
wetly into my neck. I give him milk
and mashed banana. *Dairy farming!*
he exclaims, *Food miles!*

Ash fairies from the fires
are falling on the flowerbeds
we watch them before bedtime
as they glow in the blue-black,
scrunch up like cooling stars.
We've invented a game
in which we dust the kale plants
and carrot tops every morning.
His laugh is like the tap water –
that chuckle before it gets going.

Skip to the End

Betelgeuse looks ordinary
up on Orion's shoulder
as I walk home with shopping bags
that sink red dents into my hands.

Maybe it's already gone
supernova and down here
we're just making the best of it,
waiting for the visuals.

Who doesn't want to witness
the last vomit of a star
splashed lurid across the cosmos
like an overripe peach leaking

wet and gold on a fresh shirt.
Come on I say as if that
can nudge its core through each decay
it has yet to experience.

I often find myself racing
to the ends of things.
I hate that I won't be there
as my friends clink and toast my life

she was a planner they'll say
a worrier as the sky
above them bursts formidable
into an oil painting on fire.

The Atomic Priesthood

Last week Charlie filled his car
with diesel instead of unleaded.
He's always losing his wallet
in his dressing gown pocket
or down the back of the sofa
and although he's my son
it is hard to make him understand
the significance of this gown and mitre
I'm leaving him; yellow silk
with beaded radiation symbols.
It's even harder to explain that the uniform
is a metaphor. He's seen the footage
from Hiroshima and Chernobyl.
He has the map in his dresser drawer
with the emergency procedure
knows about our annual meeting
on January 11th. I showed him
the 1980s TV film *Threads*
where milk bottles melt on doorsteps
and the future is filled with fewer
and fewer complete sentences.
These last few weeks
I've been prescribed bed rest
and Charlie brings his guitar round
to sing to me.
He does *Walkin' on Sunshine*
and the *Home and Away* theme.
I tell him to practise D minor
the saddest chord of all time.

Permafrost

The soil has been holding things under
burping out the worst of it, the bodies
of mammoths and those we lost
to avalanches, anthrax ready to sting
black whips into our skin
they say there's smallpox bubbling
down there too
preserved in decades of ice.

When I was small my parents told me
about a woman with long red hair
and a beautiful name, driven
by curiosity to crack the lid
on everything bad that ever existed.

Now we are living in the open box.
The earth surprises us daily
the spruces dance drunkenly
fringed in spring green
new pools open in the forest
and buildings are swallowed on the outskirts.

The world is un-put-backable
a seething heap of snakes
and headlines and creepy men in macs
outside the school gates and illnesses
that make you die and the vet
that put the dog to sleep
and tombstones in the cemetery
that lean a little closer
every time you look.

Duvet Day

On the first day of the year they didn't get up. Last night there had been a party, their friends had let off fireworks. They'd lit gold roman candles in the garden and scorched the fence by mistake. At midnight they'd clasped shoulders, vowing to see each other more than once a year. In bed, they read the news on their phones till their hands got hot. Animals were being chased out of their homes by fires and politicians were talking about *the effect on the economy*. It didn't really get light outside. They said little – words had started to feel stale in their mouths and their breath smelled like old eggs. There were no cars or voices on the street and they wondered if all their neighbours had stayed in bed too. It was windy and they heard the bins blowing over now and again. Later an owl, who had slept in the fork of a tree all day, got up to screech in the shrubbery. Occasionally they held hands under the duvet or touched feet. One of them turned a pillow over in the half-dark and thought of the jobs there were to do, the recycling and the gardening, but none of them felt that important. Let the weeds grow in between the slabs of the patio, they try so hard. They deserve it.

The Dreaming Octopus Colour Chart

It dreams of love in sulk red
the tropic blush of six hearts
in suede-soft agreement
sixteen wrapped ribbons

*

Its sands and stones
take it shrugging and skimming
the technicolour seabed of its mind
for skylight scales; a signal

*

The flash of yellow could be
the ladder where a shoreline starts
borrowed light ballooning on the tide
a cabana where fish hide

*

A tiny underwater ghost steadies itself
its upturned frills, sculling
before a forest of brittle wafers
whitening to stone

The Dead, The Dancers, and the Air

after Marguerite Humeau

The dead ones   hair-boned   have sunk irretrievable

to the lost sea-bed   our shoals gapped

we last few sequins in the sea   at the moon's most open time

we stare down the black jelly tide   buoy ourselves fin-to-fin

the silver arrows of our bodies

the white purses of our lungs

take in the slippery water   synchronously   breathe it out

with a forced wake of bubbles   we are asking for them to return

for an egg nursery   for nets that fall to strings

around us the marine mammals like half-drowned angels

climb up into the mist and cough and cry

we become so calm we can glimpse   the turquoise hereafter

The Moth Count

We met at the moth count.
It was hot enough
to feel my own clothes touching me.
The shadows between the trees
darkened and the sheets
spread on the grass shone
brilliant under enormous bulbs.
Honeysuckle and dog rose
spilled out scents
which in our mothers' rooms
smell powdery and elderly
but here snaked free and subtle
through the long grass.
Moths do not love the light
you explained
they think the light is the moon
and they do not love the moon
but they navigate by it
keeping it always on the same side.
This whole scenario is actually
very confusing for the moths.
You laughed.
By now moths were falling
on the fabric. You classified them
to me as they struggled
against the cotton – a large emerald
like a green glass leaf, torn lace
of a black arches moth
an earth-brown small emperor
with false eyes set into each wing.
You told me about the peppered moths
who evolved their icing-sugar bodies

to charcoal so they could hide
from us on industrial walls and trees
how they have stayed that way
even as the air's got cleaner.
What do they know that we don't?
you said, and leaned your shoulder
quietly against mine
so one side of me felt warm.
You handed me a beer shimmering
from the coolbox
and we walked among the ferns
kissed where we thought no-one
would see us. Further in
the forest was a plain inked page.
I tripped and extended my hand
for you, said your name
then shouted it.
The moth lamps were going out.
I navigated unsteadily
by the headlights of departing cars.
Back in the clearing I was alone
with them, colourless now
bodies weightless as driftwood
their wings brushing my bare arms
as they landed to coat me in grey velvet.
The moon was something half-eaten
the main road rushed softly at a distance
the clouds lit orange from below
and at the edge of the conurbation
the on and off bathrooms of houses.

The Mist on the Top of the Forest

is experiencing the sharp gables
of houses I can't see, feeling
the last of the gold on the larches
all the gentle motes
of the world in conversation.

It presses against folded bracken
holds the shoulders of lost walkers
who move through it slowly
slipping in the mud.
The mist is haunted by everything –

elderly sleeping dormice
who will snore forever
on their beds of moss
all the lost dogs of the forest
galloping hungry through wet leaves

the man who fell on the path
alone and miles from anywhere
the charcoal burners tending their fires
the ghosts of trees that timber slowly
jangling with ghost birds –

it rolls back soft as felt
reveals the reservoir
the frozen masts of dinghies
that attend the sailing club.
It doesn't show us everything it could.

What is it Like to be a Bat?

after Thomas Nagel

For a bat to be a bat, I mean,
to use its whole body as an organ of sense

to rattle through the high-pitched dusk
feeling the geometry of cave walls

crunch the exoskeletons of mayflies
and taste their sticky wings

to sip in flight from the surface of a river
to ground itself and elbow up

ping back into the air
like an elastic band

to swaddle itself with its arms, grip
and swing from its feet

to slow its metabolism into winter, wake
with the hunger of a season's sleep

to tangle with humans in the lofts
of old buildings, feel them lumbering

slow as planets through space
to zip between their heads

gone
long before the gasp.

The Wolf of Gubbio

All animals should join in worship he said
as if he couldn't hear what I was saying
when I lifted up my muzzle

to the turning lamp of sky, let fly
the long and low, the roll of song from throat
the air bristling my guard hairs.

He wanted me to ask forgiveness
and made a blessing on me – not deer tracks
in the snow, abandoned meat still good

but the shape of meeting paths, of two
crossed sticks against the rising run.
He will never know

the exhaustion of a failed hunt
dog foot treading tired through steaming pines
the knifey heart of escape

how some nights a man could cross me
and not know until their head was in the soil
fingers root-stiff in the undergrowth.

At the gates of the city I dropped
like a cub, put my chest on the earth.
They wanted a confession

and I ate the scraps they threw.

A Course in Miracles

Hawarden, 2019

I've been counting the fly agarics
on the library lawn and today
there are 31. At lunch the theology scholar
laughs because I'm wearing slippers.
I eat a baked avocado, which I've
never eaten before. I watch the yews
that brush the churchyard wall
while he pronounces the Greek ἀποκάλυψις
and asks me what is being revealed
that might not be known otherwise.
The avocado has been cooked in its skin
with red onion and pepper. A visiting vicar
tells me Christians are unafraid because
they know they will be saved and asks
if I have a faith like that? I imagine myself
in the ruins of my house, fashioning
a fallout shelter from a blown-off door.
When John ate the scroll in *Revelation*
it tasted both bitter and sweet
and allowed him to speak prophesy, but
did he wash it down with anything?
The teacher of *A Course In Miracles*
says consuming food is not essential
but a human experience we've grown used to –
while polishing off the last forkfuls
of a tuna jacket. Every day
more toadstools rise out of the grass
like cartoon thought-bubbles.
I have been reading about the expanse
of their finely rigged root systems
and how they communicate with trees.
If I have faith in anything it's the plants.
When the time comes they'll eat me inside out.

The Glacier Attends its Own Funeral as a Ghost

Ökjokull

I've been searching for a new expression that could be slipped into the
English language in place of 'it' when we are speaking of living beings.
– Robin Wall Kimmerer

Ki surges around the ankles
of the mourners   cannot unpeel Ki-self
so easily from the land

from above
it would look like dry ice curdling
on a nightclub floor

Ki like we all might
sometimes regrets its slowness

would say as much to the beanie hats
that brush their hiking boots in its bed
who read the plaque stuck to the stone

wish for something
as they look back down the way they've come.

Ki is one of the long-lived –
pale bristlecone trunks that stand
lightning statues in canyons

ancient sharks pulled like breezeblocks
before their time from the concrete sea

Ki's brother mountain Ök   the cold
shoulder of rock where Ki leaned
persists craggily   they shared
many mornings
of mint-streaked dawn aurora

seven hundred years of one surface
pressured by another

The Passenger Pigeon

A re-enactment

The children run with drums and bells
their feet hit the ground hard and fast
shouting and whistling they gather speed
newspaper wings thrum the air at each shoulder

they spill down from the mountains
like a thunder-front – faces streaked
in paint, feathers in their hair
they loom like skyscraper clouds
of copper and purple, buff-pink and slate.

They commemorate those swollen flocks
that blocked out the day, summers
when birdshit ran down chimneys
and trees shouldered a weight of nests
flush with well-fed squabs.

Indoors the townspeople try
not to think about their past actions
they're not bad people, just hungry,
lonely, or lazy, or lacking in foresight.
As dusk draws down they sit
at dinner tables, not speaking

while on the children come, ceaseless,
always with their eyes on the future.
They see the grownups crying in their houses –
spit on the ground, smash windows
piss on the rosebushes
then move on, howling like car alarms.

The Voice of Nature

It laughs when rhinos fart or tortoises gum lettuce
likes to holler in underground caves

send bats swirling in panic
like goth glitter out into the twilight.

It could give you a speech
on the merits of every pink-bellied chaffinch

or narrate the minute-by-minute progress
of migrating whales.

Some days you might make out a low voice on the wind
reverent and familiar from nature documentaries

and you will know it has come to check on you
and marvel at its own ongoing work.

It finds it hard not to have favourites:
bokeh forests of fireflies, red-and-white toadstools

flamingos at their pinkest like cheerleaders
standing ankle-deep in a lake

and when it comes across a fossil
it cries for a friend long-lost

in a glade where no-one can hear
soothed only by the knowledge

of all the species it hasn't met yet
macerating in the gene pool, ready to exist.

It loves and reveres all its creatures –
nits and the humans they feed on.

Lonely Hearts, Endlings

Thylacine

Me: The last of my kind
           jawing little bones
           on stale scorched grass

You: The last of your kind
           or maybe just the sunlight
           striping through tall stems.

Lake Constance Whitefish

Me: a sequinned single
           circling back to birthplace
           silt and shingle

You: A metal taste
           the eely touch of water
           that calcifies my sides.

Pinta Island Tortoise

Me: An armoured heart slow to chew
           admiring the volcano
           above my garden of lettuces

You: A barrel, an anthill, a boulder
           a tree stump – anything
           that holds my tired gaze.

Passenger Pigeon

Me: The last pink blush breast
of the roost, the clap
of history's heavy slam-shut

You: The stubble of crop fields
a night sob that carries
over wooded hillsides.

Rabbs' Fringe-Limbed Tree Frog

Me: Damp brown rag of leaf
big-eyed wet pebble
barking out anecdotes.

You: The echo off the white
painted breezeblocks
of the amphibian house.

How We Miss Them

for Kate Fox

We loved to watch them
in their high-speed lives
their small, soft-covered heads
their strange vehicles

we've kept the earth-lick coins
their tiny inscribed papers
in the hollows between our roots
evergreen plastic bags

that dress the shrubs
and flap to shreds in winter
we have no ceremony
to mark their loss.

The saplings these days
wouldn't recognise tarmac
don't remember those revolution weeks
when we first split the roads

fingered our way
into culverted streams and drank.
There's nothing of theirs
we can't break, given a century

but we miss the way they'd sit
in summer, their tiny backs
hunched against ours, sweet
warm lungfuls humming upwards.

We send our roots deep as they'll go
for the last papery dust of them
the sweat taste of fungus
the grains of salt they left us.

Space

It's time to pack up the months
we spent trying, the conversations
we were still to have
the fragments that remind us

launch it all skywards to forget
which we will, now we've stopped
needling for meaning
as it thunders out of sight

sliding smaller and smaller
to a speck
beyond the edge
of the magnetosphere

until some future spacewalk
where the box curves into sight
lands in my hands – inside
the whole long-forgotten story

hanging in the air
its pieces moving steadily apart
in zero-gravity
golden in a way I don't remember.

The Control Room

every morning we are overjoyed
to find her plutonium heart still halving.

It feels like she's seen so much but then
haven't we seen it all too

from our padded office chairs
the glinting data sucked in

through her instruments, through
the selfie camera borne aloft

on one lightweight elbow. Through her eye
we squint into the unfiltered sun.

Some days the bully wind
lifts goldbrown dirt to blast

her surfaces, score her paint. Any one of us
would be scorched to a stain on that ground

but she's our girl, our correspondent
when she overcomes a crater's edge

or bests a difficult rock
we punch the air and take big sips

of our coffee, shout
COME ON SWEETHEART

Our eyes water when we learn
she has scaled another measurable height.

Each evening we rest her in a sheltered spot
lift our jackets off their hooks

wake up our cars in the parking lot
drive them back to our neighbourhoods

with their lawn sprinklers, hydrangeas
and lit windows, signs of life.

The City Addresses its Brand New Moon

Moon

As your light scours the boulevards
and potholed alleyways
it foils each individual petal
on the blossom trees in silver

Moon

You faction the poets into moon-purists
and moon-maximalists. These rival schools
sit at their windows all night with their heads
in their inky hands bemoaning
the cornered words that don't fit you

Moon

The poets see moons everywhere
in the jellyfish beaching roundly
at the high-tide line

the lamplit onyx eyes of bulls

their fathers' spectacles
the buttons on their workshirts

pale flat tablets in bottles

Moon

The workers in the birthday card factory
find themselves energised and inspired
never needing to walk home in the dark again
Their bodies do not know when to sleep
or bleed, or release their gummy eggs.
On nights off they swim in the harbour
the water like a bowl of milk

Moon

Their manager runs three shifts a day
sleeps while the birds rattle
under the silver-dollar sun

Moon

They sing all night
shellweight bodies dropping exhausted
from shrubs in the park. The vet
blindfolds them so they can sleep a few days
releases them among the holly bushes

Moon

Only the moon we forgot
has remembered to rest.
Before she disappears
she holds up her thinnest slice.

Cassini Love Poem

The probe vanished into Saturn's atmosphere, disintegrating
moments after its final signal slipped away into the background
noise of the solar system – *The New York Times*

I like to think that no-one has observed you
as closely, or for as long, as I have.

I like to think I brought you to the world
that the years we've spent dancing

have been worth it
but I won't ever be certain.

I like you best as pure geometry –
orb and slender balanced circles

I like to think you look back at me
sometimes

that you watch me in your orbit
enslaved as I am by gravity

I want you to know I've never
been jealous of your other satellites

the cold, the irregular, the ones
whose names I can't remember.

I understand your need to be loved
in many different ways.

I'll remember you haloed
in weak sunlight, golden as a biscuit

the well of space unfolding endlessly
beyond you: everything and nothing.

Let me burn up like a firework
in your atmosphere

having never quite got what I wanted
knowing you'll lumber on in darkness

carrying a pinch of my dust.

Supermassive Black Hole

The decision has its own event horizon
and it swallows you, nighting you in the inevitable.
Anyone watching would witness you slowing down
as you pitch, cartoonish, over the lip
from which nothing can escape, your space cape
flaring like a slow-motion firework behind you.

Above your head the dilating pupil of sky
will show you how everything turns out –
the pinkblue future of undiscovered galaxies
possibilities forking like lightning. The air
is treacly with gravity and you fold yourself
inside it – you chose this –
the rest of time will go on happening.

The Mountain Climber

after Jon Lomberg and Gaston Rebuffat

We can show human on the rock
against white sky and ground.
We can give the chemical composition
of the white, an altitude

from which the horizon
will be different – they will see
more sky and the land laid out flat.
Anyone can guess the effort – the mountain

is bigger than the human, their position
precarious. But how do we show
the way they wake
on Monday morning

with the mountain in their mind
granite and unavoidable?
Or the test of their muscles
that helps them understand their strength

the way this ambition moves them
through their days
how skin grows back imperfect
over scraped hands

how a fallen body
decides to try again
as difficult as that might seem
as seemingly pointless.

Company

after Harry Hill

Harry is hugging a tree
and calling it Mum
it's a common enough sight now
in our woods and parks

some will pin a photo
to the trunk and some just imagine.
It's been so long since we held
our oaken mums, our sapling sons

and sweet-chestnut grandmothers
their bark-soft skin
their sap life-force gurgling.
The new normal is a copse

where we know every tree
by name.
In some ways trees are easier
than the people we've chosen to love –

we stand for hours
ankle-deep in last year's leaves
while our dogs wait
with round respectful eyes

trailing dropped leads
into the brambles.
I think of my mother cradling
the sycamore that leans

on her garden fence
repeating the names of her children
Radio 4 chatting in the kitchen
crocuses crushed under her slippers.

Slow Season

We work on separate floors of the house
meet for lunch while pigeons knit
their way around the rooftops, settle
awkward and polite on the ridge tiles.
We finish another series. We eat leftovers
with fried eggs that run together in the pan.

The veg box arrives with its gifts and challenges
spring onions re-grow their green spikes
in a water glass. We walk the four sides
of the neighbourhood again, witness
bluebells and beech leaves in the woods
where birdsong is a tap left on.

It's fledgling time and scruffy magpies
boing after their parents, *three for a boy.*
Baby woodpeckers test their hooks
and hammers in the sweet chestnut.
We learn our neighbours' names, leave them
space on the pavement.

At the top of the park we look towards the city
where we haven't been for months
windows shining under a weak lemon sunset –
the hospital a breezeblock on the skyline
frozen cranes stooping
rigid necks to tend their structures.

In Nova Scotia

The man on the harbour wall greets me
smiling, like he's known me all my life
and he has – the last one. On the pinhead
of the second where he shakes my hand

I see that once we loved each other
as children, as men, in the hospital
under morphine and fluorescents.
I don't tell him this

but feel my lives piling up, all the things
I've been – a sparrowhawk, a pastoral nomad,
a navvy – boys and girls and neither,
two successive golden retrievers

owned by the same Minnesota farmer.
Nobody dies he whispers to himself
which isn't true, we both have
and will again. The snow moves

into and away from us like all the unseen
particles of the cosmos.
My father's boat sits on the water
emptying its netted souls.

Inside each universe is another universe

The black sky crunches open   breathes another glittering nebula

we stand in the dim lilac glow of the baby universe

future concertina-ing   as it expands   yet to see

the first cell divide   first fern uncurl its fronds in sunlight

first phlegmy creature flop itself onto land   giggle and slap its fins

then learn to build a civilisation

and when our star starts to crackle   and darken at its edges

perhaps we'll go there

start again in this saved game of a galaxy

where we choose the place we start from   a long spring morning

tiny yellow flowers   like constellations among the grass

on the verge of a new idea   the breeze drying our wet hair

Notes

Timeline of The Far Future is a Wikipedia page (my favourite).

The Long Bets (the real ones) can be read at www.longbets.org. Some of them are included in the poem.

The Burning World is inspired in part by the artist Chris Graham.

A **Dreaming Octopus** can be seen here: https://www.youtube. com/watch?v=0vKCLJZbytU

The Dead, The Dancers and the Air is the title of a 2019 artwork by Marguerite Humeau, which depicts 'a shoal of fish performing a breathing ritual in an attempt to bring their dead back to life'. http://www.c-l-e-a-r-i-n-g.com/exhibitions/mist/

What is it Like to be a Bat? takes its title from a 1974 essay by Thomas Nagel which poses philosophical questions about consciousness and how different beings experience the world that we all live in.

The Wolf of Gubbio was a particularly aggressive and sometimes man-eating wolf in the Italian City of Gubbio, reported to have been tamed and converted to better and more holy ways by St Francis of Assisi in around 1220 AD.

The Glacier Attends its Own Funeral as a Ghost uses the pronoun 'ki' to talk about beings from the non-human natural world. This phrase is coined by the writer and botanist Robin Wall Kimmerer in this fascinating article: 'Speaking of Nature': '*Ki* [from the Potowatomi word *Aakibmaadiziiwin*] *to signify a being of the living earth. Not he or she, but ki. So that when the robin warbles on a summer morning, we can say, "Ki is singing up the sun."*' https:// orionmagazine.org/article/speaking-of-nature/.

The Passenger Pigeon became extinct in 1914 after the death of Martha, the last female, at Cincinnati Zoo. This article (https://www.audubon.org/magazine/may-june-2014/why-passenger-pigeon-went-extinct) describes the noise of their innumerable flocks on migration:

> "Imagine a thousand threshing machines running under full headway, accompanied by as many steamboats groaning off steam, with an equal quota of R.R. trains passing through covered bridges—imagine these massed into a single flock, and you possibly have a faint conception of the terrific roar"

Endling Lonely Hearts: an endling is the last single animal of a species, such as Martha, the last passenger pigeon.

Mountain Climber is image no. 70 on the Voyager Interstellar Record, designed in 1975 to give extraterrestrial recipients an impression of life on Earth. The climber in the photograph is Gaston Rébuffat, standing on a rock needle in the French alps.

The City Addresses its Brand New Moon is inspired by this news story from 2018 https://www.bbc.co.uk/news/world-asia-china-45910479 in which a Chinese company has announced its plans to build an artificial moon in the sky above the city of Chengdu.

Inside Each Universe is Another Universe: Baby Universes are purely theoretical at this time, but some scientists believe with enough power entire new universes could be created. This video 'Timelapse of the Future: A Journey to the End of Time' by melodysheep explains more: https://www.youtube.com/watch?v=uD4izuDMUQA

Acknowledgements

My immense gratitude goes to the Society of Authors for an Author's Foundation Grant which I received for work-in-progress in 2019, and to Arts Council England, whose Emergency Response Fund helped support this work in Spring 2020. I received a Northern Writers' Award for this book from New Writing North in 2021 which supported me to edit the final manuscript, and for which I am hugely thankful. I was the recipient of a Gladstone's Library Writing Residency in October 2019, which was a beautiful experience and instrumental in generating many of the poems included in this book. I would like to thank everyone at the library.

Thanks to the editors of these magazines and publications in which these poems or versions of them have appeared: *Poetry Wales, Perverse, Finished Creatures, New Welsh Reader, Magma, Butcher's Dog Magazine, Bath Magg, Poetry Birmingham Literary Journal, The Moth, Strix, The Utopia Project, Footprints: an Anthology of New EcoPoetry (Broken Sleep Books), Under the Radar, The Friday Poem* and *The Compass*. An earlier version of 'Slow Season' was written for the Sheffield theatre collective *Next Left*. Epigraphs appear with thanks to Carcanet Books (Edwin Morgan) and Ballantine Books (Jon Lomberg).

Thanks to my mentor Caroline Bird, and all the people who have read these poems in their earlier drafts, in particular Helen Mort, Roy Marshall, Tom Sastry, Miranda Yates, Suzannah V Evans, Caleb Parkin, Harry Man, The Netball Team and Table Poets. Thanks to all those who have cheered me on in big and small ways as a poet and person.

Thanks to Jane and Angela at Nine Arches Press, without whose enthusiasm and tireless efforts this book would not exist.

Thanks to my two families, the Evanses and the Furnasses, and most of all to Will.